Learn Unity for Android Game Development

A Guide to Game Design, Development, and Marketing

Adam Sinicki

Apress®

Learn Unity for Android Game Development: A Guide to Game Design, Development, and Marketing

Adam Sinicki
Guildford, Surrey, United Kingdom

ISBN-13 (pbk): 978-1-4842-2703-9   ISBN-13 (electronic): 978-1-4842-2704-6
DOI 10.1007/978-1-4842-2704-6

Library of Congress Control Number: 2017948866

Cover image by Freepik (`www.freepik.com`)

Managing Director: Welmoed Spahr
Editorial Director: Todd Green
Acquisitions Editor: Steve Anglin
Development Editor: Matthew Moodie
Technical Reviewer: Wallace Jackson
Coordinating Editor: Mark Powers
Copy Editor: Corbin Collins

Distributed to the book trade worldwide by Springer Science+Business Media New York, 233 Spring Street, 6th Floor, New York, NY 10013. Phone 1-800-SPRINGER, fax (201) 348-4505, e-mail orders-ny@springer-sbm.com, or visit `www.springeronline.com`. Apress Media, LLC is a California LLC and the sole member (owner) is Springer Science + Business Media Finance Inc (SSBM Finance Inc). SSBM Finance Inc is a **Delaware** corporation.

For information on translations, please e-mail rights@apress.com, or visit `http://www.apress.com/rights-permissions`.

Apress titles may be purchased in bulk for academic, corporate, or promotional use. eBook versions and licenses are also available for most titles. For more information, reference our Print and eBook Bulk Sales web page at `http://www.apress.com/bulk-sales`.

Any source code or other supplementary material referenced by the author in this book is available to readers on GitHub via the book's product page, located at `www.apress.com/9781484227039`. For more detailed information, please visit `http://www.apress.com/source-code`.

Printed on acid-free paper

Contents at a Glance

Contents

About the Author

Adam Sinicki is a developer and health and fitness writer from Bournemouth, England. He now lives in Bicester with his wife Hannah and spends most of his days sitting in coffee shops around Oxford and London, listening to 80s music while writing and drinking coffee.

Career highlights include releasing the high-grossing Android app *Multiscreen Multitasking* and working with Coldfusion on *Voxis launcher*. *Multiscreen Multitasking* came as pre-installed software on over 60,000 handsets from Indian OEMs Intex and Celkon. More recently, he has been working with Android Authority, providing development articles as well as video reviews for their YouTube channel. He has also worked as a writer for the U.K. magazine *Writers' News* and has a bachelor's degree in psychology from the University of Surrey.

Adam runs his own blog and YouTube channel called The Bioneer, where he discusses technology, weight lifting, brain training, nootropics, and more. You can stay up-to-date with his latest projects and learn about things like muscle fiber recruitment by visiting www.thebioneer.com, or following him on Twitter and Instagram at @thebioneer, or finding him on Facebook at facebook.com/thebioneer. Stop by and say hi!

Adam's other interests include weight lifting, travel, 80s action movies, comic books, computer games, and a good tuna sandwich.

About the Technical Reviewer

Wallace Jackson has been writing for leading multimedia publications about his work in new media content development since the advent of *Multimedia Producer* magazine nearly two decades ago. He has authored a half dozen Android book titles for Apress, including four titles in the popular Pro Android series. Wallace received his undergraduate degree in business economics from the University of California at Los Angeles and a graduate degree in MIS design and implementation from the University of Southern California. He is currently the CEO of Mind Taffy Design, a new media content production and digital campaign design and development agency.

Acknowledgments

I would like to thank my wonderful wife Hannah Sinicki for supporting me always and for proofreading sections of this book specifically. Another shout out to my Mum, Sister (Kathryn "Squig" Sinicki) and Pete Hunt. One more to Goof (Chris Hanlon) because I always thank him in these kinds of things whether it's deserved or not (usually it isn't). And to Nathan Wallace for play-testing my games and always sharing words of encouragement. And to Byron the dog.

More thanks to Apress for seeking me out and being awesome throughout the creation of this book. And thanks to you reader, for picking up this book and giving me a chance to rock your world! Or at least give you some coding tips ... which I realize is not the same thing.

Introduction

Thank you for picking up this book and making the decision to try your hand at Android development with Unity. You've made a great choice for a number of reasons. Not only is Android a fantastic, open platform for indie developers to build games for, but Unity also makes the process quick, easy, and *enjoyable.* Hopefully, you'll be surprised at just how easy it is to get something that looks quite professional up and running and to share that with a huge audience of millions of users—for fun *or* for profit.

That said, I know that getting started with any kind of development can be daunting, especially if you're completely new to coding. That's why this book walks you through every step in a simple and easy manner, from setting up the development environment and installing all the necessary software, right down to releasing the completed APK to the Google Play Store. You'll learn the basics of programming with C#, as well as how to design a game that people will actually enjoy playing. No prior experience required. Oh, and we'll take a brief look at virtual reality apps too, because that's a subject that is *super* exciting.

Whether you plan to unleash the next big hit or are just looking for a creative outlet, Android development with Unity has a *lot* to offer, and I hope you'll find it as rewarding as I have. Android has opened all kinds of doors for me and given me a wealth of great experiences and opportunities—including the chance to write this book! I hope it will do the same for you.

CHAPTER 1

▣ ▣ ▣

Why This Is an Incredibly Exciting Time to Develop Games for Android

This is a golden age for independent games developers.

There was a time like this once before. It was during the early days of the home computer—the days of the ZX Spectrum and Amstrad. Back then games were very simple, owing to the limitations in technology. No matter how big your dev team or your budget, there was only so much you could do with that hardware! This put everyone on a level playing field and meant that a keen programmer could have a veritable hit like *Arkanoid* from the comfort of their basement (see Figure 1-1).

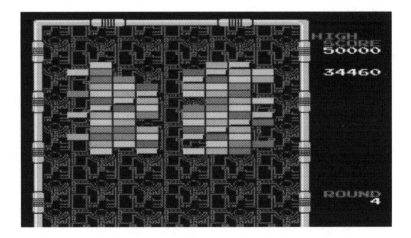

Figure 1-1. Arkanoid, *from a time when all games were indie*

Then technology moved on, the games industry grew up, and we saw the advent of the triple-A title. Games became bigger moneymakers than Hollywood films, and the hardware came on in leaps and bounds. There was no way that a single developer could ever compete with the likes of a *Halo* or a *Grand Theft Auto*. Not only does every model in a game like that need to be designed from scratch and every single line of dialog need to be recorded, but simply coding the amount of physics that determine the way things explode would be an impossible undertaking for a lone developer.

© Adam Sinicki 2017

A. Sinicki, *Learn Unity for Android Game Development*, DOI 10.1007/978-1-4842-2704-6_1

Then fate intervened. The growth in mobile devices and operating systems like iOS and Android introduced new "lower spec" devices. Meanwhile, better distribution channels like the Google Play Store, iTunes App Store, and even Steam have helped small-time developers get their creations discovered.

Slowly, more and more indie developers began releasing games to critical acclaim, and over time this eventually translated into commercial success. Early hits like *Spelunky!* showed that great gameplay and creative ideas could trump triple-A production values. Later, artistic attempts like *Limbo* or *Fotonica* have shown that stylistic visuals can be just as eye-catching as hyperreal graphics. Soon, titles like *Super Meat Boy* and *Angry Birds* began rivalling top studios for sales. In fact, *Minecraft*, a world-famous indie game and household name, is actually now the second best-selling game of all time (right behind *Tetris*). *No Man's Sky* is one of the best-selling games ever on Steam—and it also came from an indie studio.

The movement has only gained more momentum over recent years. With many gamers gradually becoming indifferent toward generic, big-budget sequels like the over-egged *Call of Duty* franchise, indie games have crafted a niche for themselves and gained a reputation for being able to offer experiences that are more creative and daring. Sometimes these experiences even challenge traditional notions of what makes a game "a game." Notable examples are the popular "walking sims" that have been gaining popularity lately.

Enter Unity

Although many factors have contributed to the rapid growth of indie games, it's also true that tools like Unity (Figure 1-2) have contributed greatly to this movement. Unity is a game engine that makes development particularly easy for beginners to get started creating their own programs.

Figure 1-2. *The Unity logo*

A *games engine* is a software backbone that provides a lot of the basic elements needed to make a game work. These elements include things like the ability to display (render) 3D and 2D graphics, handle basic physics (called a *physics engine*), detect "collisions" between GameObjects (a *collisions engine*), and even provide basic AI scripts or other ready-made assets.

Instead of creating a game from scratch, a tool like Unity allows a team of developers to focus on the elements that make *their* game unique and then simply insert them into a working environment. Unity combines this with a handy interface and cross-platform functionality and thereby saves countless thousands of hours that would otherwise be necessary to build a fully realized game from scratch and port it to Android, iOS, and Windows (Figure 1-3).

Figure 1-3. *Unity saves developers a huge amount of time*

At this point, you may be wondering whether it's in some way "cheating" to use a tool like Unity. If Unity is providing the underlying code for your physics, then did you really "make" the game? And if it's providing a user-friendly graphical interface for dragging and dropping pre-made game assets, how is it any different from a "game maker"? Is it that far removed from *Super Mario Maker*?

Make no mistake: Unity is a comprehensive tool that is used by thousands of developers, big and small. Many of your favorite games on Android (and elsewhere) are most likely built using Unity, including the following:

- *Temple Run*
- *Bad Piggies*
- *Lara Croft: GO*
- *Deus Ex: The Fall*
- *Escape Plan*
- *Battlestar Galactica Online*
- *Rust*
- *Superhot*
- *Lucky's Tale*
- *Monument Valley*
- *Cuphead*

- *Ori and the Blind Forest*
- *Broforce*
- *Tilt Brush*

In short, Unity is professional-grade software that has been used to create some of the biggest indie titles and even some of the biggest triple-A titles. Using ready-made assets is far from a sign of being less professional; in fact, it is one of the most important and encouraged strategies in coding. One of the key mantras any good programmer follows is: *don't reinvent the wheel*. In other words, don't spend large amounts of time working on something like a physics engine, AI, or even 3D models when that work already exists and is available to use. Doing so simply isn't a good use of time, and with games becoming increasingly more complex and ambitious, sharing assets and code is not only wise, it's a necessity. Professional developers know this, and amateurs should follow suit.

When Unity is such a *proven* quantity—when you *know* that it's capable of producing massive hit titles—why would you make life more difficult for yourself by ignoring it?

Sharing Assets

The ethos of sharing is an important part of modern development, and it only takes a quick Google search to realize this. Unity removes the need for much of the complex coding that you would otherwise have to handle yourself, and if you want to make a very basic 2D platformer, then you'll hardly have to write any code at all. When you *do* have to write code, you'll normally find someone willing to help you out if you ask the question in a forum or elsewhere. Of course, this book should provide you with all the basic code you need and the understanding to create more of it.

From time to time, you will need code that isn't available in Unity itself and that you don't want to have to create from scratch—for example, a particular visual effect or an advanced control scheme. Fortunately, this is where sharing comes in handy once again. Unity actually built a solution right into the software itself—there is no need to trawl the Web or download files and import them into your project. The Unity Assets Store (Figure 1-4) is a resource where you can download scripts, models, sprites, textures, special effects, and much more, all provided by the community or by Unity Technologies itself. Downloading these components automatically integrates them into your project. Better yet, many of the assets are free; others incur a relatively small price. By taking full advantage of this feature, you can create pretty much anything you can imagine while writing barely a line of code.

Figure 1-4. *The Unity Assets Store, where you can find all the scripts, sprites, effects, and more*

This open source spirit of sharing is another thing that has helped indie development take off in such a big way recently. By crowdsourcing and borrowing elements for their games, developers can build huge worlds with professional levels of polish in a fraction of the time that would otherwise be necessary.

The best bit? Unity itself is also free for hobbyists and small-time indie developers. You can download it, get started right away, and publish to Steam or the Google Play Store with no limitations until your games start raking in over $100K a year, at which point you'll need to pay for a license (which is still very reasonable). You also need to pay if you have an investment of over $200K per year, which you need to keep in mind if you plan on taking your app idea to Kickstarter. Some features are only accessible for paid accounts too, but most first-time developers don't need to worry about that (I cover this in more detail in Chapter 2).

At this point you should be excited! By using Unity, you get to build a game with precisely the same tools used by some of the biggest recent developers. Building something basic requires hardly any coding, and when you do need unique elements, you can normally obtain them online. The learning curve here is incredibly generous considering the quality of game you'll be able to develop—and it's completely free (as long as you stick within the restrictions of the free license).

If you've been dreaming of being a game developer but thought it was out of reach, think again. It has never been easier, and with Unity and this book at hand, nothing can stop you.

Why Mobile Devices Are Perfect for Indie Projects

The other great thing about Unity is that it's cross-platform. You can make a game on your Windows PC and then sell it on Android, iOS, Xbox, Playstation, Unity (Figure 1-5) and more. Some of these require that you apply for a developer license, purchase a development kit, or face other restrictions. In theory, though, the cross-platform possibilities are endless. As you'll see later in this book, Unity even supports virtual reality platforms like the Samsung Gear VR, Oculus Rift, HTC Vive, and Google Daydream. When you follow the instructions laid out for you in these pages, you'll be able to choose to port your game over to all these platforms if you so desire.

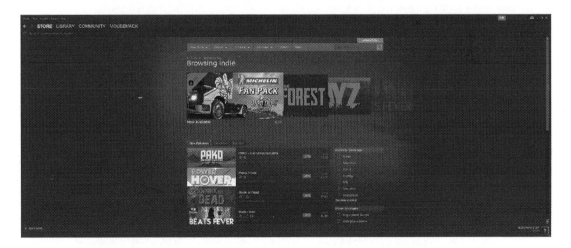

Figure 1-5. *Indie titles are highly popular on Steam*

But the focus of this book is going to be Android. That's because Android is the most open source and biggest of all these platforms. It also has the lowest barrier to entry, and you'll find it's generally the easiest platform to be successful with.

Take a look back at the list of big games made with Unity again and you'll notice that a lot of them are mobile games. One reason for this is that both Unity and mobile platforms attract indie developers. There are two reasons why mobile is ideal for indies:

- Mobile gives you access to a huge audience via a simple distribution channel.

- Mobile lowers the expectations for your game and therefore the amount of work involved in its creation.

Put simply, if you build a game for Xbox One, it's going to compete with the likes of *Call of Duty* and *Grand Theft Auto*. Although there is a thriving indie scene on Xbox, the potential graphical fidelity is still much higher, and even the input is more complex.

This is why endless runners are so popular on mobile but not very successful on other platforms. Endless runners are games where the main character runs forward ... endlessly ... and all the player has to do is hit "jump" at the right time. Occasionally they may also have to swipe to change lanes or hit another button to perform another action. But ultimately, the game consists of randomly generated obstacles, minimal input, and no "stages" in the traditional sense. On a mobile device this is acceptable because it provides an ideal two-minute distraction while you're in line at the bank. But most people wouldn't want to *sit down* to play an endless runner for any length of time, hence they're relatively rare on consoles and PCs.

Now ask yourself: as a new developer, would you rather make a hyper-real 3D role-playing game (RPG)—or an endless runner?

This doesn't mean you can produce rubbish, of course. It simply means that mobile gamers are much more lenient and prefer bite-sized entertainment. And that means you can be successful with something polished but relatively simple and short. Obviously, this bite-sized nature is often going to be reflected in the price, but that just means you can potentially sell in higher volume. And of course, if you want to be more ambitious, nothing is stopping you. Full games like several entries in the *Grand Theft Auto* series have been successfully ported to mobile, as have twin stick shooters, RPGs, and others (see Figure 1-6).

Figure 1-6. *Playing Geometry Wars 3 on an Android device*

Selling in volume, though, brings us to the next point. The other reason why mobile platforms are so popular is that they have such a massive audience. Most people these days have some kind of smartphone, probably running iOS or Android, and this includes a wide range of different demographics. Everyone from grandparents to young children can enjoy a game like *Angry Birds*, *Candy Crush*, or *Words With Friends*, and that gives you a huge audience to work with.

If you're making Android games as a hobby, you'll be able to share them with friends and get lots of feedback. If you're making them with an eye to potentially selling, then you'll have a wide audience to market them to.

Why Android Is Better than iOS for Developers

So, mobile is great, but Android *specifically* is even better. Why? Well, for starters Android apps can now also appear on a range of devices *other* than smartphones and tablets. Android is a completely open OS, meaning that OEMs (original equipment manufacturers) can modify it to run on televisions, smart watches, eReaders, washing machines, and a wide range of other hardware.

Okay, so most games aren't going to run on washing machines any time soon. But you could certainly create a game to run on a smart TV or, better yet, something like the Nvidia Shield. More likely, you'll be able to take advantage of new cross-compatibility with Chromebooks. *Chromebooks* are computers that run Chrome OS, a lightweight browser-based operating system that has been able to run Android apps natively since 2016. I talk more about how to achieve maximum compatibility with your app in a later chapter.

Practical Advantages of Android Over iOS

There are practical advantages to choosing Android over iOS as well. Apart from anything else, the process is overall *much* easier and simpler when you pick Android. Currently, uploading apps to the Play Store is still a relatively simple process that anyone can manage and that needn't take more than a couple hours. You can come up with an idea for an app, put something together, and have it live within 24 hours.

To make any real money with a game on Android, you'll want to try and get it into the Google Play Store (Figure 1-7), where users can search for apps and download them. Doing so costs a single one-off fee of $25 and is all handled automatically. You simply package and sign your APK file (Figure 1-8—don't worry, I show you how) and upload it using simple on-screen instructions. The app then uploads and goes through an automated approval process, and within a few hours people will be able to start downloading it. You can do this as many times as you like without needing to pay again, and your app will only get taken down if it violates Google's policies.

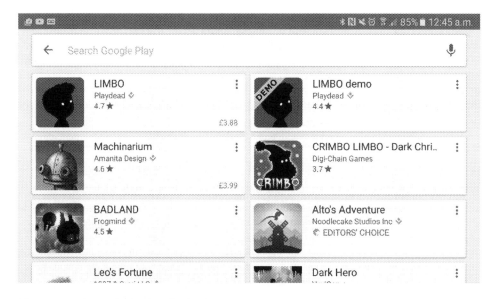

Figure 1-7. *Games in the Google Play Store*

Figure 1-8. *Success is just a click away*

This is a real breeze compared with Apple's process, which first of all requires an annual recurring fee of $99. Even if you only have one app that gets a couple downloads per month, you'll still be paying $99 each year to keep it live. Additionally, iOS apps need to go through an approval process that involves real *human* moderators and much more stringent restrictions. Many apps simply won't be allowed on iTunes, and often the reasons given are somewhat obscure or arbitrary. I know at least one developer who had a joke app rejected because it wasn't "entertaining enough." That's surely a matter of personal taste!

Of course, the Apple approach does result in a somewhat higher overall standard quality of app on the iTunes Store. In general, apps on iTunes will meet at least a minimum quality, whereas some pretty serious dross makes it onto the Play Store (not our aim here!). The risk with iOS, though, is that you spend months creating an app you're very happy with, only for it to be rejected and never see the light of day. What's more, using Android simply gives you more creative freedom and more options when it comes to the content and nature of your app.

Oh, and another thing: in order to develop for iOS, you're going to need to buy yourself a Mac computer *and* an iOS device to test on. This is in contrast to developing for Android, which you could theoretically do without even needing an Android phone by using emulators. These required purchases increase the investment necessary to get started with iOS.

Android vs. iOS for $$$

If you're interested in creating games primarily to make money, you may be less concerned with creative freedom and more focused on which platform will allow you to make the most money. In that case, Apple *does* have a slight edge.

First the good news: there are *considerably* more users on Android compared with iOS, but iOS users are likely to spend two and a half times more on apps than Android users are. Put simply, iOS users tend to have a little more money in their pockets and are somewhat more inclined to use it. In reality, that 2.5x is equivalent to $1.08 versus $0.43 per app. iOS users are also 50 percent more likely to place in-app purchases (according to *The State of In-App Spending Global & Regional Benchmarks*, published by AppsFlyer in 2016), and 7.1 percent of iOS users make at least one app-related payment per month, versus only 4.6% of Android users.

There is one category of app where Android has the advantage, but unfortunately, it's of no use to us as game devs: the category is *utilities* (Figure 1-9). Android users are more likely to spend on utility applications, most likely thanks to the greater freedom afforded to developers and app owners in this regard, which allows them to create custom launchers, memory/battery management tools, multitasking applications, and so on.

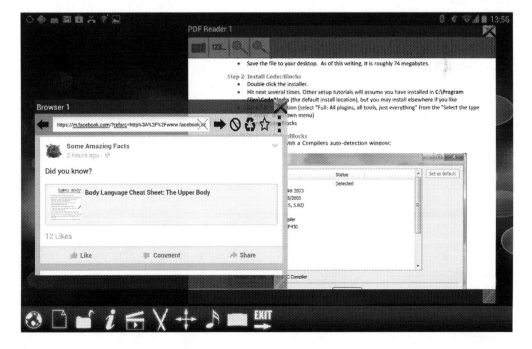

Figure 1-9. *Multiscreen Multitasking, an old utility app I developed for Android several years ago*

The AppsFlyer report also revealed other interesting data: for example, Asian users spend 40 percent more on in-app purchases compared with other territories. If you're planning on using a freemium business model, it might be a good strategy to target an Asian market. Later chapters talk more about how to maximize your earnings.

For now, the question is: should you still develop for Android, considering that iOS offers the larger earning potential? Of course, that's your call, but for many people the advantages of developing for Android outweigh the disadvantages. There is simply too much investment and risk involved in developing for iOS, and the barriers to entry are too high. Android, on the other hand, allows you to start developing games right away and reach a much larger audience with more creative freedom and less chance of your creation being rejected. On top of all that, Android's market share is constantly growing, whereas iOS's is shrinking. That stands to reason considering that thousands of OEMs are producing Android devices compared to just one manufacturing for iOS. App spending in general is also on the rise. That makes Android the more "futureproof" market, in as much as your audience (and revenue) will likely increase over time.

So, although iOS may be the slightly more lucrative platform, it is certainly *very* possible to make a lot of money from developing for Android. More important than the platform by far are the nature of the app, the marketing, and the promotion. And you're going to learn how to handle all that deftly over the rest of this book.

Android and Unity: a Match Made in Heaven

Hopefully, you're now convinced that Android is the platform of choice for indie game development. In choosing Android, you're making life incredibly easy for yourself by removing restrictions and upfront expenses and that will mean less time until you have a working app in the Play Store and you can start promoting it.

The other key part of our strategy is Unity 3D. We've already seen some of the incredible advantages that Unity offers, and by choosing to develop for Android *with* Unity, you drastically lower the barriers to entry for becoming a developer. You'll learn more about how Unity works in Chapter 2. For now, just remember that it is a game-building tool that will allow you to create much more professional games in a fraction of the time compared to other tools. With Unity, you could realistically put together an infinite runner or a space shooting game in a matter of days and it would look just as impressive as anything from a large, experienced publisher (if you play your cards right).

Unity's interface is incredibly beginner-friendly and allows you to simply drag and drop many of the elements around the screen as needed (Figure 1-10 shows a sneak preview of that UI). If you're worried about programming, consider that you can actually pretty much avoid coding entirely using the Unity Assets Store as mentioned earlier, although doing so limits what's possible to a large extent.

Figure 1-10. *Developing with Unity*

And as we've seen, Unity is also cross-platform and allows you to publish to multiple formats at the touch of a button. So, all that debate about whether to target Android or iOS is somewhat less pertinent because you can simply create a single game and then publish to *both* platforms at the touch of a button. In fact, you'll also be able to publish to PC (Windows Store *and* Steam), Windows Phone, Linux, Xbox, and more.

The process of creating your games is going to be near-enough the same across platforms, so even iOS developers can benefit from what we'll cover here.

How to Choose Your First Project

Using Unity 3D, the possibilities are pretty much endless. You can create anything from a simple puzzle game to a fully realized 3D first-person shooter. Thanks to Moore's Law, the capabilities of the average smartphone are now such that near console-quality titles are able to fit in our pockets.

But that doesn't mean you should set out to make the next *Call of Duty*. It's entirely possible to develop a highly detailed, 3D game for Android using Unity (see Figure 1-11), but that doesn't mean you should. This is where the vast majority of first-time developers go wrong, and it's one of the first and most important take-home messages you need to learn from this book.

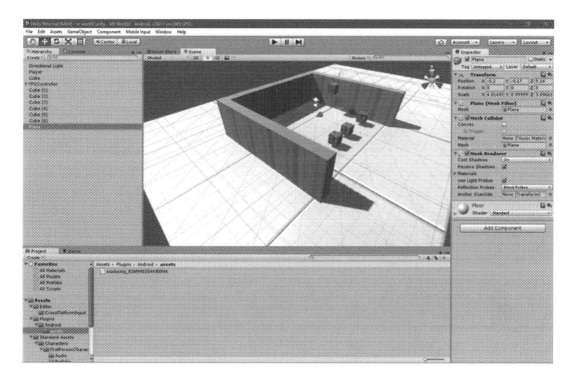

Figure 1-11. *Full 3D is also easy in Unity*

Simply put: most first-time developers have aspirations that far outstrip their capabilities—they simply overlook the need to reign in their ambitions for their first projects. I'm not looking to step on anyone's dreams here, but it's a much better strategy to set out to create an achievable and realistic goal than to commit to an impossible project that ends up taking up years of your life and never being seen through to completion.

Consider for a moment the huge undertaking that developing a triple-A-style title involves. Create a 3D level set in a city environment and you'll need to 3D model every single passer-by, every car, every lamppost, rubbish bin, letterbox, phonebox, bit of rubbish on the street, building, enemy ... the list goes on. Each of these items also needs realistic physics, fluid animations, and associated sound effects. You'll need cut-scenes, voiceovers, music, sprawling play areas, multiple levels.... For one person, this is a project that could take years and years. By which point, technology would have moved on, and everything you created would probably end up looking outdated. That's essentially what happened to *Duke Nukem: Forever*, and that was a game with a large, experienced studio behind it. This is one reason why the most successful indie games tend *not* to sport the most lifelike graphics; they instead choose original art styles that are eye-catching while simultaneously reducing the workload for the creators.

The Best Strategy for Creating a Successful Indie Title

Look at something like *Limbo*, a game available for Xbox, Playstation, Windows, and mobile. This was an early indie hit that sold incredibly well and made a big splash in the gaming community. This was possible partly thanks to the art style, which entirely used silhouettes. That suited the tone and the image of the game while also looking stunning and visually interesting. The developer (Playdead) couldn't compete with top publishers by using hyper-real graphics and took an entirely different route, coming up with something unique and very appealing. The screenshots would stand out enough during app store scrolling to pique a shopper's interest and potentially get them to buy.

Better yet, by choosing to work with silhouettes, Playdead drastically reduced the amount of detail needed for sprites and in-game elements. The game has absolutely gorgeous animation, which really helps to sell the atmosphere, but this was likely only possible because the lack of detail enabled the team to focus their attention on that area.

Of course, not every game can use silhouettes, but you're going to need to think outside the box and get creative. One option that is particularly popular is to use "pixel art." This is a retro-looking style that emulates graphics from old 8- and 16-bit consoles and has a very nostalgic appeal. Again, it limits the amount of work needed. Games like *Superbrothers: Sword & Sworcery EP* show how the style can be used to quite beautiful effect.

Considering Gameplay

The same approach should be taken to gameplay, especially for your first project. Instead of aiming to make a first-person shooter that requires you to create 3D models and large maps filled with details, it makes much more sense to attempt something 2D, ideally with procedural generation or other techniques to reduce your workload. (*Procedural* generation means that game elements are added at random according to an algorithm, removing the necessity to create levels manually.)

As mentioned, endless runners are very popular on mobile platforms thanks to their simply gameplay and lack of complex controls. Here, all you do is tap to jump while the protagonist runs forward, and this allows you to dodge upcoming obstacles and enemies. Said obstacles and platforms are generated randomly as the game scrolls forward, and the game tends to speed up the longer the player lasts. Replayability comes from trying to reach top scores and from the fact that no two "runs" will ever be identical. Games like *Rayman Fiesta Run*, *Canabalt*, and *Mario Run* have sold in huge numbers using this very simple formula. *Flappy Bird* can also be seen as a variation on the traditional infinite runner formula.

Other games use even simpler gameplay mechanics. The fantastic *Super Hexagon* by Terry Cavanagh utilizes very inventive graphics comprised of hexagons moving inward toward the center of the screen (which creates a very trippy effect) and a simple objective of pressing on the left and right sides of the screen to try and move your avatar into the small gaps in each layer. This game looks *instantly* unique and hypnotic, and the difficulty makes it highly engaging. That was enough to make it a massive hit, and Terry didn't need to design a single sprite or level map.

Or how about *Goat Simulator*? This is an indie game that does exactly what its name says: it allows you to control a goat while creating all kinds of havoc in a sandbox environment. The game is 3D, but its goofy nature means no one is expecting realistic graphics or physics or even challenging level designs. The game has been very successful nevertheless thanks to the appeal of the central concept and the very YouTuber-friendly nature of any gameplay footage. In this case, the idea alone trumped the need for any technical accomplishment. There are many games on Android claiming to be the "world's hardest games," and these are successful for the same reason: their concept is inherently intriguing, and that gets people to download.

If you want to create games as a hobby, feel free to tinker with whatever bombastic project you like. If you want to make some money, though, or at least get some positive feedback from real users, look for "easy wins"—at least to begin with.

So Here's What We're Going to Do

Put that world-changing RPG on hold for a while and instead consider taking on something smaller for your first project. Forget *Dragon Slayer 3D: An Epic Quest* and think more in terms of *Retro Catching Game*.

A simple puzzle game, a basic 2D platformer, or an infinite runner that you can make in a few weeks will give you the opportunity to actually get something concrete out into the world *and* develop your skills as you go. That way, you won't invest too much time and effort into something that may never take off and you'll be able to quickly start benefiting and honing your strategy. The good news is that Unity has a 2D "mode" that makes this strategy a lot simpler and alters the UI and features to better support 2D game development.

In business, this approach is known as *fail fast*. Instead of creating a product that takes years of research and development and thousands of dollars of investment, you instead create simple, easy products that don't *need* to succeed. If the product is a bust, you simply move on to your next idea. But if it gains traction in the marketplace, then you spend some time developing the idea and taking it further.

There's nothing more soul destroying that pouring years of your life into a game, only for it to get ten downloads and a one-star review. So, create an MVP (minimum viable product), get it into the Play Store, and then develop it *only* if it finds an audience.

If your art style is unique enough, the gameplay hook is original enough, and your marketing skills are strong enough, you'll be surprised at what an impact a relatively simple game can have.

What You Will Learn in This Book

Taking all that into account, this book is going to walk you through the entire process of designing, building, and publishing a fully functioning Android game using Unity. Specifically, it walks you through the basics of creating a 2D platformer or an endless runner, and that includes everything from building physics and sprites to signing your APK ready to be uploaded to the Play Store.

The project you'll be working on will be basic enough that you can easily adapt it to fit your own purposes, and by changing a couple of sprites and giving it a fresh title, you'll be ready to release your first game within weeks. The game will be simple but will have enough features to help you grasp the core concepts of game development with Unity so that you can apply them to future projects.

You'll discover the following:

- How to install and set up Unity

- How to use the Android SDK (Software Development Kit)

- How to find your way around the Unity IDE (Integrated Development Environment)

- How to create and add sprites

- How to add animations

- How to introduce physics using RigidBody 2D

- How to program in C++ and Java using Visual Studio

- How to add collectibles, sound effects, enemies, gameplay mechanics, and more

- How to add checkpoints, scores, level selects, menus, and more

- How to add dynamic cameras

- How to design levels to be fun and challenging

- How to create signed APK files ready to upload

- How to publish your app to the Google Play Store

- How to price your app for maximum profit

- How to promote your game and gain more downloads

Throughout this process, we'll be using a small amount of code and a fair amount of media (sprites, music, sound effects, and backgrounds)—and all of it will be available for you to use in your own projects, reverse engineer, or edit as you see fit.

During the course of this book we'll also be looking at various alternative things you can create and build with Unity. The aim is not to limit you, so you'll discover how to work in 3D and even make virtual reality applications for the Gear VR (Figure 1-12), Google Cardboard, and Google Daydream. This will give you a firm base of knowledge that will act as a jumping-off point if ever you want to expand your development and take on more challenging projects in the future.

Figure 1-12. *Developing for the Gear VR with Unity*

And yes, Unity 3D *can* be used to create apps and utilities, and the skills you learn in this book will enable you to do that too if you desire.

TLDR; this is a great time to be an indie developer. Android and Unity offer the perfect combination for beginners who want to launch something concrete in the Play Store. This book walks you through the development of a simple game and provides *everything* you need to know to get your first project off the ground and to help you grow as a developer in future.

Ready? Time to hit Start, Player 1!

CHAPTER 2

Introducing Unity and Getting Set Up

Developing for Android already makes a ton of sense for beginners and for indie developers looking to make some cash. But it's Unity 3D that makes all the difference when it comes to the ease and practicality with which this is possible. Unity is an incredibly powerful tool that makes it *considerably* quicker and easier to create some awesome games.

In this chapter, you're going to get a little better acquainted with Unity, what it is, where it came from, and how you go about getting it set up so that you can start using it.

What Is Unity?

Chapter 1 introduced Unity briefly, but now it's time to dive a little deeper into what you can expect Unity to do for you and how it's going to affect your workflow. This chapter covers what a game engine is, what an IDE is, and how to get it all set up and running. By the end of this chapter, you'll have the basics down and you'll be ready to start getting your hands dirty. If you're already familiar with Unity, though, and it's currently installed on your PC, feel free to skip this chapter.

Unity as Game Engine

Essentially, Unity is a game engine that has evolved to become an IDE/rapid development tool. If that all sounds like gobbledygook, don't worry, I'm going to break it down.

To describe it in a little more detail, a game engine is essentially a large amount of code that takes care of all the boring bits that make games function. Notably, this includes the physics as well as rendering, lighting, basic camera function, and more. Unreal Engine is another example of a game engine, as is CryENGINE 3. Others include Torque, Lumberyard, Ogre3D, Blender, JavaFX, and the list goes on.

Were you to program a game entirely from scratch without using a preexisting game engine, you would need to code every single detail yourself, which would mean a huge amount of development before you even got to start adding things like levels. There is simply no benefit to coding the way a wooden crate should fall and break when that's already been handled for you.

Again, this is why we're seeing a renaissance for indie developers. Back in the days of the ZX Spectrum and Amstrad, game engines could be *considerably* simpler, and most sprites were made of about 50 pixels. The complexity of today's games would make it impossible for one person to go it alone were it not for the existence of solutions like Unity.

© Adam Sinicki 2017
A. Sinicki, *Learn Unity for Android Game Development*, DOI 10.1007/978-1-4842-2704-6_2

Unity is also cross-compatible, meaning it can act like a bridge between your code and whatever device you're targeting. Compiling your game compresses all the assets and converts them into the right file format for adding to the respective distribution platform.

In short, Unity handles all the behind-the-scenes stuff for you and allows you to develop a great game without worrying about reinventing the wheel or worrying about how light should refract through various materials (see me happily coding in Figure 2-1). It's as if the laws of the universe have already been created, and all you have to do is fill it. Unity then handles the final legwork necessary to turn your world into an actual *game* ready for distribution.

Figure 2-1. *Unity streamlines development (photo by Sophie Bunce)*

Today, the vast majority of developers—even big studios—use ready-made IDEs like Unity or Unreal. Occasionally, a game will use a custom-built engine (such as the "rhythm violence" game *Thumper*), but these usually have unique gameplay mechanics that warrant the creation of a custom engine, and they normally spend a *long* time in development.

Because Unity makes life that much easier without introducing any major limitations, there is simply no reason *not* to use it (or a similar option like Unreal). "Going it alone" merely makes the challenge considerably more difficult, with no tangible benefit.

Unity as IDE

What makes Unity such a blessing for developers, though, is that it is at once a game engine *and* a game maker with a user-friendly interface that allows elements to be easily dragged and dropped around the screen (Figure 2-2).

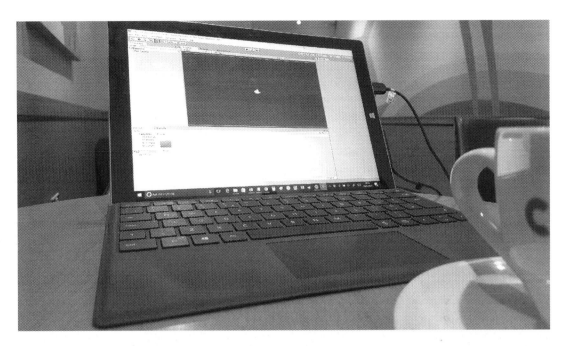

Figure 2-2. An IDE is a single environment for developers to handle every aspect of creating their game

To use more technical language, Unity is not a game maker but rather an IDE. IDE is an acronym for Integrated Development Environment, which is essentially a comprehensive set of tools used for development and arranged with a simple interface that lets you view and modify various different aspects all from one program. If you were to create an Android app without Unity, you would need to use another IDE—most likely Android Studio, which would allow you to see the code, your assets folders, debug information, graphical previews, and so on. In Unity's case, you see a view of your scene (essentially the level), a hierarchy of all the elements in said scene (called GameObjects), details for whichever item you choose to focus on, your assets folders, and more. We'll take a look at all the different windows and views that Unity presents shortly.

Unity vs. Unreal 4 (and Others)

I said there was no reason not to use Unity, but that's not *quite* true. There is one good reason you might opt not to use Unity and that's if you intend on using one of the *other* various game engines/makers out there.

Perhaps the closest comparison can be drawn with Unreal 4 (Figure 2-3), which has many similar features. Both are fully functional with very few limitations, and this—along with their relative simplicity—makes them arguably the two most popular IDEs for indie studios. So which is the better platform of the two? Why choose Unity? As ever, the answer hinges on what type of game you plan on developing. In our case, we're intending on making a 2D game for Android, and for that specific task Unity is preferred.

***Figure 2-3.** The Unreal logo (boo!)*

Although there isn't a *lot* in it—and it often just comes down to personal preference—Unity arguably has better built-in support for mobile game development and 2D game development. Unity is the most popular game engine on mobile, which reflects just how capable it is. This also ensures that there is a huge community out there to provide creators with support, as well as a near-infinite supply of custom assets in the Asset Store, which can drastically speed up development.

Many people also like the *flow* of Unity, which allows you to build games using a simple system of entities (GameObjects) and components (scripts). This is certainly a matter of opinion, but suffice to say that Unity is, for the most part, very intuitive and easy to use as a beginner. Unreal, on the other hand, has a steeper learning curve and isn't so well organized. But Unreal 4 has better graphical capabilities for developing triple-A-looking games. It's also open source, which effectively means that you can access the source code and make changes to the engine itself. Neither of these things is going to be an issue for indie developers targeting mobile devices. So Unity wins.

The Origin of Unity

Unity is developed by a company called Unity Technologies SF, which was founded in 2004 by David Helgason, Nicholas Francis, and Joachim Ante in Copenhagen, Denmark. Figure 2-4 shows the official website at the time of writing.

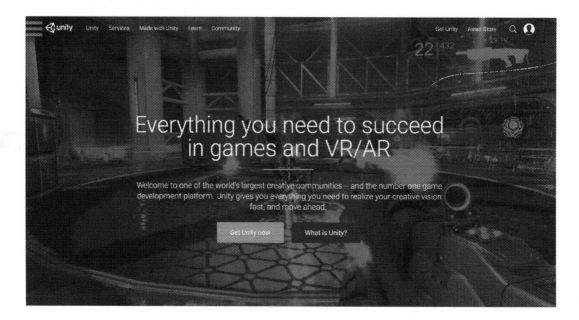

***Figure 2-4.** The Unity home page today*

Prior to this, the three developers called themselves Over the Edge Entertainment and had worked on a game for Mac called *GooBall* that had gameplay similar to *Super Monkey Ball*. Though the game failed to make a splash, the team recognized that the engine might have value to other developers. As such, they went on to announce Unity 3D for OS X at the 2006 WWDC trade show.

Since then, Unity has undergone many iterations and developments and is now far more comprehensive in terms of the platforms it supports and the features it includes. With Version 1.1 came support for creating games for Microsoft Windows and browsers, along with support for C/C++ plugins. Version 2.0 added support for Microsoft DirectX, and in 2008 Unity iPhone was released.

Version 3.0, released in 2010, was another major step, as the team wanted to get the program to run on Windows, which required it to be rebuilt from the ground up. Thus version 3.0 incorporated Windows, iPhone, as well as support for the Wii and numerous other platforms that had previously only been supported by separate standalone editors. Now the name *Unity* finally made sense. And yes, this is also when we got support for Android.

Unity version 4.3 saw another important update: the inclusion of out-of-the-box 2D support with Unity2D. Until this point, developers essentially had to "hack" the IDE to support 2D by using fixed camera angles and adding textures to flat planes to create backgrounds. Now, creators could much more quickly and easily build truly 2D games utilizing sprites and other more conventional methods.

According to Unity Technologies, it was Unity 5.0 that would be the biggest and most important release, with better performance across the board and major updates to the animation system, audio mixer, shaders, and more. Thus, many people refer to Unity as Unity5 now. The latest version of Unity at the time of writing is 5.5.0. It has a number of improvements for Android in particular that should enhance performance.

What if You Have a Newer Version of Unity?

It's important to note that Unity is constantly developing its platform and adding new features and improvements. Thus, depending on when you're reading this book, you may find that some elements are different from those described here. Maybe you're reading from the distant future and you're using Unity 200. If so, I hope you have a flying car.

More likely, though, any changes that you do encounter will be minor. Of course, middleware developers like Unity Technologies work hard to avoid breaking code with future updates, and that means most of the basic functionality should still work.

But in some rare cases, a line of code may be highlighted in Unity and described as being *deprecated*. That means it's supported but discouraged. If you notice this, a quick Google search should help you to find the new, correct way to go ahead to handle that function.

Licenses

As if Unity weren't already awesome enough, the best part of all this is that it's also completely *free* to use (for the most part). In the future, as your ambition grows, you may find yourself in need of additional features or earning above the $100K threshold, but most beginners will be fine unless their games take off in a big way. That's a pretty good worst-case scenario.

Essentially, there are a few different types of accounts you can create, as shown in Figure 2-5, with each priced differently and having different restrictions.

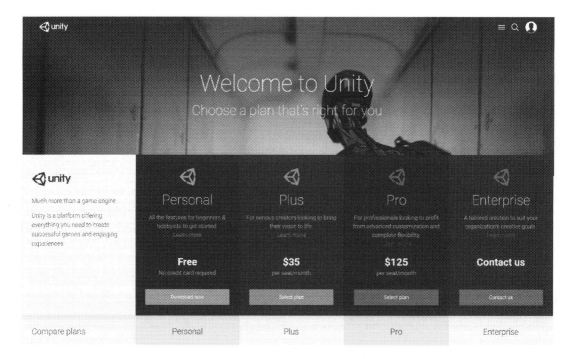

Figure 2-5. *For most people, the free personal plan will more than suffice*

Personal

The free account that you'll want to start with is the Personal account. This account costs nothing, and Unity doesn't even take royalties. The only restriction is that you're not allowed to make more than $100K per year on this license. That's fine, though, because you can simply switch to one of the other licensing agreements once you start turning over big numbers. Keep in mind that this $100K restriction also applies to money *raised*, meaning that if you raise money on Kickstarter and it exceeds $100K, then that counts. This rule also goes for profit that comes from other sources, including pay-per-click advertising or in-app purchases.

There are also a couple of missing features and restrictions with the Personal account. For instance, creators using the Personal account are required to feature the Unity splash screen when the game boots up (showing users that you made the game in Unity), and you won't have access to the real-time developer analytics or Cloud Build. For multiplayer online games, the Personal account only allows 20 players at once.

Unity Plus

Unity Plus currently costs $35 per month and removes the splash screen while increasing the revenue cap up to $200K per fiscal year. It also adds extra support and features that might be useful for larger developers, such as support for 50 concurrent users and discounted asset kits.

Unity Pro

Unity Pro hikes the price up to $125 per month and completely removes the revenue cap, meaning you can become incredibly rich without paying anything more if you so wish. It also provides a number of pro services, including support for up to 200 concurrent players, more analytics and performance, support for large teams, and more.

Unity Enterprise

Finally, Enterprise membership lets you pick and choose features to create a tailored development platform specific to your independent needs. This is the most premium option, and the price actually isn't listed at all—which rather suggests it is very expensive. In short, it's not going to be something most people reading this book need to worry about for a while yet. In fact, for the vast majority of people, the basic Personal account will more than suffice and should provide all the features and flexibility you require.

▒ **Note** These are the prices at the time of writing, but they're of course subject to change. It's also possible to save money by paying annually, and you should research this further if you're looking to pay for a more advanced account.

Here is a handy table comparing the various features:

Personal	Plus	Pro
All engine features	All engine features	All engine features
All platforms	All platforms	All platforms
Continuous updates	Continuous updates	Continuous updates
Royalty free	Royalty free	Royalty free
MWU splash screen	Custom splash screen	Custom splash screen
Revenue capped at $100K	Revenue capped at $200K	No revenue cap
Standard queue for Unity cloud build	Priority queue for Unity cloud build	Concurrent builds for Unity cloud build
Personal analytics	Plus analytics	Pro analytics
20 concurrent players	50 concurrent players	200 concurrent players
Unity in-app purchases	Unity in-app purchases	Unity in-app purchases
Unity ads	Unity ads	Unity ads
Beta access	Beta access	Beta access
	Pro editor UI skin	Pro editor UI skin
	Performance reporting	Performance reporting
	Flexible seat management	Flexible seat management
	Asset kits 20% off	Asset kits 40% off
	Unity certification courseware 1 month access	Unity certification courseware 3 month access
		Source code access ($)
		Premium support ($)

Downloading Unity and Required Components

Okay, I think I've prattled on long enough. Let's get started with the technical stuff. You're of course going to need to set up Unity and get it running on your computer. This is straightforward enough for the most part, but bear in mind that you'll also need a few additional pieces of software too. Specifically, you'll need to download and install the following:

- Unity itself

- The Android SDK (along with Android Studio 2.3)

- The Java JDK

- Visual Studio

The Android SDK is the Android Software Development Kit. This is a set of software tools provided by Google that can act like a bridge in accessing the functionality of your hardware. In other words, it provides source code that Unity needs to make your games compatible on the Android platform. It also contains a few other tools that might be useful for you in the future—including an emulator that will allow you to test Android apps right on your desktop. You also need to opt to install Android Build Support, but you do this through the Unity Installer, so there's no need to download that separately.

The Java JDK (Figure 2-6) is another development kit, this time for Java. This is what your computer needs to support Java development, and because Java is the main language of Android, you'll need it to go ahead. We'll be downloading this first.

Figure 2-6. *The Java logo*

Visual Studio is what you'll use to handle the actual programming in Unity. When you start writing scripts, you'll edit these in a separate Visual Studio window—but we can worry about that later. Note that you don't actually *need* Visual Studio, and it's possible to use alternative options such as MonoDevelop. But Visual Studio is certainly the preferred option of the two and will make your life a little easier.

Downloading Unity

To start downloading Unity, first head over to Unity3D.com (`https://unity3d.com`) and click Get Unity Now. You'll then be able to choose the plan you want (Personal, in most cases), and there you'll simply click Download Now and then Download Installer on the next page (Figure 2-7). Once you do that, the download will begin.

Figure 2-7. *This is where you will find Unity*

You don't need to download Visual Studio separately, because you can do that through the Unity Downloader. That saves you a little time and trouble.

Downloading the Java JDK

If you're feeling a little overwhelmed at this point, don't worry. Once you've installed all these bits and pieces, they'll operate on their own in the background and you can forget all about them. This is a one-off procedure (unless you set Unity up on a new computer) that you never need worry about again.

The Java JDK is what allows your computer and therefore Unity to understand and interpret Java code. Head over to `www.oracle.com/technetwork/java/javase/downloads/index-jsp-138363.html` and download the Java SE Development Kit (Figure 2-8). Make sure you select the x64 version if your computer will support it.

Figure 2-8. *The Java JDK download page*

Downloading the Android SDK

To download the Android SDK, head over to `https://developer.android.com/studio/index.html` (Figure 2-9). Click the Download Android Studio button, accept the terms and conditions, and let the download begin. If you're running a computer with a relatively small hard drive, click Download Options instead. Android Studio is the standard Android IDE used for creating regular apps, and you don't actually need this to use Unity. To save yourself a huge unnecessary file, you can just download the command line tools and then use the SDKManager included in order to download the rest of the SDK. You'll find instructions on how to do this on the Android Studio web site.

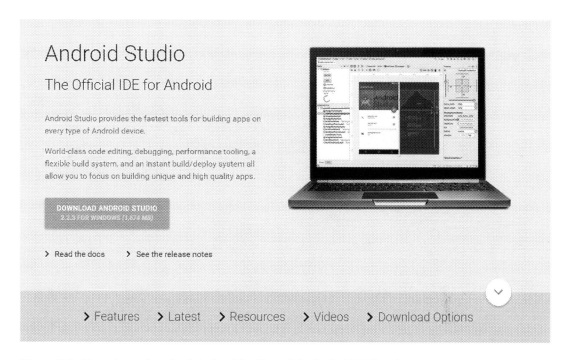

Figure 2-9. *It's easiest to download Android Studio and the Android SDK at the same time*

This is more complicated, though, and Android Studio is certainly a useful thing to have around, so if you can afford the space, I recommend just installing the whole package once you have Java.

Installing Unity 3D

Once everything is downloaded, it's an easy enough process to begin installation. Start by finding the files where you saved them and then double-clicking each one in turn. It doesn't really matter which one you start with, and all necessary steps are explained in this section.

Unity

When you double-click the Unity Installer and accept the terms of the license agreement, you'll then need to choose which version of Unity to download: 64-bit or 32-bit. The best version will depend on your version of Windows because not all computers support 64-bit. To check whether you have an x64- or x32-bit processor, head to This PC, right-click, and then go to Properties (Figure 2-10). If your computer is 64-bit, it will read: "64-bit Operating System, x64-based processor."

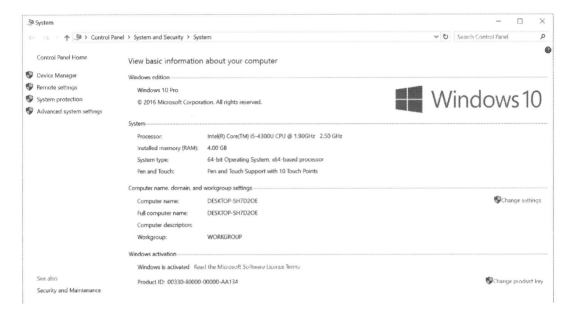

Figure 2-10. *This Surface Pro 3 is 64-bit*

If you *can* support 64-bit, then that's the one to go for because it will enable console support and other features. The next screen you'll be shown is the Download Assistant screen. This lets you choose which components you want to install along with Unity and it shows you how much space you require on your computer.

On the left, a lot of different options are ticked, and there will be some boxes that are left unticked. By default, you should find the following are selected:

- Unity 5.5 0f3

- Documentation

- Standard Assets

- Microsoft Visual Studio Community 2015

It should look like Figure 2-11. Leave all these as they are, as they're all important. Unity and Documentation are self-explanatory, whereas Microsoft Visual Studio Community 2015 is what will allow you to create and edit scripts in your game (discussed earlier). The Standard Assets option isn't compulsory but will come in very handy—this is a large selection of pre-made scripts, sprites, 3D models, textures, and more that you are free to use in your own games. If you have the space, then adding these is a *very* good idea. If you think you'll want to develop for any of the other platforms listed (and you have the space), go ahead and tick those options too.

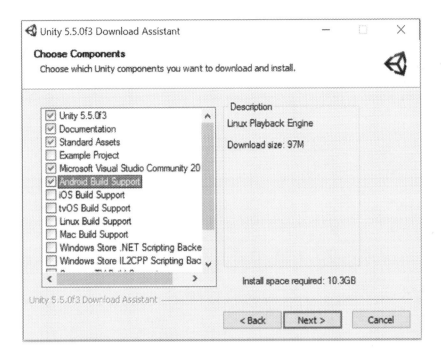

Figure 2-11. *Tick these boxes for smooth sailing later on*

There's one more that *isn't* selected by default, though, that you want to make sure you get: Android Build Support. This is what will ensure that you can create APK files to upload to the Play Store and *will* be required when you test and complete your project. Make sure it's ticked.

You'll also notice iOS Build Support here, as well as Mac Build Support, Windows Store options, and more. The good news is that you'll be able to come back and add these in later if you need to. You'll notice how much space is required (around 10.3 GB at the time of writing), and if you have that available on your hard drive, you can go ahead and click Next again.

Now choose where you want Unity to be installed on your computer. This is entirely a matter of preference, but do make a mental note of it. Accept some more terms of agreement, hit Next again, and then wait for Unity to install.

Go and make yourself a cup of coffee, as this does tend to take a fair bit of time.

The Java JDK

Installing the Java JDK is very simple. Just double-click the file and click Next twice, and it will begin (Figure 2-12).

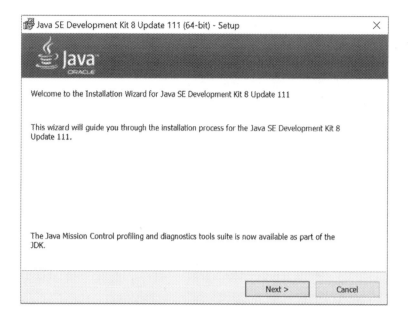

Figure 2-12. *The JDK installer*

After a few progress bars have been filled, you'll be given the option of choosing a destination folder. At the time of writing, the default is C:\Program Files\Java\jre1.8.0_111 (Figure 2-13). It's fine to leave it as this, but you may want to make a note of it for later. Click Next again, the installer will finish, and you'll be ready to take the next step: installing the Android SDK.

Figure 2-13. *Set your destination folder*

The Android SDK

Finally, you need to install the Android SDK. To do that, you install the Android-Studio-Bundle. Double-click the .exe you downloaded earlier and then click Next on the welcome screen (Figure 2-14) to get to the first set of options.

Figure 2-14. *The Android Studio installer*

Here you will choose what you want to install (Figure 2-15). Annoyingly, you can't deselect Android Studio (because Google) but you can decide whether you want the Android SDK and Virtual Device.

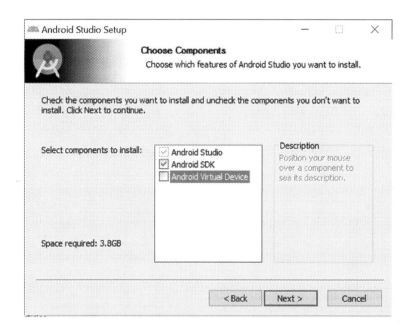

Figure 2-15. *Decide whether you need the AVD*

The SDK is the main bit we need, so make sure to leave that ticked. The Android Virtual Device meanwhile is an emulator that you're going to be able to use to run apps. Unless you're making a very simple puzzle game or you have a *seriously* beefy gaming rig (we're talking two GTX1080s with a 4 GHz CPU here), you're probably not going to be able to use this much to test your fully realized games. You can test live on your Android device too, so you may want to untick this one if you want to save yourself 1 GB of data. That said, it can be useful for other testing purposes (experimenting with screen sizes, for instance), so this is your call.

Either way, click Next and then agree to the terms and conditions. On the next screen (Figure 2-16), you can choose the location for installing both the SDK and Android Studio. If the latter is obtuse (by default, it might be: C:\Users\rushd\AppData\Local\Android\sdk), then find somewhere simpler to install it that has 3.2 GB+ of free space. Make a note of where this is, because you'll need the path later. I've chosen C:\ AndroidSDK, seeing as the path isn't allowed to include spaces (annoyingly).

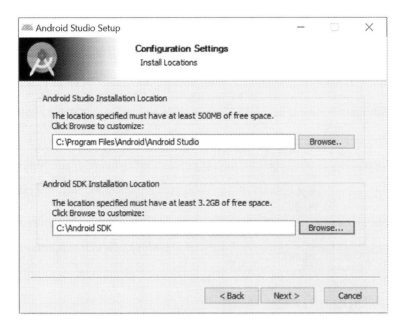

Figure 2-16. *Finally, set your destination folder*

Click Next and again on the next screen, and then the installation will begin.

Hardware and Workflow

While all this stuff downloads, let's take this brief interlude to consider the best hardware for creating your games and achieving the best setup.

The good news is, your PC doesn't need to be particularly powerful in order to handle Unity, but you will want something at least fairly modern. I personally run Unity on a Dominator Pro GT72 6RE as well as on a Surface Pro 3 (Figure 2-17). The Dominator Pro is a very new VR-ready gaming laptop with a GTX1070 GPU and has no difficulty whatsoever with Unity. The Surface Pro 3 is definitely on the lower end in terms of ideal specs for Android development with Unity. Although I've never been unable to do anything, the system does get rather hot while I'm coding, and some 3D games can see dropped frame-rates.

Figure 2-17. *A device like the Surface lets you work on the move*

Based on this, I would say the Surface Pro 3 (i5) model represents pretty much the minimum specs you'll want to work with. That means:

- 1.9 GHz Processor (turbo boost up to 2.6 GHz)

- Integrated graphics

- 4GB RAM

The Unity website recommends higher, though, and suggests that developers have at least some form of dedicated graphics card or DX11 with feature level 9.3 capabilities. More RAM would also be preferable, especially if you intend to use other software like Photoshop (or free alternatives like Fusion, DaVinci, or GIMP) for creating large images and multitasking between tools. You'll also want higher specs if you plan on testing your games with emulators, though you can struggle with this even when using extremely capable machines.

A GPU is a graphics processor that's used to render 3D scenes more quickly. This might not be a big issue if you're developing largely in 2D (which the majority of this book will be devoted to) but it certainly doesn't hurt to give yourself options. Likewise, it would be useful for the section on 3D modeling with Blender.

As well as a GPU, another useful addition is to have both HDD and SSD hard drives. SSDs are *solid state disks*—an alternative to hard disk drives—and are very fast but generally somewhat smaller than the slower, older HDDs. It's standard to get SSDs of around 128 GB or 256 GB. Because Unity, the Android SDK, and Android Studio all take up a lot of space, it may be handy to keep at least some of these files on the HDD while keeping your OS and game files on the SSD for speed. Again though, this is a preference, not a requirement.

In short, it's possible to make do with a mid-range PC but it would certainly be preferable to use a gaming rig of some kind. Apart from anything else, having a rig capable of playing games will be useful for research purposes.

Creating Your Battlestation (Work Setup)

It's also worth thinking about your actual setup and work environment because this can make a big difference to your enjoyment during development and can save you headaches later on. One big advantage, for example, is to have a large monitor and possibly even an ultrawide 21:9 display (Figure 2-18). Unity has lots of different windows and panels as we'll see in Chapter 3, and it is a big advantage to be able to see all these at the same time so you can juggle tasks more easily. A big screen will provide a big boost to your multitasking, help you avoid eye strain, and improve immersion (removing distraction).

Figure 2-18. *A superior setup*

If you prefer to work on a laptop, make sure it's one with a larger screen (18.3 inches or larger) and has enough horsepower to cope. There is something to be said for working in cafes over a cup of coffee (I find it enhances productivity), but for that you'll ideally want a newish laptop from the likes of Razer, Asus, Dell, HP, Lenovo, or Toshiba. A Surface Book or a MacBook will also do the job nicely. Of course, our installation instructions are aimed at Windows users, so if you'll be running on a Mac, you'll need to go through a slightly different process to get up and running.

You'll want a comfortable keyboard, of course, and a precise mouse for typing and dragging and dropping. A wired keyboard is preferable to improve responsiveness when testing games on the computer. If you're shelling out in order to create the best possible setup, something like a Corsair Gaming keyboard will be a joy not only to type on but also to test and play games on.

Otherwise, make sure you have a comfortable chair, ideally a large desk space to spread out and arrange notes and sketches, and a room that's as free from distraction as possible. If you manage all that, you'll be good to get started and you should find that your work goes as smoothly and as enjoyably as possible. If you plan on doing a lot of development, investing in a good space for work is a good way to spend your money and will result in a better end product completed more quickly.

Starting Your First Project

Installation finished? Great!

At this point, you should have Unity and all the necessary components you need for it installed on your computer and ready to go. And hopefully you're eager to jump in and get started. In that case, let's launch Unity for the first time and do just one last bit of setup.

First you'll need to sign in to the account you created on the web site. If you haven't done that already, click the link (Create One) and you'll be taken to the relevant page where you can set one up. You can then log in using your new Unity ID and you'll need to confirm that your company is making less than the threshold if you want to stick with the free account.

Once you're past that screen, you'll be greeted by window that lets you select from existing projects or start a new one. You'll probably have nothing here for now, seeing as this is your first ever time using it. So click New and choose a name and location for your project (Figure 2-19). You also need to make sure that you choose 2D so the game will automatically support a 2D format.

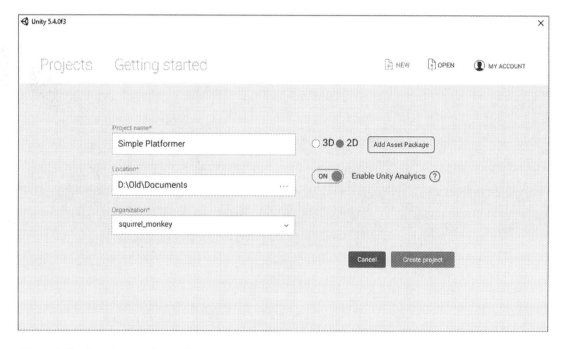

Figure 2-19. *Starting your first project*

It doesn't matter what you call the game at this point—this is only the name of the folder. You can change the name of the APK to whatever you like later on. For now, let's just call it Simple Platformer. Enter that, tick 2D, and then click Create Project. Give it a second and you'll be greeted by a rather empty Unity project. There are lots of windows, and it probably looks a little confusing at this point, but don't worry, we're going to go through what everything does in the very next chapter.

Setting Paths

Let's do one last bit of setup by telling Unity where the Android SDK is located on our system. Head to the top menu and find Edit ➤ Preferences ➤ External Tools. You'll then find a space to input the location of the Android SDK (main folder) and the Java JDK (file), as shown in Figure 2-20. If you made a note of these paths earlier on, copy and paste them into here. Otherwise, hit Browse and navigate to the right locations. If your folder is located in AppData, it may be hidden, so tell File Explorer to Show Hidden Items (under the View tab) and then track it down manually. It's there somewhere—just keep looking.

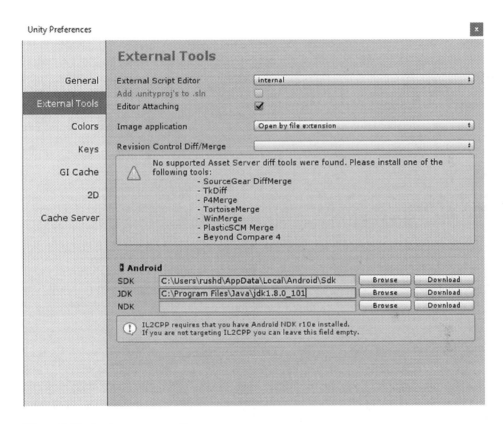

Figure 2-20. *Setting up your paths*

You won't actually need to worry about this until you come to test your app for the first time, but it's good to have everything set up before we begin. If you want, you can skip this stage for now but just be sure to come back to it when it comes to the first launch of your game.

With that done, Unity is now set up and ready to go. It's time to get excited because in Chapter 3 we're going to start actually using it, arranging some GameObjects, and even introducing very basic physics.

■ ■ ■

Finding Your Way Around Unity

So Unity is now up and running, and there's nothing left standing in your way. Time to get going.

Before you build anything, let's first get you acquainted with the different UI elements, controls, and options. You're going to be spending a lot of time here, so it's a good idea to familiarize yourself.

What's All This Then? Getting Acquainted with the IDE

When you get your first look at Unity (Figure 3-1), it can all appear rather confusing with lots of different windows, menus, and options. Fortunately, it's all a lot simpler than it looks once you get going. We'll go over what each of these different views is for over the course of this chapter and at the same time we'll be able to test our first very simple application.

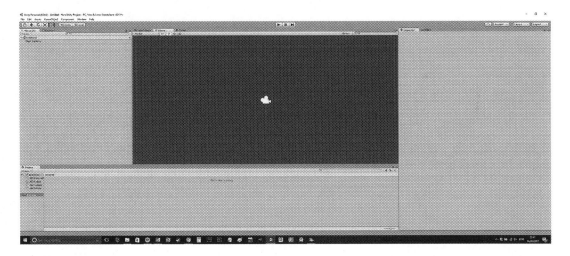

Figure 3-1. *Welcome to Unity! You'll be spending a lot of time here*

First, the views.

© Adam Sinicki 2017

A. Sinicki, *Learn Unity for Android Game Development*, DOI 10.1007/978-1-4842-2704-6_3

Scene

Right in the center of Unity is a view called Scene. This is where a lot of your work is going to get done and is essentially the window where you'll move your various GameObjects and arrange everything. This shows you a view of the level/menu screen that you're working on at any given time and lets you select and reposition elements around the screen. You can zoom in and out and if you were in 3D mode you'd also be able to move the camera around 360 degrees.

Asset Store

At the top of the Scene window (Figure 3-2) are two tabs that allow you to change between two different functions. Hit the Asset Store tab, and as you might expect, the Scene view will be changed for the Asset Store view. The Asset Store is where you browse for various assets—scripts, GameObjects, sprites, effects, and more—to include in your own application. These assets are developed by other Unity developers, as well as by Unity Technologies. Some are free and others cost money; some are very simple additions to existing projects, whereas others are practically entire ready-made games for you to edit as you like.

Figure 3-2. *Scene, Game, and Asset Store tabs*

In short, the Asset Store makes your life considerably easier by ensuring that you won't need to create every single script and sprite by hand.

That said, this isn't something you're going to be needing for a while, so for now keep the tab on Scene and don't worry about it.

Game

There may be a third tab on this window, as shown in the preceding figure, called Game. This view is where you'll see the actual game as it will appear when it's live. And when you play the game, this is where it will be located (unless you choose to maximize the game as you play it).

If Game isn't located in the same place, it will be around there somewhere. You have freedom to change the positions of the windows, and sometimes after an update, the default setup can get moved around. Most people should find that everything is in the same place and they can follow along with these instructions. If not, you should be able to locate each element pretty quickly.

You can't drag and drop elements into the Game view (as you can in the Scene view) and you can't select them or move them around either. That said, for the most part Game view will mirror what you're seeing in the Scene view with a few differences. For one, the perspective will be fixed to the in-game camera, meaning you'll see what your players will see when they launch the game. Likewise, when there are multiple items sharing the same X and Y coordinates, the item on top will be the one closest to the camera along the Z axis, rather than the one selected.

If this all sound a little confusing, don't worry about it—it will make sense once you see how it all works (and that applies to all the windows).

Services

Usually located to the right of the Scene view is the Services tab, which shares a window with the Inspector. This includes such things as ads for monetization, analytics for learning about how your players are enjoying your games, multiplayer, and so forth. Note that some of these features will be missing or limited if you have the free version.

For now, you can completely ignore this window. These services will mainly come into effect for more ambitious projects and only once those apps are live in the Play Store.

Inspector

Next comes the tab that often shares its window with Services: the Inspector (Figure 3-3). The Inspector is what you will use to see and edit details of GameObjects. So when you select a GameObject like a sprite in the Scene view, you'll then be able to use the Inspector in order to view things like the name of the object, the dimensions, any scripts that might be attached, and so on.

41

Figure 3-3. Inspector and Services

You'll be using the Inspector a *lot*, so keep this where you can see it. Right now, though, it will be completely blank.

Project

Normally located along the bottom of the screen is a window for the Project and Console tabs (and sometimes Game will be here too). The Project tab should be open by default and is where you can see all the individual files associated with your project. Along the left portion of the window is the directory where you can select a folder, and on the right are the contents of that folder. Right now, your project only has one folder called Assets. And in that folder is ... nothing.

This will be a useful window as you work because it will allow you to find sprites that you've created with other software and rename or delete files that you need for your game.

Console

Next to the Project tab is the Console tab (Figure 3-4). This is where you can get information regarding the status of Unity and your app. You'll be able to see debug information, crash reports, and errors, and this can help you identify issues in your code or work out just why your game won't run or compile. This will come in handy, but we won't need to worry about it for a little while, so keep Project visible in front of it for now.

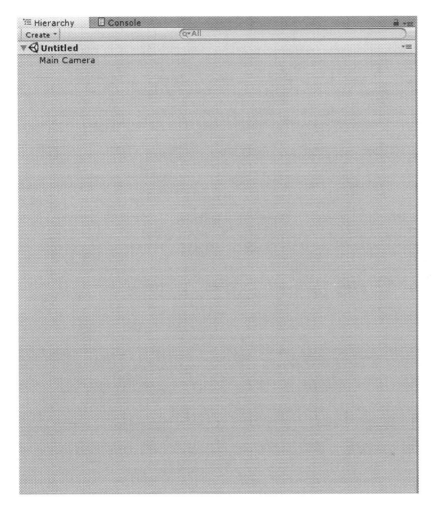

Figure 3-4. *The Hierarchy and Console*

Hierarchy

Finally, one of the most important elements in the UI is the Hierarchy (shown in Figure 3-4), which is almost always found on the left of the Scene view. Hierarchy shows a list of all the GameObjects in your scene at any given time, and when you select one of them the Scene view will center on it; it will also be opened in the Inspector. This lets you quickly find specific GameObjects to make edits, and it's also the only way you can select "invisible" objects like checkpoints. The Hierarchy can also be very handy when you want to select multiple objects (maybe all of your collectibles, for example) and has a useful search utility for quickly retrieving specific items.

Keeping a tidy Hierarchy is good practice and will help you to work a lot more quickly and efficiently going forward.

Housekeeping

I recommend that you leave the windows in their default configuration in most cases. They have been arranged like that for a reason (it works), and this will make it easier for you to follow along with the instructions in this book. The Console or others might not be in precisely the same place, but we'll mainly be using the Scene, Game, Project, and Inspector windows for now. Don't worry about the rest.

But if you find that the UI feels cramped or you just don't like the way it's arranged at any point, you can hover the mouse pointer over any of the dividing lines to change the relative sizes. You can also drag tabs from one window to another, close them entirely, or bring them back using the options in the Window menu. You may have already noticed that there are additional windows that you can open, found in the Window menu, including the likes of Audio Mixer, Animator, and Sprite Packer. Some of these we'll be using later, but for now you don't need to worry about them; you should be able to do mostly everything with the Hierarchy, Scene, Project, Game, Asset Store, Console, and Inspector windows.

Getting Your Toes Wet with Objects and Scenes

That's enough theory—time to get practical. To really understand how these windows work and what you need to do to get started, the best thing to do is to start building something. Once you do that, you will see firsthand how everything works together and how you'll manage your workflow once you get developing.

Adding Sprites

To get started then, let's begin by adding our first GameObject. That is going to be a simple 2D square.

Unlike working with 3D objects, there are no simple shapes for you to insert in 2D. That means that any 2D objects you introduce must be created first as sprites. Creating a square is simple enough, though: we can literally start a new MSPaint file, resize it to 50 x 50 pixels, and then just fill the space with a single block color. Save that as a PNG file and drag it from wherever you saved it into your project folder. Call it Square for simplicity. You can see my Square in Figure 3-5.

Figure 3-5. *Square. Not quite triple-A graphics.*

To help us get into good habits early on, we'll first create a folder in our project specifically for sprites. And in the spirit of good habits and good nomenclature, we'll call the folder Sprites. To do this, right-click your Assets folder in the Project window and then go to Create ➤ Folder (Figure 3-6) and name the folder Sprites. It should look like Figure 3-7 once you're finished.

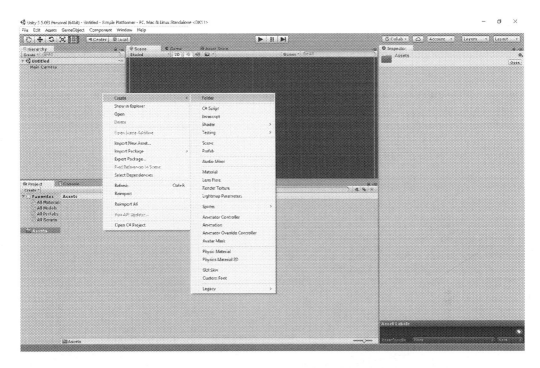

Figure 3-6. *Creating new folders is very simple*

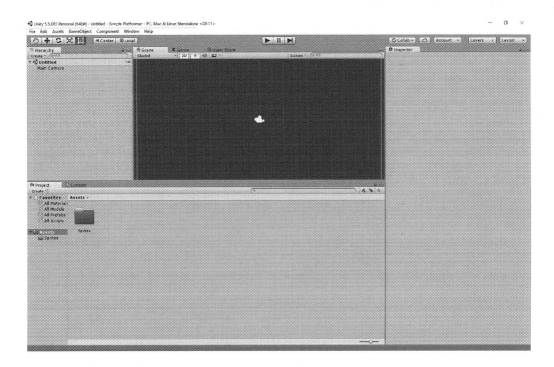

Figure 3-7. *Your Sprites folder should look like this. It's a folder. Called sprites.*

As we go, we'll be creating more folders for our scripts, sounds, scenes, and more—it's smart to create lots of folders to help keep everything separate and so we can quickly retrieve the type of file we need at any given time.

Once you've made that folder, you can simply drag the square.png file from Windows Explorer into your Sprites folder. Note that at any time, you'll also be able to right-click your Project window and select Show in Explorer. This will show you the Assets directory within your project, and anything you put in here will show up in the Project window once you refresh the view.

With that, the sprite is now a part of your project. And you can use the exact same process whether you want to add sprites of trees, collectibles, enemies, or anything else into your levels. It really is that simple.

Two Ways to Introduce GameObjects

There are two ways to add this simple GameObject into the scene, and we're going to go through both of them here because I feel it's a good learning opportunity.

The most straightforward way is simply to click the sprite in your Project window and then drag it straight into your scene and drop it. You'll then see that it appears in your Scene view and also that it's listed in your Hierarchy on the right (Figure 3-8). If it's selected, details about the square will show in your Inspector window as well. Click your Game view and you'll see that square against a different shade of blue in the background.

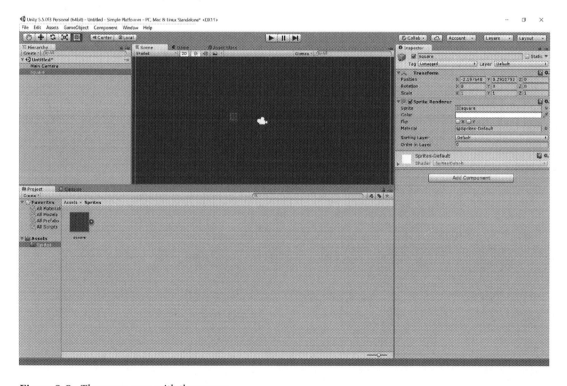

Figure 3-8. *The scene, now with the square*

The other way to add sprites like this to your Scene is to head over to the top menu and then click GameObject ➤ 2D Object ➤ Sprite (Figure 3-9). When you do this, a New Sprite will appear in your Hierarchy window, but you won't be able to see it in the Scene view because it currently doesn't have an image file associated with it. It will have a translucent circle around its coordinates, however, whenever it's selected.

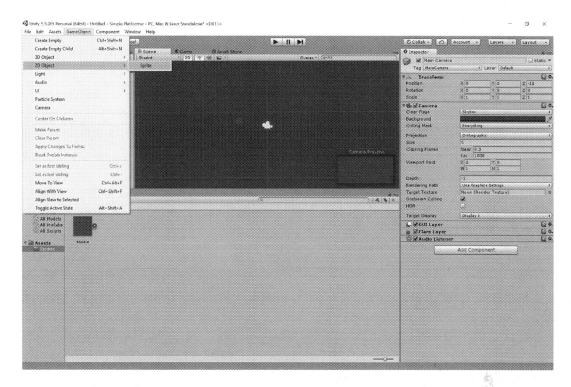

Figure 3-9. *The second way to insert your sprite*

With New Sprite selected in the Hierarchy, open up the Inspector window and notice the section called Sprite Rendered. In here, the first line says "Sprite: None (Sprite)." You can simply drag and drop your Square file into here or you can click the small circular button next to the box to choose it from a file selector dialog (Figure 3-10).

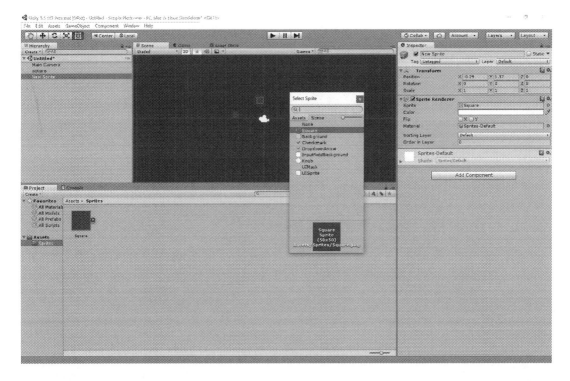

Figure 3-10. *Using the Sprite Renderer*

While you're in the Inspector, why not also take this opportunity to change the name of your second sprite (currently New Sprite) to something more interesting … like Square 2.

Try both these methods and you'll have two different sprites on the screen in your Scene window: Square 1 and Square 2. It should look like Figure 3-11.

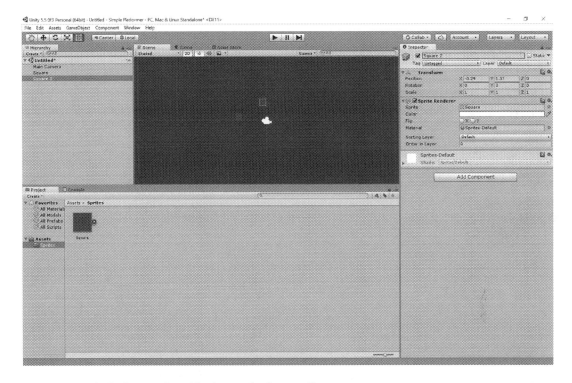

Figure 3-11. *If it looks something like this, you're doing well*

Manipulating GameObjects

As you might have guessed already, you can very easily move your new sprites around in the Scene view simply by clicking them and dragging them around the screen. As you do this, you'll notice that the coordinates change in the Inspector. Under Transform, the X and Y values of Position change as you move the square, as I have done in Figure 3-12.

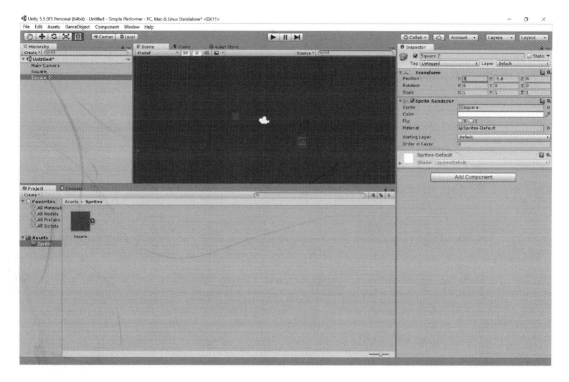

Figure 3-12. *Change the X and Y coordinates in the Inspector to move your sprites*

That means you can just as easily change the positions by entering numbers in the Inspector. This will come in handy if you need to line things up perfectly or set them in a very specific position (something you'll do a lot of). We'll see later on though that there are also more effective ways to ensure that everything stays nicely lined up and snapped to a grid while we work.

"What about Z?" I hear you ask! Well, the Z axis is largely redundant when creating 2D games, though not entirely. We'll see later on that you can use this option to create a parallax scrolling effect and that it can also be useful for defining which sprite should be rendered for the player to see when there are multiple located in the same place. This can also be controlled by changing the Z order, which we'll also look at later on.

Rotation and Scale

You may have noticed that you also have two more interesting options under Transform here in the Inspector: these are Rotation and Scale. They pretty much do what they say and allow you to alter the rotation and the size of your sprites. We'll ignore Rotation for now because we won't be needing that for a while. But you'll find that if you change Scale X and Y from 1 to 2, your sprite doubles in size.

Manipulating GameObjects in the Scene View

If you wanted to do this freehand, you could opt to alternatively use the tools along the top of screen, on the left just above the Hierarchy window. These tools include a hand and various arrows doing different things, as shown in Figure 3-13.

Figure 3-13. *The tools you'll be using in the Scene view*

These tools change the way you interact with the Scene view. You simply click the tool you want to indent it and select it:

- The hand at the furthest left lets you drag the screen around and move your view, which is useful for scrolling through a large level.

- The tool that looks like four arrows on a compass is what you use to move specific GameObjects around the screen (see Figure 3-14). You can simply click the GameObject and start moving it around freely in the Scene view, or you can select it and then drag either the red or green arrow to move it solely in the X or Y axis respectively.

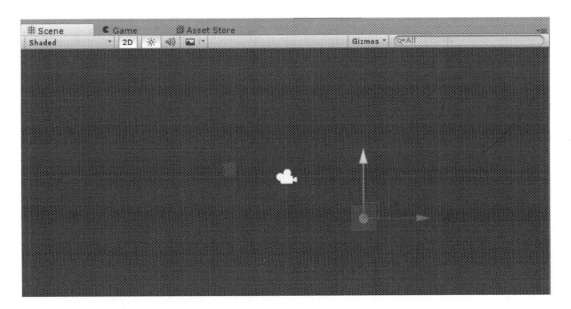

Figure 3-14. *The drag tool*

- The two curved arrows indicate the rotation tool. Select this and a circle will appear around the selected game object that will allow you to rotate it in two dimensions.

- Then you have the scale tool, which again gives you two arrows that you can use to scale the object along each axis.

- The final tool is your jack of all trades. It lets you drag GameObjects, resize them by pulling on the corner, or draw squares to select multiple objects in one go.

Whether you move your objects around freehand with the tools or by changing numbers in the Inspector, you can arrange your sprites however you like and conceivably create some nice-looking landscapes.

But let's not get ahead of ourselves....

Testing the Game and Using the Camera

If there's one control in the UI that's likely to have caught your eye, it's the play button. The good news is that this does exactly what you would hope: it allows you to test the game.

Hit the play button and your game will run in the Game window, showing you two squares located on a light blue background. It's probably not going to take the world by storm, but congratulations, you just ran your first working program (Figure 3-15)! This is our "Hello World," and things only get a lot more fun from here.

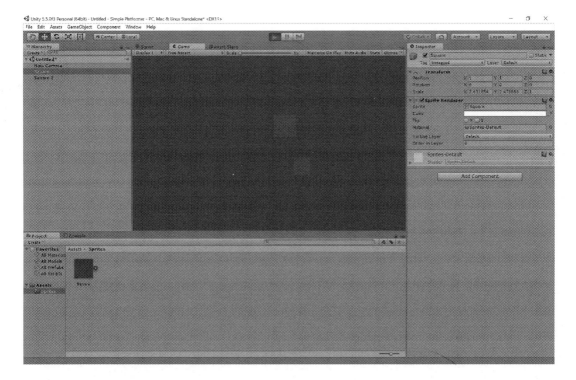

Figure 3-15. *Your first "game"—congrats!*

While the game is playing, you can view it in the Game view (Figure 3-15) and you can continue to make edits via the Inspector or in the Scene window. Just keep in mind that when you do this, nothing will save. If you move a sprite while the game is running, it will then jump back to the position where it last was as soon as you stop it again. Use this for previewing changes "live" but not for making permanent alterations to your code. Try and drum this into your head right now. It's not uncommon to move a bunch of things around and change a bunch of code, only to find out that you forgot to stop the game from running first and lose it all.

To stop the game at any time, just hit the play button again. Note that if you want the game to be full screen when you hit play, you can click Maximize On Play. This is useful when you're testing your game properly, or you just want to have a good go at it. Figure 3-16 is what our game currently looks like when blown up.

Figure 3-16. *The same game, only massive*

The Camera

The observant among readers may have noticed that there are more than just two GameObjects in the Hierarchy view. The third object is called Main Camera, and if you select it, you'll see that this is the white camera icon that is floating in your Scene view.

Main Camera is a GameObject, like your sprites, but with a Camera component rather than a sprite. When you add one of these to a scene, it defines where the player's perspective is and what they're going to see on the screen. Try moving the camera around and then hitting play, and you'll find that it changes where the squares appear on the screen—the squares haven't moved, but your perspective has changed.

It may feel odd that your camera is treated in the exact same way as a sprite, but this is what you need to understand about Unity: *everything* is a GameObject. Scripts do not run unless they are attached to GameObjects, and this may require you to rethink the way you approach your code if you're used to other languages. But once you get to grips with it, it's a powerful and flexible way of working.

P.S. This is *not* what is meant by object-oriented programming. It's related... but I'll explain more in a subsequent chapter.

Since we're looking at the camera, let's edit something that you may be finding frustrating: the background color of your Game view. Click the camera and you'll see a setting called Background in the Inspector, which is currently blue. If you select the color, you'll be given the chance to set this to a new color. Choose black—that way your blue squares will stand out a lot more clearly.

Saving Your Project and Scene

Seeing as you're probably incredibly pleased with this amazing creation, it's time you go about saving it to make sure nothing bad comes to it.

There are actually two things you need to save here: the project and the scene. The scene is what you are viewing through your Scene window and it encompasses everything in your Hierarchy right now (two squares and a camera). For all extents and purposes, a scene is a level in most cases, though it could also refer to a title screen or an options menu. It is essentially any collection of GameObjects and scripts that you'll want to load at some point in your game.

To save your project, use the menu along the top and choose File ➤ Save Project.

To save the scene, you'll first want to create a new subfolder in your Assets folder—call it Scenes. Now go to File ➤ Save Scene (Figure 3-17). When the dialog comes up, select the Scenes folder you just created and call the file Level 1. When you have multiple scenes in your project, you'll be able to switch between them simply by double-clicking them from the Scenes folder.

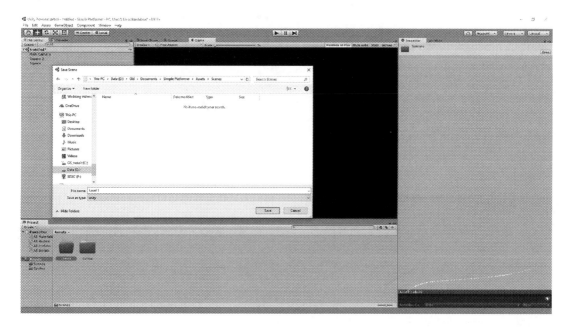

Figure 3-17. *Saving our scene*

A Little More Organization

As we're being so organized and getting into good habits early on, let's make one more sort-of-folder before we move on. Right-click any blank space in your Hierarchy and click Create Empty. This will create an "empty" GameObject, called GameObject. It should already be selected, so head over to the Hierarchy and rename it Squares. You could theoretically turn this empty GameObject into any other kind of GameObject by clicking Add Component and then choosing the Camera component or the Sprite Renderer, for example. Instead we're keeping it empty, which will let us attach other GameObjects to it and thereby use it as a makeshift grouping (Figure 3-18).

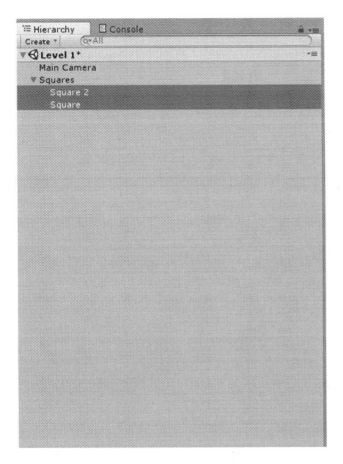

Figure 3-18. *Start organizing your Hierarchy now and you'll be very glad you did*

Drag your two squares from where they are onto your empty GameObject, and they will now be filed underneath it. The arrow just next to the empty GameObject will also now allow you to expand and collapse those items. This isn't really necessary at this point, but trust me, when you have 200 collectible coins, 30 enemies, and 700 tiles on your screen, you'll be glad for the organization.

One Last Thing to Set Up: Snap Grid Settings

In Chapter 4 things are going to get exciting: we're going to add physics to our squares so that they can fall and bounce around, and that's just the start. Before we do that, though, we should handle one more bit of setup and explain one more piece of the UI.

You may have noticed that there is a grid in your Scene view and wondered what all that was about. This grid is made up of *units*, which can represent whatever you want them to in order to help you organize your sprites around the screen. What do you call a program full of units? Unity! (Okay, this isn't really where the name comes from....)

Right now, you'll notice that your squares and units bear no relation. To change that, first set the scale X and scale Y on both squares back to 1. Now open up your Sprites folder and select the Square sprite so that it opens in your Inspector (don't just click one of the Square GameObjects, because that won't work).

You should notice an option for Pixels Per Unit, which may be set to 100 by default. Change that to 50—don't forget to click Apply in the bottom right—and you should find that both squares now immediately change to become the same size as the squares on the grid (as in Figure 3-19). Remember, when we made these sprites, we made them 50 x 50 pixels. By making it so that 1 unit = 50 pixels, we now have perfectly sized squares.

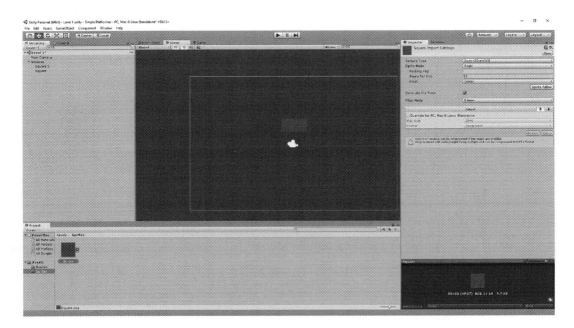

Figure 3-19. *Make sure to set your pixels per unit for every new sprite*

Another useful trick we can use now is to *snap* our sprites into place. While dragging a sprite, hold Ctrl and you will find that it jumps from point to point rather than moving smoothly. You can change how far apart those points are by choosing Edit ➤ Snap Settings. You'll find that this is probably set to 1 for the X and Y axes respectively. If it isn't, change it so that it is (see Figure 3-20).

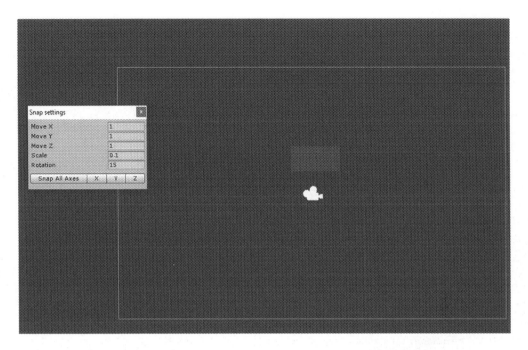

Figure 3-20. *Snap settings*

Close that dialog and free-move one of your squares so that it is positioned exactly within the bounds of one of the grid squares. Now press Ctrl + C (copy) and then Ctrl + V (paste). This will duplicate your Square GameObject to create an exact copy in the exact same place. Hold down Ctrl and drag your square to the right. It should move exactly one tile's width to sit flush next to your previous tile. You can also copy and paste GameObjects by right-clicking and selecting Copy from the Hierarchy view. Do this a few times and you can create stairs and other structures.

This might feel pretty unexciting at this point, but it's actually a very important skill. When creating levels in games, it's really important that all your tiles are perfectly positioned right next to each other and that they don't have tiny pixel-wide gaps between them.

Why not try using a slightly more elaborate sprite and making something that looks like the basics of a level? I've made some grassy steps in Figure 3-21.

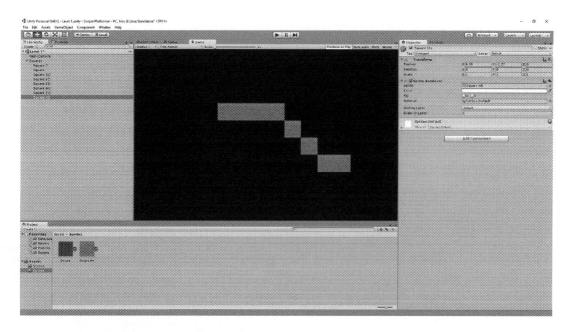

Figure 3-21. *We'll learn how to create sprites and even pixel art in future chapters*

Hey, would you look at that ... we're getting somewhere.

Now let's bring this world to life, shall we?

CHAPTER 4

Adding Physics and Getting Started With Coding

At this point, you now have a world that is starting to look a little bit like a conventional computer game level. In this chapter, we're going to make it *play* like a conventional computer game level by adding some basic physics and movement. For this, you're going to be trying your hand at coding for the first time. Good luck!

So, we have tiled sprites that have a grassy pattern, and to mix things up a little, I've also created a sprite to represent the ground underneath the grass, so that I can get a bit more creative with my level design (see Figures 4-1 and 4-2).

Figure 4-1. *The second ground tile*

Figure 4-2. *Some tiles just ready to be climbed on!*

© Adam Sinicki 2017
A. Sinicki, *Learn Unity for Android Game Development*, DOI 10.1007/978-1-4842-2704-6_4

I created the second dirt sprite the exact same way as the first one and then just copied it around wherever I needed ground underneath the surface of my grass. You can do the same—just remember to hold down Ctrl to keep the distances perfect using the snap to grid feature.

Now we're going to do something even more exciting: create a game character and drop him into our world. To begin with, we're going to make the simplest character sprite we possibly can, which would be another square. In the interest of making things a bit more interesting, we'll also give him eyes.

Meet Squarey (Figure 4-3).

Figure 4-3. *Squarey, mate, you don't look so good*

Squarey can be any size you like, but for simplicity I recommend keeping the same dimensions as you used for the ground tiles.

Now add Squarey into your Sprites folder just as you did with the others. Make sure that you remember to set the Pixels Per Unit to 50 again and then drag him into your scene. Name this new Game Object Player and keep it separate from the Squares folder. It doesn't matter where in the level you want to drag him, but I chose to put him at the top of the hill I created (Figure 4-4).

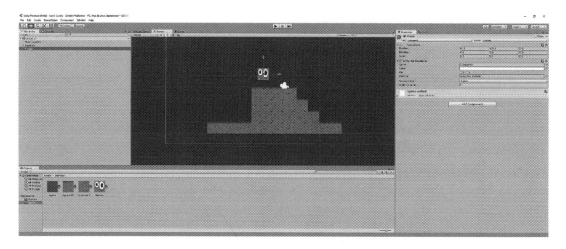

Figure 4-4. *Squarey surveys his domain*

Congratulations! You now have a main character. Problem is, he doesn't actually do anything yet.

So, the next thing we want to do is to apply some physics so that gravity and other things will affect our character. And you won't believe how easy Unity makes this bit.

Using RigidBody 2D

As mentioned, the whole point of using a physics engine like Unity is so that we can access ready-made scripts and elements to avoid coding everything ourselves from scratch. This makes it *incredibly* simple to add something like gravity: all we have to do is drag a script onto our GameObject for it to take effect.

While your player is selected, click Add Component in the Inspector. Now click Physics 2D ➤ RigidBody 2D. RigidBody 2D is the name of a script that works on 2D sprites and applies all the basic physics we could want, such as gravity, friction, momentum, collision, and more.

The easiest way to see what this does, though, is to put it into action. So drag Squarey a little higher in the Scene window and then click play. If everything goes according to plan, we now have a sad-looking Squarey who simply falls from the top of the screen and off the bottom. Squarey, meet gravity!

Using Colliders

The astute will note that there's something missing here. Of course, we don't actually want Squarey to fall through the ground underneath him; we want him to land on it. Fortunately, this is an easy fix too.

Just click Squarey again and then Add Component ➤ Physics 2D ➤ Box Collider. You should now be able to see both RigidBody 2D *and* Box Collider 2D in the Inspector.

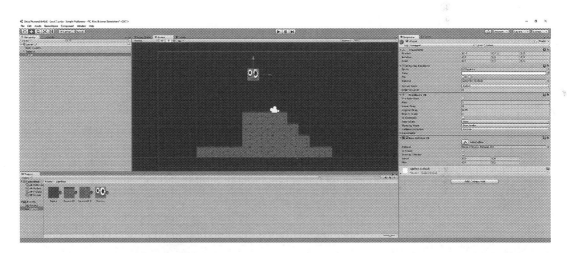

Figure 4-5. *The green outline shows Squarey's collider*

What's more, you should also notice a thin green outline around Squarey. This is the *collider*, which essentially defines the boundaries of your sprite and tells RigidBody 2D where the physical mass that makes up the character starts and stops.

Click play and you'll see that the character still falls through the ground below. Hopefully, you've guessed already that this is because our tiles *also* need to have colliders attached. To do this, drag a square around the tiles in your Scene view using the mouse in order to select them all at once. You can do this just the same way you would select a bunch of icons on your desktop (Figure 4-6), or by clicking the first item in the hierarchy and then the last item while holding down Shift. You can also use Ctrl for making bulk selections, just as you would in most Windows programs. This is a trick that will often come in handy, although there's another method for making mass changes that we will look at shortly. Make sure to deselect the camera and then add a collider in the Inspector. This will now be applied to every GameObject selected all at once.

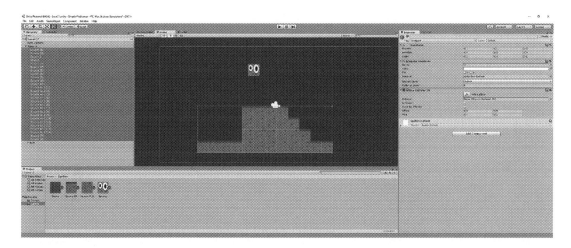

Figure 4-6. *Later we will discuss using prefabs to avoid having to select multiple GameObjects*

Notice that we're not adding the RigidBody 2D to our ground tiles. That's because we don't want them to fall off the screen.

Now click play, and if everything goes according to plan our character will fall and land on the ground (Figure 4-7).

Figure 4-7. *Success!*

If you want to test just how detailed RigidBody 2D is, position Squarey so that he's partly hanging over the edge of one of the steps and then click play again. When he lands, he should tip and actually roll down the stairs.

At this point, we now *already* have a game that acts the way we expect it to. The next step should probably be to make it interactive. Get ready: this is where the actual coding comes in.

Getting Started with Coding in C#

Before you begin coding, we first need to make a folder to contain all of our scripts within the Assets directory. Right-click in the Project view and select Create ➤ Folder, just as you did when you created the Sprites and Scenes folders. Call this new folder Scripts and then open it up.

In here, you're again going to right-click and this time select Create ➤ C# Script. Call this Player and then double-click it to open it. You'll now be opening Visual Studio for the first time. But first, you need to sign in. To do that, you can just use your Microsoft account (the one you probably use to log into Windows and Hotmail). If you don't have one, you'll be given the opportunity to create one.

Once you're in, the UI should look something like Figure 4-8.

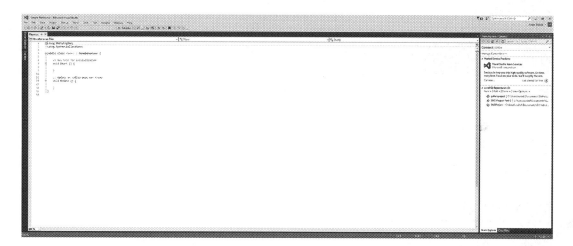

Figure 4-8. *Welcome to Visual Studio*

For now, we're concentrating on that big window in the middle, which is where we can input and edit code. We're choosing to code in C# here because it's somewhat similar to Java—the language used in most Android development—only slightly simpler. One thing to keep in mind when coding in C# is that every line needs to end with a semicolon or an open or closed curly bracket. If you miss this, you'll get an error. You'll probably find that it's surprisingly easy to miss this crucial detail and then spend ages routing through your code trying to find out why it won't run.

What you might also notice here is that the document actually isn't empty but instead has several lines of code already within it. These are *functions*, which are standalone collections of code that are called at specific times. The two functions we have here will be present in every script we create and help to provide a little bit of structure for what we're about to do.

The whole thing should look like the following:

```
using UnityEngine;
using System.Collections;

public class Player : MonoBehaviour {

    // Use this for initialization
    void Start () {
    }
```

```
    // Update is called once per frame
    void Update () {
    }
}
```

Don't worry about the top two lines just yet. The third line that reads `public class` is really just naming the script we've created, and the following two sections (`void Start` and `void Update`) are our functions.

Two other things to note are the forward slashes. Whenever a line starts with two forward slashes in C#, that means it's a comment and that it won't have any effect on the way the code runs. In other words, this is how you can write yourself messages in case you forget what a line of code does. When teams of programmers work together, commenting like this is immensely important to ensure that every member knows what everything does.

The two comments that are already here describe what the functions do. The first one says "`Use this for initialization`", so `void Start` will run whenever the script is first introduced into the scene. The second comment says "`Update is called once per frame`", so `void Update` runs repeatedly at a very fast speed as the game refreshes.

To demonstrate this, let's try and make our character move right across the screen. To do that, we first need to refer to some important elements that we're going to be working with in the code. In this case, we need to work with the RigidBody 2D script that is attached to our `Player` GameObject. And to do that, we need to add the following code:

```
public class Controls : MonoBehaviour {
    public Rigidbody2D rb;

    void Start () {
        rb = GetComponent<Rigidbody2D>();
    }
```

What's happening here is that we're creating a reference to *a* RigidBody 2D and calling it `rb` (short for RigidBody). Then, when the script initializes, we're telling it that the *instance* of RigidBody 2D to work with is the GameObject that our script is attached to (in a moment, we'll be attaching this to the `Player` GameObject).

Don't worry if this is all a little confusing: you can just copy and paste the code for now and it will make more sense later on.

Finally, we're going to add the following line of code to our `Update` function:

```
void Update () {
        rb.velocity = new Vector2(1, rb.velocity.y);
    }
```

This is simply adding a veleocity with the value 1 to the horizontal X coordinate of the RigidBody (Vector is a coordinate). Because this is in `Update`, that means that it should run each time the scene refreshes—which happens incredibly quickly. The whole thing should look like the following:

```
using UnityEngine;
using System.Collections;

public class Player : MonoBehaviour {
    public Rigidbody2D rb;
```

```
    // Use this for initialization
    void Start () {
        rb = GetComponent<Rigidbody2D>();
        }

        // Update is called once per frame
        void Update () {
            rb.velocity = new Vector2(1, rb.velocity.y);
    }
}
```

Make sure you remember to save your work!

Now all that is left to do is to head back to Unity and add the Player script to the Player character. We do this just the same as we added RigidBody 2D: select the Player GameObject, click Add Component, and then Scripts ➤ Player. Now click play and you should find that Squarey moves continually to the right and then falls down the steps to his ultimate doom (Figure 4-9).

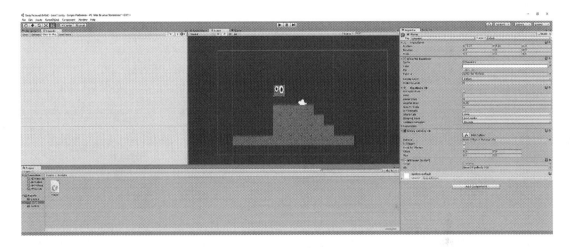

Figure 4-9. *Squarey now has Lemming AI*

Only once you've attached the script to your GameObject will it have any effect, and you could just as easily have added this to a ground tile for the same effect.

Introducing Variables

Now it's time for us to play with some variables. Variables are a very important concept in coding and are where a lot of the logic and versatility come in.

Essentially, *variable* is a shorthand for a piece of data that can be used to represent that data (such as health or a player's name) in the future. Chances are, if you can think back to math at school, you will find you have encountered variables in the past. Remember puzzles like these?

$$10 + x = 13, find\ x$$

Well, in this case, x is a variable that happens to represent 3. But if we were to write it like this

$$10 + x = ?$$

that would allow us to alter the outcome, simply by changing the value of *x* using a key or something similar. We can do the precise same thing when working with variables in C#. For example, we can change the speed that our character moves at by replacing the 1 with a variable called movespeed. But first, we need to define what movespeed means by initializing it. So now our code looks like this:

```
using UnityEngine;
using System.Collections;

public class Player : MonoBehaviour {
    public Rigidbody2D rb;
    public int movespeed;

    // Use this for initialization
    void Start () {
        rb = GetComponent<Rigidbody2D>();
        movespeed = 2;
    }

        // Update is called once per frame
        void Update () {
        rb.velocity = new Vector2(movespeed, rb.velocity.y);
    }
}
```

Squarey will move just the same before, but this time at twice the speed.

When we created our variable, I used some terminology that will be useful to understand. Int, for example, is short for *integer*, which is a type of variable that stores whole numbers. Whenever you define a variable, you always need to tell C# what type of variable you're working with. A few useful ones to know at this point are:

- *Integer*: Any whole number

- *Float*: A *floating point* variable is a number with a decimal point

- *Boolean*: A variable that can be true or false, or 1 or 0

- *String*: A text variable

Meanwhile, public means that the variable can be accessed from outside the script. In fact, this means that we can even edit our movespeed from the Unity UI.

To do that, delete the line that says movespeed = 2 and then select the Player GameObject in Unity. You should see that there's now a Movespeed box in the Inspector, as in Figure 4-10.

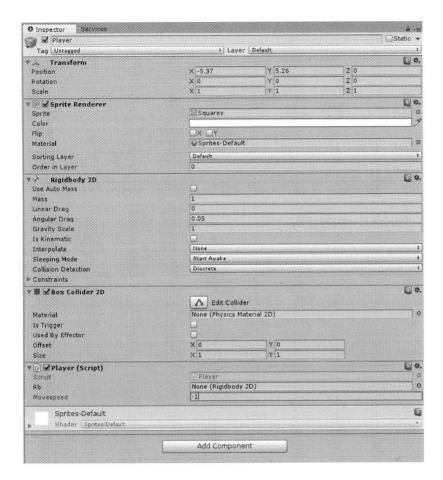

Figure 4-10. *Changing Movespeed in the Inspector*

Try setting this value to –1 and you'll see that Squarey now moves in the opposite direction, away from the stairs and toward the sudden drop. If you don't delete the movespeed = 2 line from the script, this will simply be overwritten every time that the Start function is called. If you don't want the variable to be accessible outside of your code, then simply use the word private instead of public.

For now, let's leave movespeed as 3, because we want Squarey to be a bit faster for the next bit. Although you could have done the same thing without using a variable, this is all very useful to know and you'll see it comes in handy repeatedly as you add more elements to your scenes.

Controlling the Player Character

Seeing our character move around the level and interact with the scenery is pretty exciting, but really we want to be able to *control* the character. The good news is that this is something we can do quite easily by only slightly changing the code we already have. All we need to do is add a couple of if statements, as in the following code:

```
void Update () {
        if (Input.GetKey(KeyCode.LeftArrow))
        {
            rb.velocity = new Vector2(-movespeed, rb.velocity.y);

        }
        if (Input.GetKey(KeyCode.RightArrow))
        {
            rb.velocity = new Vector2(movespeed, rb.velocity.y);

        }
}
```

What's happening here is that the script is checking to see whether there's an input each time the game updates. Of course, KeyCode.LeftArrow and KeyCode.RightArrow refer to the respective keyboard inputs, and we then move the character by movespeed or –movespeed depending on which one was pressed. "If" statements essentially tell a section of code to run only when a specific argument is true. The code inside the curly brackets will run only if the line inside the parentheses is true.

If we were to write this in *pseudo code* (fake "code" that uses normal English terminology to be more easily understandable), then it would translate as follows:

```
If (Player is pressing right) {
Move character to the right
}
```

It's always important that you remember to close the curly bracket at the end of the if statement. If you have any experience with Excel or other spreadsheet software, using if statements like these might be familiar.

■ **Note**   If you were to create an APK (app package for Android - more on this later) and run this on Android right now, it would actually work with a Bluetooth keyboard. Later on though, we'll look at how to implement touchscreen controls.

If you click play now, you should have the exciting opportunity to actually try controlling Squarey—like a real game. Although we've had to write a little bit of code here, hopefully you agree that this is *remarkably* simple all things considered: with just a few lines, we now have a good-looking game world and a character that we can control within it.

More Advanced Logic and Introducing Jumping

Squarey can move left and right like a pro now and is pretty adept at jumping off of things too. You should be feeling like a proud parent. But in order to platform with Mario, Sonic, and the best of them, he's also going to need to learn some jumping skills. Unfortunately, that's a little more complex than moving left and right.

You *could* try and implement jumping the same way you handled moving left and right. The following code would allow our hero to jump:

```
if (Input.GetKey(KeyCode.Space))
        {
            rb.velocity = new Vector2(rb.velocity.x, 5);

        }
```

The only problem is that this code would also allow him to *fly*. That's because we'd be adding more upward velocity *every time* we pressed the spacebar, regardless of whether he was on the ground or in the air. This is no good.

So instead we need to check that he's on terra firma first. And that's a tiny bit more complicated.

First, we'll need to create a new transform. A *transform* is a point in space that has its own coordinates and rotation (angle). This point is also going to have a radius (which will be a float), and we'll also need a *layer mask*. We're now also creating our first Boolean variable called onGround.

In short, you're adding all the following code to your script:

```
public Transform groundCheck;
public float groundCheckRadius;
public LayerMask whatIsGround;
private bool onGround;
```

Now, that might seem rather complicated, but don't worry, I'll explain what each bit is and what it does as we go.

In case that wasn't all daunting enough at this stage, we're also going to add another function to our code, called FixedUpdate. FixedUpdate is a function just like Update except that whereas Update is tied to the refresh rate of the screen, FixedUpdate is more consistent and therefore more reliable for code relating to physics.

Inside this function, you are going to add the following:

```
void FixedUpdate()
{
    onGround = Physics2D.OverlapCircle(groundCheck.position, groundCheckRadius,
whatIsGround);
}
```

Don't worry about what this does just yet. Head back to Unity where you can now see the new public float, Bool, and layer mask that we created in the Inspector.

Here you're going to create a new empty GameObject. This is a GameObject just like a sprite or the camera but with no components. Right-click in the Hierarchy and select Create Empty. You're going to call this empty GameObject Check Ground and make it a *child* of Player (by dragging it on top of Player in the Hierarchy—see Figure 4-11).

Figure 4-11. *Check Ground is an empty GameObject and child of Player (more on what that means later)*

Now select the player again and in the Hierarchy find where it says Ground Check. Currently it will say None (Transform), but you're going to change that by dragging the Check Ground game object and dropping it into that box. It should look like Figure 4-12.

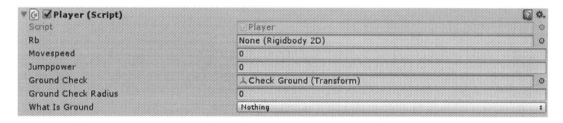

Figure 4-12. *Ground Check is a transform that is now defined as the coordinates of Check Ground*

Remember: Ground Check is a transform, meaning a set of coordinates. By dropping an empty GameObject into here, we are now telling our script to set those coordinates to be those attached to Check Ground. In other words, we have defined a "point," and this is how we're going to look at whether or not Squarey is standing on solid ground. Now set the radius value to 0.1, meaning that it will be a very small point. Finally, select Check Ground in the Scene view and use the move tool to position it just below Squarey so that it's checking the space directly below him.

One more thing we need to do is create a new layer and call it Ground. Drag and select all of your floor tiles again and then look for the Layer menu at the top left of the Inspector. At the bottom of the dropdown, you'll see the option to Add Layer (Figure 4-13).

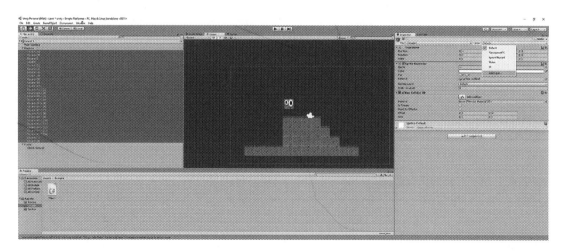

Figure 4-13. *Adding the Ground layer*

You'll then be given the opportunity to create your new layer simply by typing its name into the next available space (several layers are already defined by Unity), as in Figure 4-14).

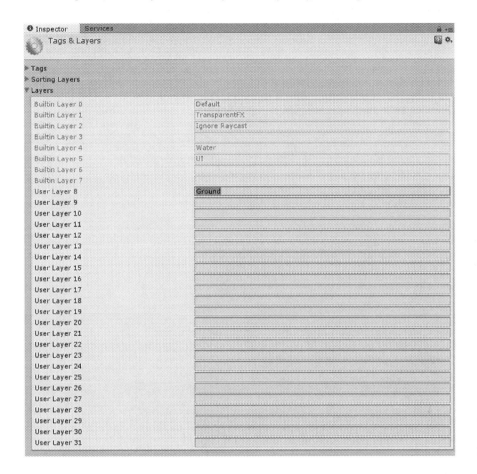

Figure 4-14. *Call the new layer Ground*

Type *Ground* into the empty space. Then go back to the Inspector for your Square tiles and this time select Ground from the dropdown menu to set them all to that value.

Now view the Player GameObject in the Inspector again and this time set What is Ground to Ground by using the dropdown menu. This basically means that anything that is set to the Ground layer will now be treated as *ground* in our script— meaning Squarey can jump off of it.

With all this done, we can now simply add the final line of code to our script:

```
if (Input.GetKey(KeyCode.Space) && onGround)
        {
            rb.velocity = new Vector2(rb.velocity.x, 5);
        }
```

Now hit play and you'll find that Squarey can jump—but only if he's on solid ground. This means he won't be able to jump continuously in the air, and it means that in Chapter 5 we can start introducing some actual platforming challenges.

A Little Bit of Further Explanation

You may still be a little confused at what has actually happened here. Let's recap what's going on.

The key is this line, which we have placed in our FixedUpdate function:

```
onGround = Physics2D.OverlapCircle(groundCheck.position, groundCheckRadius, whatIsGround);
```

The statement Physics2D.OverlapCircle(groundCheck.position, groundCheckRadius, whatIsGround) is a true or false statement that is asking whether the groundCheck transform is overlapping with anything that we defined as Ground (whatIsGround). onGround is true if there is an overlap and false if there is no overlap—remember, this is a variable that can only be either true or false. Because this line is in FixedUpdate, it's going to continually change its value depending on what's going on in the game.

In pseudo code, we are saying this:

```
If the circle underneath the player is overlapping with ground material, then onGround is
true. Otherwise, onGround is false.
```

Then, in our Update function, we check whether onGround is true whenever the player presses space: in C#, && simply means *and*. By using && inside an if statement, we're testing whether *two* arguments are true. So

```
if (Input.GetKey(KeyCode.Space) && onGround)
{
    rb.velocity = new Vector2(rb.velocity.x, 5);
}
```

actually means

```
If player presses jump and 'onGround' is true then add upward velocity.
```

We could also replace 5 with a variable as we did with movespeed. Call it jumppower.

For your convenience, the entire Player script should now look like so:

```
using UnityEngine;
using System.Collections;

public class Player : MonoBehaviour {
    public Rigidbody2D rb;
    public int movespeed;
    public int jumppower;
    public Transform groundCheck;
    public float groundCheckRadius;
    public LayerMask whatIsGround;
    private bool onGround;

    void Start () {
        rb = GetComponent<Rigidbody2D>();
        movespeed = 3;
        jumppower = 5;
    }
```

```
    void FixedUpdate()
    {
        onGround = Physics2D.OverlapCircle(groundCheck.position, groundCheckRadius,
        whatIsGround);
    }

    void Update () {
        if (Input.GetKey(KeyCode.LeftArrow))
        {
            rb.velocity = new Vector2(-movespeed, rb.velocity.y);

        }
        if (Input.GetKey(KeyCode.RightArrow))
        {
            rb.velocity = new Vector2(movespeed, rb.velocity.y);

        }

        if (Input.GetKey(KeyCode.Space) && onGround)
        {
            rb.velocity = new Vector2(rb.velocity.x, jumppower);

        }

    }
}
```

If you copy this for now, you can always try tweaking lines and reverse engineering it as you try and understand it. You should find that a lot of it is actually quite self-explanatory.

One Final Touch: Keeping the Player Upright

Except there is *one* small problem: Squarey currently tumbles and spins down stairs as though he's had a few too many vodkas. If you jump and then land on your head, you won't be able to take off again because the Check Ground GameObject will now be pointing up in the air.

To fix this, click Squarey and find the Constraints option underneath the Rigidbody component in the Inspector. Here, you'll find the option to Freeze Rotation Z. Tick that box and Squarey's angle will now be locked in place (Figure 4-15).

▼⇲ **Rigidbody 2D**		▣ ✿,
Use Auto Mass	☐	
Mass	1	
Linear Drag	0	
Angular Drag	0.05	
Gravity Scale	1	
Is Kinematic	☐	
Interpolate	None	⬍
Sleeping Mode	Start Awake	⬍
Collision Detection	Discrete	⬍
▼ Constraints		
Freeze Position	☐X ☐Y	
Freeze Rotation	☑Z	

Figure 4-15. *Tick Freeze Rotation and your character will stop falling over*

You'll notice a few other options here too, such as Gravity Scale (which controls how Squarey is affected by gravity) and a few others. We'll be playing around with these in Chapter 5.

Now you can try creating a few floating platforms and having a little fun trying to cross them without falling off the screen. You might need to adjust your jumppower a little for that or your Gravity Scale, so just have some fun with it. And take a moment now to reflect on what you've already accomplished: only a short way in and you already have a character that can jump around the screen and a level that's quite fun to navigate (Figure 4-16). We've barely gotten started, so just think what else you'll be able to do before we're finished!

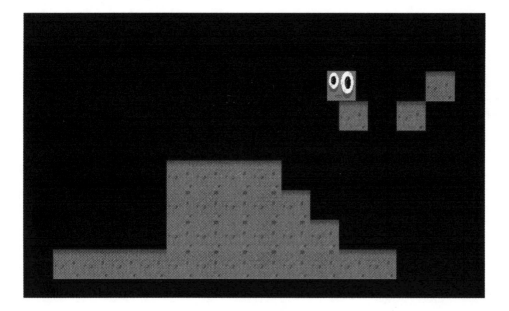

Figure 4-16. *Only Chapter 4 and our game is already almost fun!*

In Chapter 5, we'll be looking at how to create better platforms with prefabs and affectors and we'll be doing some more interesting things with our camera. We'll even be able to start putting in collectibles and hazards.

■ ■ ■

Filling the World with Prefabs, Effectors, and Collectibles

At this point, things are starting to come together and feel a *bit* like an actual game. We have a very basic 2D level, we have a character that we can move around with the arrow keys and the spacebar, and we have working physics.

But a few things are still a little *off* at the moment, and we're not following all the best practices. The world is also rather empty, devoid of any collectibles, scenery, or even a sky.

In this chapter then, we'll be looking at how we can begin adding things like trees, coins, and platforms that have special properties. We'll also see how to keep better track of all these new elements and streamline our game design process with *prefabs*. By the end, your game world will look a *lot* more colorful, and you'll even be able to start creating some basic platform challenges.

Using Effectors

One thing you may have noticed that isn't quite right at the moment is the fact that we can stick to walls. If we run Squarey into a wall and keep holding the arrow keys in that direction, then he will glue himself to the surface and stop falling. That's pretty odd behavior for a platform game, so let's stop that from happening.

First, click the platform you want to edit and then view it in the Inspector. Now click Add Component ➤ Physics 2D ➤ Area Effector 2D. You'll then be prompted that you need to tick the box under the Box Collider 2D that says Used By Effector.

This will then show a semicircle around the box and bring up some more options in the Inspector. You should have something that looks like Figure 5-1.

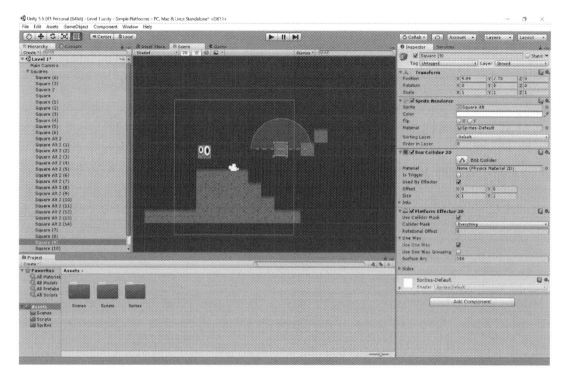

Figure 5-1. *Platform Effector added to one of our tiles*

Now try and stick the character to the block and you'll find he simply slips off. In short, Platform Effector has caused the platform to behave like a platform.

Try and jump into the platform from underneath and you'll notice something else: Squarey can pass through them. You might have played platformers with this feature before, but at the moment we want to turn it off. The reason for this is that as of now, performing this move will break the game. Holding jump will currently cause Squarey to jump a second time as he passes through the floor, which looks very strange.

There are plenty of ways to fix this: by using *raycasts* to check for the ground instead of the system we're currently using, for example, or by simply making the player tap spacebar a second time before they can jump again. Right now, though, it's easiest just to untick the Use One Way box (Figure 5-2), which will also allow for some gameplay features like caves and dead-ends.

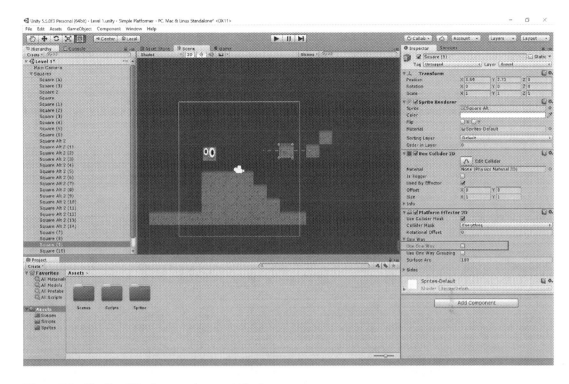

Figure 5-2. *Use One Way has now been unticked*

This is a very early example of how your gameplay is going to dictate decisions you make regarding your physics and code. You can't build a game engine and design your levels separately: the way the game world behaves should be informed by your game design and vice versa. Form should follow function.

In this case, the question is whether you want to design a more fast-paced game that allows the player to seamlessly scale through platforms by tapping jump, or whether you want something a little more puzzle/exploration based and maintain the ability to trap them in different sections.

(Of course, you can also have multiple types of platform that behave in different ways, but then the challenge of your game design is to make sure the differences are clearly communicated from the start of the game.)

For our purposes, we're going to keep things simple though and switch this feature off.

More Effectors

Effectors are a great way to quickly and easily get your game elements to behave in specific ways. When you chose the Platform Effector, you may have noticed that there were also a few other effectors you could have chosen.

For example, you may have spotted Buoyancy Effector. This is an effector that allows us to make tiles behave like water.

To demonstrate how useful Effectors are, let's design some new tiles that look like water (Figure 5-3), keeping our same 50 x 50 dimensions.

77

Figure 5-3. *A square of water*

Now add this to your Sprites folder and create a new game asset called Water Square (or whatever you want to call it). Remember to set the Pixels Per Unit to 50 for this sprite and make sure that it has a collider. Now choose Add Compontent ➤ Physics 2D ➤ Buoyancy Effector 2D. Remember to tick Used by Effector, and this time you're also going to click Is Trigger (I'll explain what this means later). Copy and paste a few water squares and surround them with banks on either side to create a pool. Now jump into it and watch Squarey bob up and down just below the surface (see Figure 5-4).

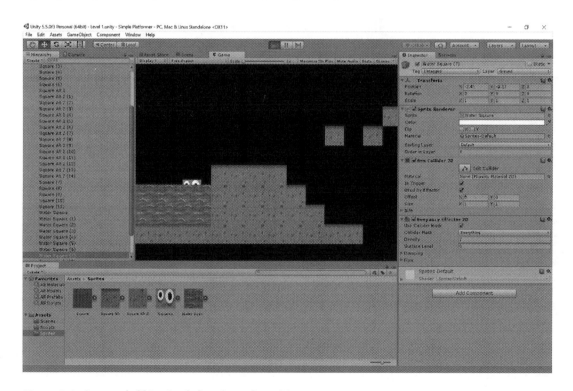

Figure 5-4. *Squarey bobbing just below the surface of the water*

Other effectors can let you create wind, conveyor belts, and more.

Prefabs and More Organization

Nope, I didn't forget. Right now, we have a pool of water that's a lot of fun, but only *one* of our tiles works the way it's supposed to.

You *could* go and change every square tile in the scene in order to apply the Platform Effector. And actually, this wouldn't even be that bad considering that we can select multiple GameObjects at once and add compontents or change settings in that way. But now imagine that you have multiple levels, tons of different GameObjects, and huge, intricate layouts. If you decide that you want to change a value now, all that is going to make life extremely difficult for you.

What we're going to do instead is to create a prefab. *Prefab* is short for *prefabricated* and is essentially a GameObject with predefined properties. We can drop prefabs into a scene just as we've been dropping sprites into our scenes, but they'll carry all of the ready-made components and values.

Better yet, when we change the effector in our folder, those changes will be reflected across every instance of the object in the game. That will let us change our minds about aspects of our game design and be able to quickly implement those changes.

First, create a new folder inside Assets and call it Prefabs. This is the same process as it was for the Sprites folder and Scripts folder (right-click ➤ Create ➤ Folder). Now find the ground tile you made that included the effector and drag it from the Inspector into the Prefabs folder. Then do the same thing with the other ground tile and one of the water tiles (Figure 5-5).

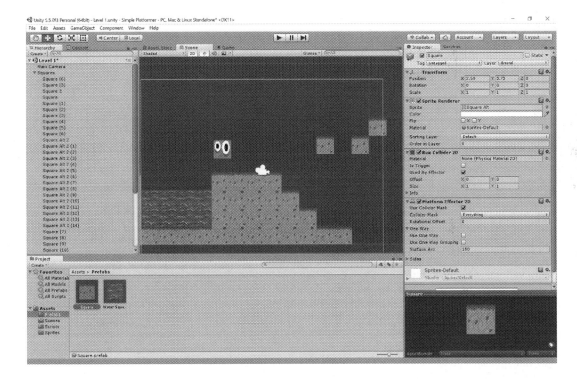

Figure 5-5. *Two prefabs down, one to go*

Now comes the scary part—you're going to *delete* all the tiles in Scene view, leaving nothing except for the Player and the Camera. All that hard work has not gone to waste, though, because now you're going to be able to simply drag and drop one of each tile into your game world again.

This is a nice opportunity to create some even better organization and redesign our level. Before you start dropping tiles in again, first select the prefabs and view them in the Inspector. In here, change the names to something that will be easily recognizable. I've gone with water, dirt, and grass. This won't change the name of the prefab itself but will change the names of the GameObjects once they're in situ.

You can also take this opportunity to create separate empty GameObjects to serve as groupings for each of the three elements you have on the go. Mine are `Top Soil` for the grass, `Ground` for the dirt, and `Water` for the water.

Now drag one of each tile back into the scene, holding Ctrl to snap to the grid. Make sure the first instance of each item goes in the correct group so that duplicates will also appear in here. Start by dragging the item out from the Prefabs folder and into the correct category—then you'll be able to simply copy and paste the elements within the Scene view. Here you're making copies that will conform to the rules of the prefab. Don't forget to hold Ctrl to space your tiles out and snap them to the grid. Now you can redesign the level layout as you like. You can see mine in Figure 5-6.

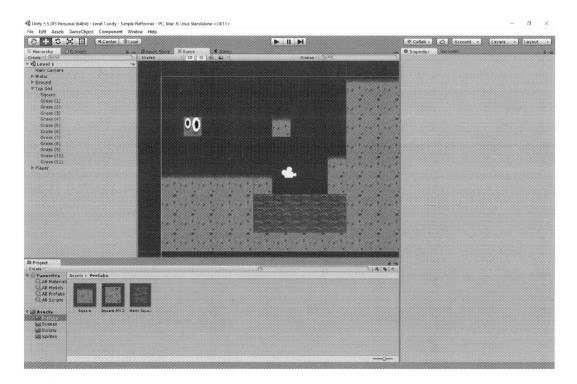

Figure 5-6. *A new, more organized setup using prefabs*

Finally, create one more empty GameObject and call it `Tiles` or something similar.

To demonstrate the power of the prefab, you can now try selecting the Grass tile in the Prefab folder and selecting Use One Way. Click play and you'll find that you can now jump through any instance of the grass block from underneath. Untick it and they will all change back.

This will make our workflow much easier as we move forward and so too will the way we've arranged our Hierarachy. Try clicking the Water group for instance, and you'll see that every single water tile gets highlighted (Figure 5-7). Click Tiles and all the water tiles, grass tiles, *and* dirt tiles will be selected (Figure 5-8).

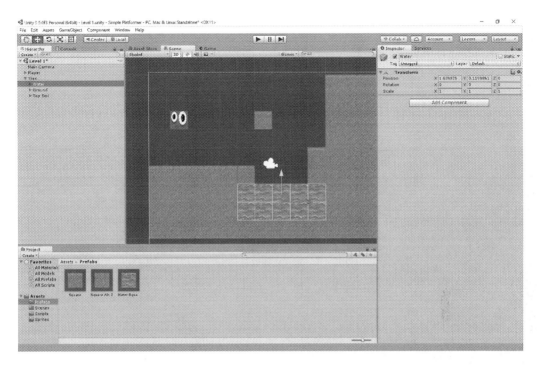

Figure 5-7. *Water selected*

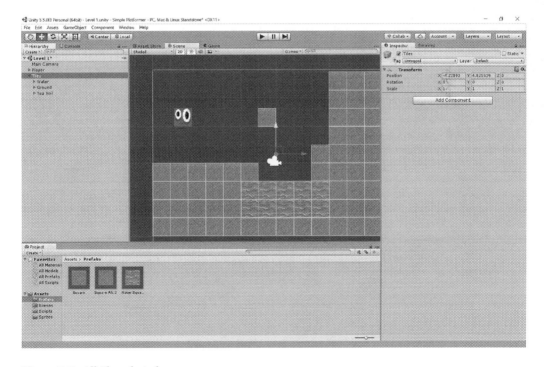

Figure 5-8. *All tiles selected*

This means you could easily delete an entire category of tile, and in the future, this is going to help us to manage things like collectibles, enemies, and decorative items. Good timing—the next part of this chapter is going to start adding more variety.

Troubleshooting: Help! Squarey Keeps Getting Stuck!

One of the joys of software engineering (yep, that's what this is) is that things will constantly go wrong and you'll be forced to try and deal with them. Sometimes there will be a simple fix (and Google is your friend in this instance). Other times, the issue might be outside your control, forcing you to come up with a novel solution.

Right now, if you're using box colliders on your tiles *and* on your player character, you might find that you occasionally get stuck on things that you shouldn't—your character may stop moving and press against thin air. The problem normally occurs at the vertices between the closely positioned tiles, and unfortunately, it seems that this is a slight issue with Unity itself rather than anything you can fix (apparently, it was introduced in 4.3.1 and has yet to be resolved as of the time of writing).

If you do encounter this problem, just try using a polygon collider for Squarey himself, changing the shape slightly by clicking Edit Collider, and then creating a small bump in the outline as in Figure 5-9 so that you can "slide" over these imagined obstacles.

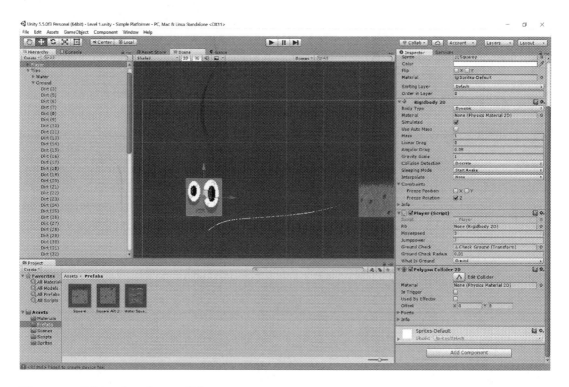

Figure 5-9. *Editing the polygon collider*

Welcome to development!

Understanding Parents and Making a Moving Camera

One other thing that is useful to understand is the relationship between *parents* and *children*.

These groupings in your Hierarchy are not really folders as such. Rather, the empty GameObjects are called *parents* and the items your group under them are called *children*. Like real parents and children, children in this case will *inheret* the properties of the adult. For example, were you to move Top Soil to the right, then all of its children would move right by the same amount, ensuring they all remained within relative distance from one another. This can be a useful feature in a range of scenarios—for instance, if you wanted two GameObjects to move at the same speed in the same direction.

Why might that be something you want to do? Well, how about if we use this to stick our camera to our player? Right now, Squarey is only able to explore within the confines of the screen, which is rather limiting in terms of the kinds of level designs we can make. But if we go to the Hierarchy and select the camera, we can then drop it onto Player, thereby making it a child of that GameObject. Now, the camera will always move relative to the player! Move it onto the center of the player to make sure it's in a good position where you can see obstacles from the left and right. Why not add some more level off to the right to celebrate?

In Figure 5-10 you can see how the camera should look, as well as some extra level design I've added.

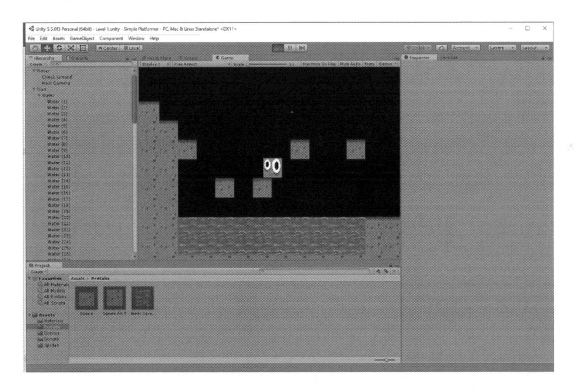

Figure 5-10. *With his camera attached, Squarey is now free to explore foreign lands*

Just note that this is very much a quick hack rather than the way we really want to handle the camera. In a finished game, a camera should do much more than just blindly follow the player. Rather, it will speed up or slow down, zoom in and out, and behave differently depending on the type of game. This can benefit the gameplay or provide added drama and excitement depending on the circumstaces. We'll discuss all of this in more detail in a later chapter.

Decorating the Scene Using Z Order

Right now, our level looks very gamey—it's very clearly a computer game level and doesn't feel very lifelike, seeing as the only objects in it are clearly platforms designed to be jumped on. To change this, we need to add some decoration to make the world feel like a living, breathing place.

To do that, you first need to create some elements that you can use for decoration. I've created a tree (Figure 5-11) and a bush (Figure 5-12).

Figure 5-11. *Tree*

Figure 5-12. *Bush*

Note that both of these images are PNG files and have a transparency around the edge. I did this using the free image-editing software GIMP, and we'll discuss how you can do the same in more detail in chapter 10.

For now, you want to add these into the game as you've done several times before. Put them in your Sprites folder, make sure to change the pixels per unit, and group them under an empty GameObject called Plants. You may want to create prefabs again too, although this is much less important on this occasion as they'll all going to look and behave a little differently anyway.

Now scatter your plants and trees around the world a little. You can feel free to mix up the size, and it's not important to stick within the grid. In fact, it's a good thing to make the positioning look a little random, because that will appear more natural and help remove some of the gamey aesthetic.

Try playing the game now and you'll find that when you walk past the bushes and trees, you might go in front of them or behind them. In fact, you might even flicker in and out of view if you have an older version of Unity.

The problem is that two things are being drawn in the same place, and you haven't defined which should go on top. To fix this, you need to change the *Z order*, which you do in the Inspector by changing the option called Order in Layer. By default, this is set to 0 when you add a new GameObject, but you can change this in order to create various effects.

If you make the number lower, that means the object will be drawn earlier—behind the other elements. Likewise, if you make the number higher, that means it will be drawn at the end, on top of everything else.

My recommendation is to make some of the bushes and trees appear behind Squarey (set them to –1) and make some appear *in front* of Squarey (set them to 1). This creates an interesting effect where he appears to be walking through thick foliage (Figure 5-13), though it's important as you build the game to ensure that this doesn't become confusing for the player.

Figure 5-13. *Squarey peeping out from behind some bushes*

Likewise, you also need to try and avoid making things confusing for yourself. My recommendation is to keep your player as 0 and to use this as your reference point. I also recommend making sure that the tiles will stay in front unless you specifically intend to add decoration to them. This will allow you to tuck GameObjects like trees a little below the surface without worrying about ugly gaps. You can do this by setting their Order in Layer to something like 10.

Why would you ever want to put something *on top* of your platforms? One reason is if you want to add a little more natural, random-looking detail. For example, I've created this creeper (Figure 5-14) and then set the Z order to 11. By changing the scale to –1 on the X and Y axes respectively, I can flip the image horizontally and vertically too (Figure 5-15).

Figure 5-14. *This creeper adds a little detail to the game world*

Figure 5-15. *This is how it looks when it's in place*

You can add as many details like this as you like. Personally, I feel that these little touches make a huge difference to the way a world looks and feels. I recommend getting a bit creative and seeing what you come up with.

And of course, now that we're able to add different layers, that means it's time to add in a backdrop, which will make a big difference to the aesthetic. I've drawn a cloudy sky (Figure 5-16) and made it fairly large so that it can cover the space with no dark borders around the edge.

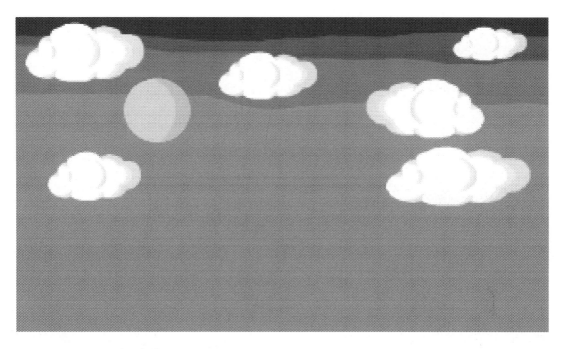

Figure 5-16. *A nice cloudy sky*

You can use large images like this or you can tile your background—the choice is yours. Just make sure you never run out of sky. Obviously, using larger images is going to mean the following for your app:

- It takes up more memory
- It takes a little longer to load levels

Set the background to a Z order of something like –10 just to ensure that you never accidentally put something behind it, and create a group in your Hierarchy called Backdrop.

We're left with what you see in Figure 5-17. Now doesn't that look much better?

Figure 5-17. *Much better!*

Parallax Scrolling with Perspective

If you want to get really fancy, you might decide to use *another* extra trick: *parallax scrolling*.

You may have noticed that the Inspector allows you to change not only the X and Y coordinates of objects, but also the Z coordinate. This may strike you as odd, seeing as you're using Unity in 2D mode. Why not just remove this option altogether?

The simple answer is that under some circumstances, you may want to change the Z position of an element in order to create 3D effects. To demonstrate, select the backdrop you just created and change the Z coordinate in the inspector to 30. Now select the camera and in the Inspector and click the dropdown menu called Projection. Change this from Orthographic to Perspective.

Now click play and see what happens. You should find that the sky now appears further away and moves much more slowly than the rest of the level. You just created a parallax scrolling effect!

The best way to illustrate what's happening here is to switch the Scene window into 3D mode. Click the 2D button along the top to toggle between the two modes, and you should see something like Figure 5-18.

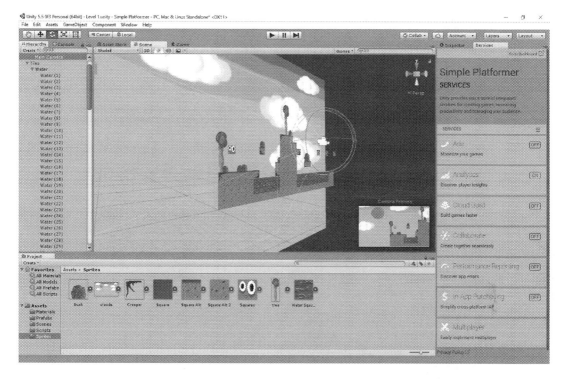

Figure 5-18. *This is what the camera "really" sees*

In short, we now have a 3D perspective looking head-on at purely 2D elements arranged in a 3D space. There are a lot of cool things you can do with this, and you can add as many layers and elements as you like. You could even have translucent clouds passing in the foreground, or rolling hills moving at another speed in the middle distance. All this can add depth and beauty to your scenes, but just make sure you don't get carried away at the expense of clarity or performance. If you have too much going on at any one time, your players won't know what they can jump on or walk through, and it can even get borderline headache-inducing.

Later on, we'll be looking more at how to design your levels to look great and get rid of some of those sharp edges. Until then, let's keep things fairly basic.

Adding Collectibles and Hazards

Now that you've added some inanimate objects and decoration, it's time to consider adding some elements that you will actually be able to interact with. And a good place for us to start would be with some collectibles.

To do this, we of course need to start by designing something that we can collect. A popular choice in this regard is a gold coin, so let's start with that. Mine is shown in Figure 5-19.

Figure 5-19. *A gold coin. Don't you just want to collect it?*

89

Now we're going to once again add it to our scene the way we've added other GameObjects to our scene. That means we need to import the sprite, set the Pixels Per Unit, and then make it into a prefab. Any coins we scatter around our scene we're going to put into the following Hierarchy: Collectibles ➤ Coins ➤ Gold Coin. This time we're also going to create a collider though, and we're going to tick the Is Trigger box in the Inspector.

A *trigger* is basically a collider that doesn't act like a physics object. In other words, our coin won't be something we can walk into or jump off of—rather, we'll pass right through it as though it were made of air. At the same time, though, Unity will "flag up" the fact that this has happened, allowing us to add code that tells the game how to respond to this event.

Drop one or two of your new gold coin prefabs into the scene, and you should have something that looks like Figure 5-20.

Figure 5-20. *The scene with some added gold coins*

Now we need to create a new script, which you should remember how to do. Head down to your Assets ➤ Scripts folder, right-click, and select Create C# Script. Name this CollectCoin (script names can't have spaces) and double-click on it to open Visual Studio for just a little more coding.

In here, we're going to use a function called OnTriggerEnter2D. This function is called any time the attached GameObject is triggered, so anything you place in here will happen once the player touches that GameObject.

In this case, we want the coin to disappear, so we need to destroy it. We do this by saying Destroy(gameObject). When using Unity, gameObject with a lowercase *g* refers to the specific GameObject that the script is attached to.

The full script should look like so:

```
public class CollectCoin : MonoBehaviour {

        // Use this for initialization
        void Start () {

        }

        // Update is called once per frame
        void Update () {

        }

    private void OnTriggerEnter2D(Collider2D other)
    {
        if (other.tag == "Player")
        {
            Destroy(gameObject);
        }
    }
}
```

In pseudo code, this is saying: *when something comes into contact with the 2D collider, if that thing has the tag player, self-destruct.* As you may have already guessed, that means we now also need to hop into Unity and add that tag to Squarey. Select Squarey and then find the Tag option at the top of the Inspector. It should currently say Untagged, and all you're going to do is click the dropdown menu and choose Player.

Finally, don't forget to attach the CollectCoin script to your coins. Do this by clicking Add Component ➤ Scripts ➤ CollectCoin.

Hit play, and now when you walk into the coins, they should instantly disappear. In Figure 5-21 you can see how I've arranged my coins, as well as how I've added the Player tag to Squarey.

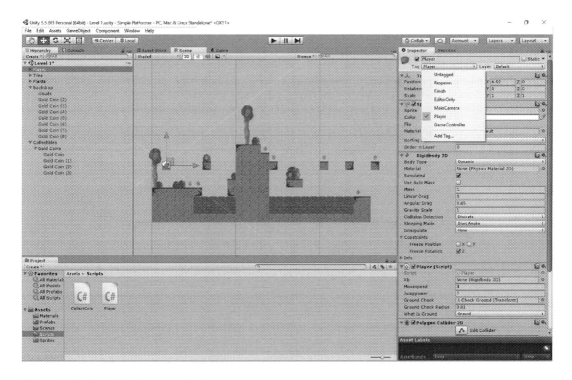

Figure 5-21. *Ready to do some collecting*

What if we want to create some hazards? In that case, we could do the precise same thing, except we'd want to move our player back to the starting position or possibly end the game.

To do this, we'll need a new sprite (Figure 5-22).

Figure 5-22. *Spikes*

Now add the sprite and make a prefab just as you've done before. Remember to set the Pixels Per Unit and add a polygon collider. You'll probably need to shape it yourself to fit around the spikes nicely too.

You'll be adding a script just like last time. And the code will be very similar this time around too, with a slight twist. Now it will say the following:

```
public class Hazards : MonoBehaviour
{
    private Player player;

    // Use this for initialization
    void Start()
    {
        player = FindObjectOfType<Player>();
    }

    // Update is called once per frame
    void Update()
    {

    }

    private void OnTriggerEnter2D(Collider2D other)
    {
        if (other.tag == "Player")
        {
            player.transform.position = new Vector2(-6, 8);
        }
    }
}
```

Attach this script component to the Spikes prefab, remember to tick Is Trigger, and then you're good to go. This script works very similarly to the last one except instead of destroying the GameObject, we're *moving* the player. First, we have to define what we mean by "player," which we do by looking for objects attached to the Player script. From there, we can then change the transform (position) of the Player to a new Vector2 (a coordinate with two axes). We're moving the Player to position (–6, 8) because that's where Squarey starts out in my scene. Take a look at the starting position of your version of Squarey and change the coordinates to match.

Finally, place some spikes in a logical position in your level as I've done in Figure 5-23. I also recommend organizing them under an empty GameObject called Hazards.

Figure 5-23. *Beware the spike pit!*

Now when you hit play, falling on the spikes should automatically teleport you back to the starting position. That's not very glamorous, but it does the job and illustrates the point. In future chapters we'll look at how to kill and respawn the player properly, as well as how to tally up points for collectibles. For now, though, this gives you a very good idea of how you can use triggers in order to make all kinds of effects work. We could use the precise same code to make a portal or doorway to transport the player to the next part of the level! Or we could use it to create some enemies....

Introducing Enemies

Essentially, all *enemies* are hazards that move. You know the drill by now: start out by creating a new sprite, ideally something that looks a bit menacing, as in Figure 5-24.

Figure 5-24. *Not sure who this guy is but he looks menacing*

Give him a collider, make him a trigger, and create a prefab. Then attach the Hazard script so he's functionally the same as the spikes. The difference is that we're also going to be adding another script called BackAndForth. Go and make that just the same as you've made your previous scripts (right-click in the Scripts folder) and then add this code:

```
public class BackAndForth : MonoBehaviour
{

    public double amountToMove;
    public float speed;
    private float startx;
    private int direction;

    // Use this for initialization
    void Start()
    {
        direction = 0;
        startx = gameObject.transform.position.x;

    }

    // Update is called once per frame
    void Update()
    {
        if (gameObject.transform.position.x < startx + amountToMove && direction == 0)
        {
            gameObject.transform.position = new Vector2(gameObject.transform.position.x +
            speed, gameObject.transform.position.y);

        }
        else if (gameObject.transform.position.x >= startx + amountToMove && direction == 0)
        {
            direction = 1;
        }
        else if (gameObject.transform.position.x > startx && direction == 1)
        {
            gameObject.transform.position = new Vector2(gameObject.transform.position.x -
            speed, gameObject.transform.position.y);
        }
        else if (gameObject.transform.position.x <= startx && direction == 1)
        {
            direction = 0;
        }
    }
}
```

Take a read through that and see if you can work out how it works. Got it? Of course you did. But just in case ... essentially, we have two public variables that we can set from the Inspector: the speed (called speed) and the distance that the object will move (called amountToMove). When the object is created at runtime, it also checks to get its current x coordinate. The direction can be 1 or 0 and—like all integers—is set to 0 by default when the script starts.

So, the script then asks *if the current position is smaller than my start point* plus *the distance I have to move, move to the right at speed—but only if I'm moving right*. Once the object goes past that point (>= means "bigger than or equal to"), it will then change the direction to 1. When direction is 1, the reverse logic is applied until the character is equal to or smaller than the start position—at which point direction switches back to 0 and we go right again.

Now if you add this script to the bad guy *along* with the Hazard script, you should have a GameObject that moves left and right and kills the player when it comes into contact with them. Just remember to set the variables in the Inspector first (see Figure 5-25).

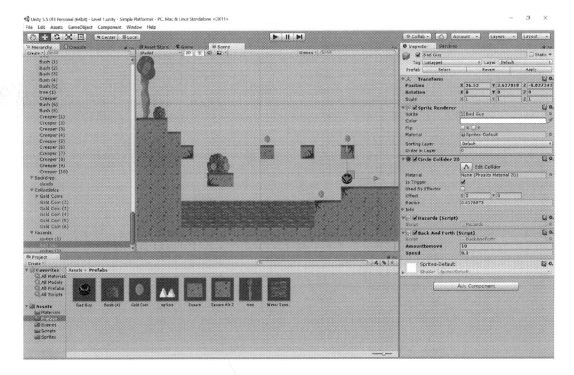

Figure 5-25. *The bad guy in his starting position*

Notice how you can achieve impressive results without having to rewrite out lots of code—just combine multiple scripts in unique ways. The sky's the limit.

Pushable Objects

While we're adding all these different kinds of objects and elements, let's add one more that's really nice and simple: a pushable crate (Figure 5-26).

Figure 5-26. *Crate to finally meet you…*

All you need to do is introduce a GameObject that has a collider and Rigidbody (just like the Player). This will then allow you to interact with that object by pushing it or even dropping it into the water to watch it bob up and down (Figure 5-27). This creates a lot of potential gameplay mechanics and challenges, and it couldn't be simpler.

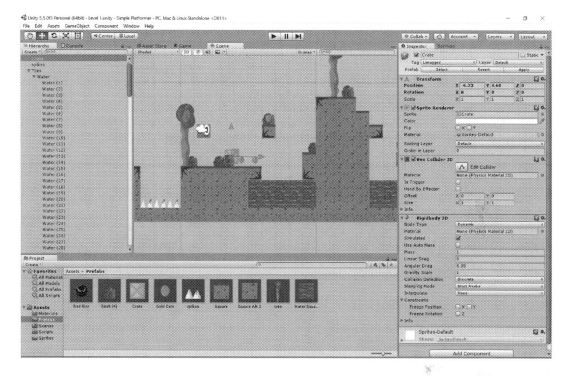

Figure 5-27. *Push the crate into the water and see what happens*

Remember, though: if your character is going to be able to jump off the crates, they need to have their layer set to Ground.

Using Materials

Before I close this chapter, let me address one small thing that still isn't quite right with the objects in our game world: the slidiness. You've probably noticed that Squarey likes to slide around all over the place like he's on ice, which doesn't look right and is rather hard to control.

To fix this, we're going to create a *material* and apply it to Top Soil. To do this, you're going to create a folder called Materials and then a new Physics Material 2D (RMB ➤ Create ➤ Physics Material 2D). Call this Ground.

Now select that material to view it in the Inspector and you'll see that you can change two properties: Bounciness and Friction. As you might have guessed already, Friction controls how much friction a particular surface has. Change this to 0.6 for a bit more ground control and change the Bounciness to 0.1 for an imperceptible judder when Squarey lands (Figure 5-28).

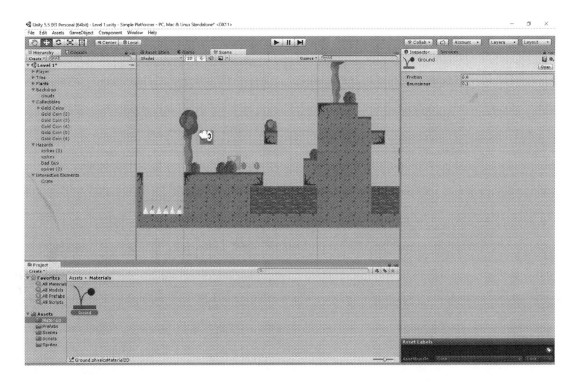

Figure 5-28. *Squarey lives in a material world*

Now select the topsoil prefab and in the Inspector and find the Material option beneath Box Collider 2D (not the one under Sprite Renderer). Choose the Ground material you just created, and it should automatically apply to all the grassy tiles in your game. Try running and jumping now, and things should be easier to control.

Materials like this provide a useful way to add properties to various GameObjects, and we'll see more uses for them later on.

For now, this is more than enough to start crafting a world filled with platform challenges, obstacles, and things to collect. We still have much to do, though, and over the next couple of chapters we'll be looking at how to tally up scores, add UI elements, and even introduce fancy animations. Once all *that* is in place, we can start trying it all out on an actual Android device.

It's all coming together now!

■ ■ ■

CHAPTER 6

Adding Animations, Effects, and a HUD

Okay, so I am aware that we are now six chapters into the book and at this point we still haven't actually touched an Android phone! That's the irony of coding with a desktop IDE, but don't worry if you're feeling impatient—in the very next chapter you'll get to try deploying your game on an actual Android phone or tablet. For now, though, we're going to add a few more touches that will give us the foundations for our future game development—touches like animations, particle effects, and a heads up display (HUD). When we get to Chapter 7, it will make sense why we did this first.

And don't fret. There's a lot to be excited about right now too: adding simple things like animations is what will allow you to really add character and charm to your game and elevate it to a point where it starts to look really rather professional.

Handling Death and Using Particles

Everyone has their own way of handling their mortality. Right now, Squarey's way is not particularly elegant. Not only does he just kind of "appear" back at the start of the game instantly, but he also doesn't give us any brief pause while that happens. The whole thing is a little too brief to let it really sink in.

It would be nice if we had some kind of death animation, or better yet, a gory explosion.

To do that, we're going to use the *particle system*, an effect that lets you scatter pixels all around the screen and get them to behave in different ways. We're going to make a particle effect that will look like an explosion of blood—but you could just as easily use this to make regular explosions, fireworks, fountains, electricity, and more.

To create your first particle system, choose Game Object ➤ Particle System. You should see a fountain of slow moving white blobs appear in your scene with options on the righthand side in the Inspector (Figure 6-1).

© Adam Sinicki 2017
A. Sinicki, *Learn Unity for Android Game Development*, DOI 10.1007/978-1-4842-2704-6_6

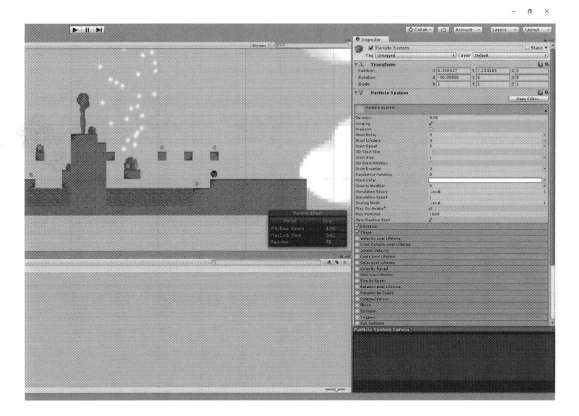

Figure 6-1. *Your first particle effect*

You need to tweak some of the settings here in order to make the effect look a little more like blood. We can start by changing the Start Color to red (click the white bar) and Start Size to 0.2. Then click the Shape option below that and choose Sphere instead of Cone. Under Emission, change Rate over Time to read 300.

Now expand the Renderer menu option and click the circle next to the Material option. Choose Sprites – Default, and the red blobs should change into red squares.

Next, expand Size over Lifetime (note that you need to tick the bullet box first) and drag the righthand side so that the line is a downward slope. This means the particles will get smaller as they travel through the air, allowing them to disappear in a way that looks natural rather than suddenly blinking out of existence. Similarly, you can also do the same for Color over Lifetime. I've made my blood get slightly darker as it expands outward, just to keep things interesting.

I also applied .2 gravity (so that the particles fall downward). Feel free to play around with the other options as you want—they're generally pretty self-explanatory.

One thing you *need* to do, though, is to untick the Looping box at the top and change the duration to 0.30. Now the effect will play just once and end, rather than looping instantly. At any time, you can still test the animation by clicking the Simulate button that floats over the Scene view when the particle effect is selected. You should have something that looks like Figure 6-2 once you're done.

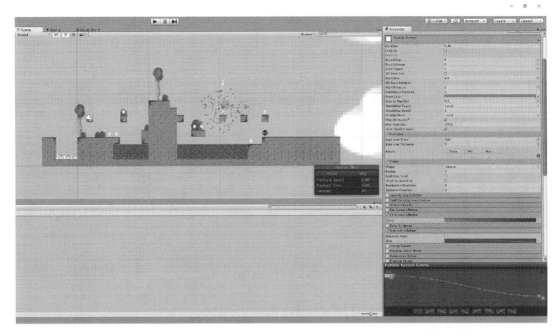

Figure 6-2. *A lovely cloud of blood*

Destroying the Particle System

We're going to put this to one side for a moment now while we write another new script. Create this in the Scripts folder, as ever, and call it DestroyParticleSystem. Can you guess what it is yet? (Ah good, a Rolf Harriss reference...)

The script is going to look like this:

```
using System.Collections.Generic;
using UnityEngine;

public class DestroyParticleEffect : MonoBehaviour {

    private ParticleSystem thisParticleSystem;

    void Start()
    {
        thisParticleSystem = GetComponent<ParticleSystem>();
    }

    void Update()
    {
        if (thisParticleSystem.isPlaying)
        {
            return;
        }
        Destroy(gameObject);
    }
}
```

The purpose of this script is simply to destroy the particle effect once it has finished playing. First we look for the particular instance of our particle system (which in object-oriented programming is often referred to as "this") and then we check to see if the particle system is playing during the Update method.

Finally, once the effect has finished playing, we destroy it.

Why is this important? Because otherwise, we would have countless instances of our particle held in memory, which could eventually start to bog things down. This will make a little more sense in a moment. For now, just take my word for it, save the script, and add it as a component to the particle effect object you created earlier.

Rename said particle system as Blood and then drop it into the Prefabs folder. Now delete Blood from your Hierarchy and your scene.

Making Hazards Hazardous

We're not quite done yet, though. Next, you need to add additional code to your Hazards script, which will look like so:

```
public class Hazards : MonoBehaviour
{

    private Player player;
    public GameObject Blood;

    void Start()
    {
        player = FindObjectOfType<Player>();
    }
    void Update()
    {

    }

    private void OnTriggerEnter2D(Collider2D other)
    {
        if (other.tag == "Player")
        {
            Instantiate(Blood, player.transform.position, player.transform.rotation);
            player.transform.position = new Vector2(-6, 8);
        }
    }
}
```

First, we're looking for a public GameObject that will be referred to as Blood and then we're *instantiating* that GameObject. That means we're creating an instance of said GameObject, and in this case we're using the same coordinates as we have for the player. It's important that we do this *before* we move the player, though.

Make sure you also remember to set the Blood prefab as the GameObject in the Hierarchy for each of your hazards. You need to do this in the Prefab folder so that it will be reflected across each subsequent instance of a spike or an enemy (rather than just that particular one). See Figure 6-3.

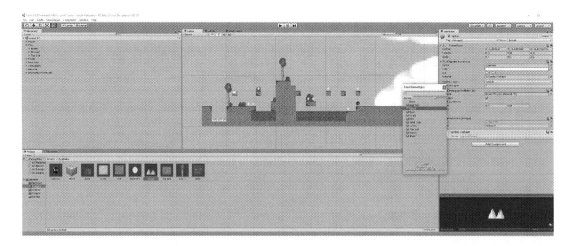

Figure 6-3. *Adding the blood particle system to the Hazards script attached to the Spikes prefab*

With all that in place, you can now try playing the game and testing the new effect. Only try watching the game as it plays in the Scene view rather choosing the full-screen Game view. This way, you should be able to see what happens: when Squarey walks onto a pit of spikes, he explodes, and an instance of the blood particle effect is created at that location. You'll see it appear in the Hierarchy at this point. The effect will then play itself out before disappearing once the sequence has finished.

And that's why we needed that DestroyParticleEffect script—otherwise, we would have lots of "finished" particle effects all in the Hierarchy from all the times we died, and this would take up unnecessary memory.

We can likewise use similar scripts if we create bullets or enemies, so that data is destroyed as we use it up. In this case, we might have a script that destroys objects after a set amount of time or after a certain interaction with the player.

Why not try doing something similar for the coins in your game? Create a new particle effect and call it Sparkle, make sure to add the DestroyParticleEffect script, and then apply it to the coins in the game. Don't forget to add the necessary line to the CollectCoin script either. You also want to make the sparkle appear at the location of the coin, not the location of the player, but I'll leave you to figure that out.

Two More Added Touches

We're going to add two more little touches to our handling of death. The first is to introduce a short pause between Squarey being killed and Squarey appearing in his new location. We do this with the following bit of code added to the Hazards script:

```
void OnTriggerEnter2D(Collider2D other)
{
    if (other.tag == "Player")
    {
        StartCoroutine("respawndelay");
    }
}
```

```
public IEnumerator respawndelay()
{
    Instantiate(Blood, player.transform.position, player.transform.rotation);
    player.enabled = false;
    player.GetComponent<Rigidbody2D>().velocity = Vector3.zero;
    player.GetComponent<Renderer>().enabled = false;
    yield return new WaitForSeconds(1);
    player.transform.position =new Vector2(-6, 8);
    player.GetComponent<Renderer>().enabled = true;
    player.enabled = true;
}
```

You don't need to worry too much about what's going on in this code for now, but suffice to say we're adding a delay. Respawndelay is a routine that can occur while other things are going on, which means we can include a pause without making it look as though the game has crashed. We're instantiating our explosion, waiting for 1 second (WaitForSeconds(1)), and *then* moving the player to the new position.

Between these events we're also turning off the visibility for our player (*player.GetComponent <Renderer>().enabled = false*) and we're removing all momentum so that the player won't be moving when they respawn (*player.GetComponent<Rigidbody2D>().velocity = Vector3.zero;*).

Hit play and give this a try. You should find that Squarey's death is now a little more convincing as he explodes, the game pauses, and he then appears back at the start (Figure 6-4). In an upcoming chapter, we'll be taking a look at how to implement checkpoints, but for now, this should do the trick just nicely.

Figure 6-4. *Ouch, that has got to smart!*

The last little touch we're going to make for now regarding death is to stop Squarey from falling infinitely when he drops off the edge of our level. This is *very* easy to do—all we're going to do is to create an invisible GameObject with a box collider and attach the Hazard script. Then we'll stretch it out to create a barrier underneath the level (see Figure 6-5). Remember to make sure that the GameObject is a trigger.

Figure 6-5. *Adding our barrier underneath the level*

Animating the Player

Adding particle effects like this has done something important for our game: it has added a basic animation, which makes the world feel much more dynamic.

But not every animation involves lots of little dots being scattered all over the place. In a conventional platformer, objects are animated like cartoons so that they look like they're really running, jumping, or blowing in the wind. It's high time we added this kind of dynamic animation to our player character, so with that in mind, I've created a little spaceman who can explore the alien worlds we're going to be designing. We will call him Kevin, after Kevin Spacey. His sprite is shown in Figure 6-6, below.

Figure 6-6. *Kevin, your typical derivative platform hero!*

You may notice that Kevin's sprite is a little different from your regular sprite. Specifically, Kevin is not *one* sprite, but several sprites—except all those sprites are in a single file. You can either use Kevin in your own game or you can create a different set of sprites; just be sure to keep them all in one image file.

This is what we call a *sprite sheet*, which is just a single image containing all the frames of animation for a single character or object in the game. This is simply a more efficient way of handling sprites, and you can likewise make sprite sheets for any other elements in a game. Import this into the game as you usually would but then open it in the Inspector and after setting Pixels Per Unit to 50, set Sprite Mode to Multiple. This is telling Unity that the file contains *multiple* different frames of animation in a single image. The checkerboard pattern behind the sprites represents transparent areas in the image.

Now click Sprite Editor and then Slice (in the top left). See Figure 6-7 for reference.

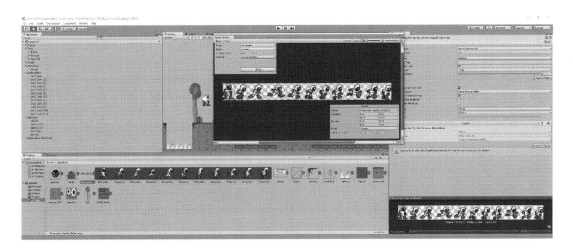

Figure 6-7. *The Sprite Editor*

This slice button is great because it automatically detects all the frames in our image and crops them for us into multiple different images. You'll see the individual frames outlined by boxes and you'll have the option to adjust this manually if you prefer. Once you're happy, just click Apply along the top.

Now you can select the first image from the sequence in your Sprites folder (clicking the little arrow next to the sprites will show the individual frames) and drop it into the sprite box for the Player character. Now we have replaced Squarey with Kevin (you will be missed, Squarey), but he will still kind of slide along the floor when we run (Figure 6-8).

Figure 6-8. *Kevin enters the world*

The next step is to open up two more windows in Unity. These are Animation and Animator. You'll do this by selecting Window ➤ Animation and then Window ➤ Animator using the top menu. This will open up the two new windows that will be floating on top of the UI to start with. Drag these by the tabs into place where you want them in Unity. I've put Animation in the same position as Scene and Game, and I've put Animator down the bottom along with the Project tab (see Figure 6-9).

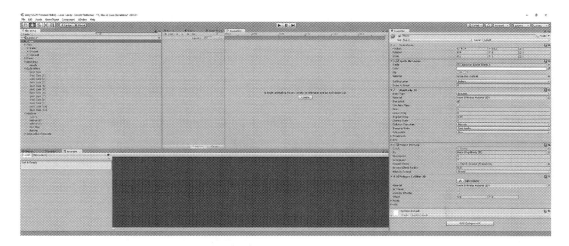

Figure 6-9. *Animation and Animator windows in place*

You'll see I've selected the player, which you should do too. In the Animation window you should now see a Create button, which we can use to create our first animation. We'll call this one Idle, and when the dialog opens up for you to define this, you'll also want to create a new folder to store it in called Animations.

You'll notice that once you've done this, a timeline appears in the Animation window, along with a kind of "mind-map" in the Animation window. We'll get to that in a second; for now, all you're going to do is drag and drop the first sprite (of Kevin standing completely still) into the start of the timeline so that you have something that looks like Figure 6-10.

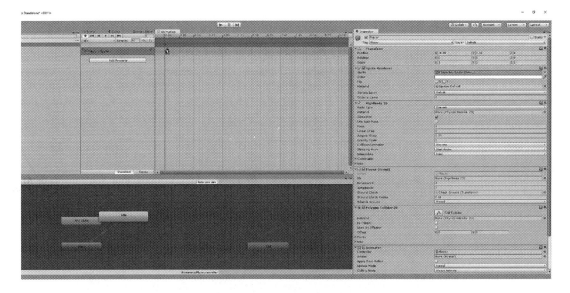

Figure 6-10. *An idle Kevin*

Believe it or not, you just created your first animation. It doesn't feel like much of an animation, seeing as it only has a single frame. But if you watch the Animation window while the game is playing, you'll see that the same image is looping over and over.

Walking With the Animator

Our more interesting animation of course is going to be the walking animation. To make this, you need to find the word Idle in the Animation window with the up and down arrow next to it (it's in the top left). Click that and then click Create New Clip. Call this one Walking and make sure it's in the Animation folder again.

Now drop each frame of the walking animation from the sprite sheet into the timeline, making sure they're more or less evenly spaced. If you need to create more space, you can do so by scrolling down on the mouse, which will zoom out the view. It should look something like Figure 6-11.

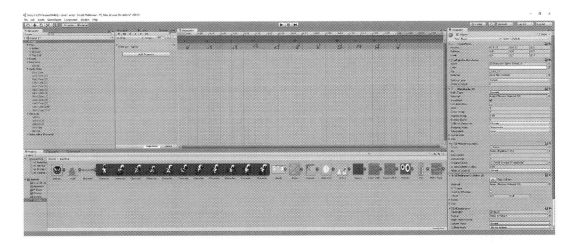

Figure 6-11. *Kevin's running animation, ready to go*

Now we have two separate animations, but at the moment Unity doesn't know when we want to switch between them. With that in mind, we need to head into the flow chart in the Animator, which currently goes straight from Entry into Idle (ignore Any State for now—this comes in handy only for more complex interactions of animations).

What we need to do is to add a condition under which our flow chart moves from Idle into Walking. To do this, right-click Idle and choose New Transition. This will create an arrow that you can drag onto the Walking state. Now your chart goes Entry ➤ Idle ➤ Walking.

Make sure the transition itself (the arrow) is selected and then find the little tab that reads Parameter and switch to that. You'll see a plus button next to Name, and if you click that, you'll be able to choose from different types of variables. Remember: variables are containers that represent data like numbers and strings. We're creating a new *bool*, short for Boolean—a variable that can be either true or false, 1 or 0. Once you've clicked plus, you'll be able to name this and you should call it Walking. It will look like Figure 6-12 if you've done everything correctly.

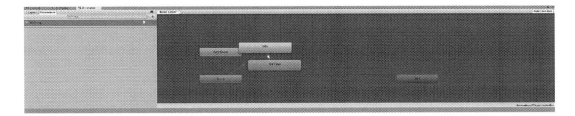

Figure 6-12. *Adding the walking Boolean*

Code for Animation

We need to do a little coding again now, so open up the Player script and create a new Animator reference, which we will call `anim`. Then we're going to add a little code in the `Update` method that will check to see if either the left or right keys are being pressed and set the Walking bool appropriately.

109

Once finished, your Player script should read as follows:

```
public class Player : MonoBehaviour {
    public Rigidbody2D rb;
    public int movespeed;
    public int jumppower;
    public Transform groundCheck;
    public float groundCheckRadius;
    public LayerMask whatIsGround;
    private bool onGround;
    private Animator anim;

    void Start () {
        rb = GetComponent<Rigidbody2D>();
        anim = GetComponent<Animator>();
    }

    void FixedUpdate()
    {
        onGround = Physics2D.OverlapCircle(groundCheck.position, groundCheckRadius,
        whatIsGround);
    }

    void Update () {

if (Input.GetKey(KeyCode.LeftArrow))
        {
            rb.velocity = new Vector2(-movespeed, rb.velocity.y);
            anim.SetBool("Walking", true);

        } else if (Input.GetKey(KeyCode.RightArrow))
        {
            rb.velocity = new Vector2(movespeed, rb.velocity.y);
            anim.SetBool("Walking", true);

        } else
        {
            anim.SetBool("Walking", false);
        }

        if (Input.GetKey(KeyCode.Space) && onGround)
        {
            rb.velocity = new Vector2(rb.velocity.x, jumppower);

        }
    }
}
```

Notice we are using an `"else if"` statement. When this statement follows immediately after an `if` statement, it means that the following code runs if the previous statement is *false* and the following statement is *true*. This allows us to set `Walking` to false only in scenarios where neither button is being pressed, while leaving our logic intact.

We could alternatively do something similar with the line *anim.SetBool("Walking", rb.velocity.x 1=0)*, meaning that the `Walking` variable will equal true if the statement that follows is true—if the velocity of the player along the X axis is zero. However, this can leave Kevin jogging on the spot while he slides forward on pure momentum.

With that done, return to Unity, select the transition that goes from Idle to Walking, and find the heading that says Conditions in the Inspector. Click +, use the dropdown menu to choose Walking as the condition, and to set the value to True. This essentially means that the transition will occur as long as the Walking is true.

Untick the box that says Has Exit Time while you're here. That means that Unity won't wait until the whole animation has played out before transitioning from one to the other.

Now repeat these steps in reverse so that you have a transition going from Walking back to Idle whenever `Walking = false`. Once everything is in place, it should look like Figure 6-13.

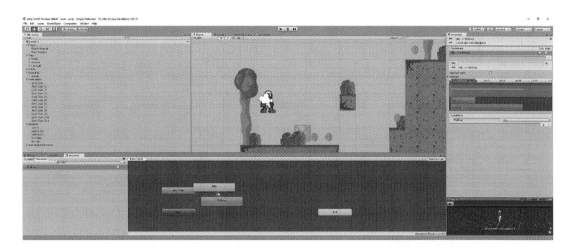

Figure 6-13. *Our flow chart is complete*

As you may have already gathered, there's nothing to stop us from adding more branches to our flow diagram so that the character has animations for jumping, falling, or any other actions we add later in the game. Likewise, we could add animations so that trees blow in the wind and coins spin in situ. Water could even wave gently on the top layer.

Flippin' Kevin

Of course, there's one rather glaring omission here currently, which is that Kevin only has an animation for running right. Oh no! We forgot to create sprites for running left.

Psych! Fortunately, there's no need for us to make everything twice, and we can very easily create animations for running left by simply *flipping* the image when Kevin turns around. To do that, we need to create a private integer variable in our Player script and call it `facing`. Set `facing` to 1 in the `Start` method (it makes some sense to have the forward direction correspond with the positive value, so 1 is going to = right). Then update this section of code in the Update method like so:

```
if (Input.GetKey(KeyCode.LeftArrow))
    {
        rb.velocity = new Vector2(-movespeed, rb.velocity.y);s
        anim.SetBool("Walking", true);
        if (facing == 1)
        {
            transform.localScale = new Vector3(-1f, 1f, 1f);
            facing = 0;
        }

    } else if (Input.GetKey(KeyCode.RightArrow))
    {
        rb.velocity = new Vector2(movespeed, rb.velocity.y);
        anim.SetBool("Walking", true);
        if (facing == 0)
        {
            transform.localScale = new Vector3(1f, 1f, 1f);
            facing = 1;
        }

    } else
    {
        anim.SetBool("Walking", false);
    }
```

The key lines here are the ones that read transform.localscale—this is the one that is flipping the Player sprite by setting the scale to 1 or –1. We also need to ensure that we're changing the value of facing so that this only happens the first time the player changes direction each way. The code should look like Figure 6-14.

```
Simple Platformer - Microsoft Visual Studio
File   Edit   View   Project   Debug   Team   Tools   Test   Analyze   Window   Help
                                                        Attach... ▼

Player.cs ⊕ ✕  Hazards.cs        CollectCoin.cs
⌗ Miscellaneous Files                                                              ⚙ Player

    7       public int jumppower;
    8       public Transform groundCheck;
    9       public float groundCheckRadius;
   10       public LayerMask whatIsGround;
   11       private bool onGround;
   12       private Animator anim;
   13       private int facing;
   14
   15       void Start () {
   16           rb = GetComponent<Rigidbody2D>();
   17           anim = GetComponent<Animator>();
   18           facing = 1;
   19       }
   20
   21       void FixedUpdate()
   22       {
   23           onGround = Physics2D.OverlapCircle(groundCheck.position, groundCheckRadius, whatIsGround);
   24       }
   25
   26       void Update () {
   27
   28
   29
   30           if (Input.GetKey(KeyCode.LeftArrow))
   31           {
   32               rb.velocity = new Vector2(-movespeed, rb.velocity.y);
   33               anim.SetBool("Walking", true);
   34               if (facing == 1)
   35               {
   36                   transform.localScale = new Vector3(-1f, 1f, 1f);
   37                   facing = 0;
   38               }
   39
   40           } else if (Input.GetKey(KeyCode.RightArrow))
   41           {
   42               rb.velocity = new Vector2(movespeed, rb.velocity.y);
   43               anim.SetBool("Walking", true);
   44               if (facing == 0)
   45               {
   46                   transform.localScale = new Vector3(1f, 1f, 1f);
   47                   facing = 1;
   48               }
   49
   50           } else
   51           {
   52               anim.SetBool("Walking", false);
   53           }
   54
   55
   56           if (Input.GetKey(KeyCode.Space) && onGround)
   57           {
   58               rb.velocity = new Vector2(rb.velocity.x, jumppower);
   59
   60           }
100 %  ▼
```

Figure 6-14. *The new Player script*

Now hit play and you should find that Kevin has a nice little running animation and can switch direction. Make sure that your Camera object has the coordinates of precisely 0 and 0—otherwise, the view will jolt slightly as Kevin flips left and right.

Of course, this is far from perfect right now. We're lacking animations for jumping, the movement is a little stilted, and the camera is rigidly following us around the screen. Don't worry, you can fix all this later. For now, I'm just giving you the nuts and bolts so you can start playing around yourself. Feel free to start animating all your game elements. Figure 6-15 shows how much more action-packed Kevin already looks as he grabs a coin and prepares to leap into the abyss.

Figure 6-15. *You go, Kevin*

Adding a HUD

In this chapter we've been focusing on using effects and animations to add more feedback for the player. Now it's time to focus on the more direct and fundamental kind of feedback: the player's score and progress.

In other words, it's time that we started letting the player know how they're doing at the game we've made for them and keeping a tally of things like the level, their score, and so on. This will be accomplished via a HUD that shows the player important details. Later, we'll be able to use this overlay to show all kinds of other things too.

To start with, let's begin by keeping track of how many coins the player has collected. To do that, we want to create a new public integer called coins in the Player script. We don't need to say coins = 0 in the Start method, because all numerical variables are set to zero by default when they're created.

Now we're going to open up our CollectCoin script and add a reference to player. Then, in the OnTriggerEnter2D event, we will add the line: player.coins++. This is shorthand for player.coins = player.coins + 1. In other words, we are increasing the value of player's coins by one.

The whole thing will read as follows:

```
public class CollectCoin : MonoBehaviour {

    // Use this for initialization
    public GameObject Sparkle;
    private Player player;

        void Start () {
        player = FindObjectOfType<Player>();
    }

        // Update is called once per frame
        void Update () {

        }
```

```
private void OnTriggerEnter2D(Collider2D other)
{
    if (other.tag == "Player")
    {
        player.coins++;
        Instantiate(Sparkle, gameObject.transform.position, gameObject.transform.
        rotation);
        Destroy(gameObject);
    }
}
```

If you try playing the game while watching the Coins variable in the Inspector (with Player selected), you'll see it goes up each time we collect a new coin.

We now know the number of coins our player has collected, but at the moment the player doesn't. To rectify this, we're going to create something called a *canvas*.

Adding and Using Canvases

Head up to that top menu again and create a new GameObject. This time select GameObject ➤ UI ➤ Canvas. Double-click it in your Hierarchy and you'll see your scene suddenly zooms out to show you a large white box. This is the *canvas*, which is where you can add UI elements to your game, such as a HUD and touch controls. That, incidentally, is why it was pertinent to focus on graphics before creating the first APK.

Now right-click the canvas in your Hierarchy and choose UI ➤ Text to create a new text object. Here, let's write Level 1 in the Inspector and set Font Size to 20 and bold. We could change the font if we wanted simply by finding the relevant ODF or TTF file (by downloading a font, in other words) and dropping it into the box here as we would do a sprite. We can worry about that later, though.

The most important thing we need to do at this point is anchor this UI element to the top left of the screen. Do that by clicking the picture of the square in the top left of the Inspector and then selecting the top left option from the dropdown menu. Now position the text where you want it, and it will always stay locked to the top lefthand corner of the screen. It should look like Figure 6-16.

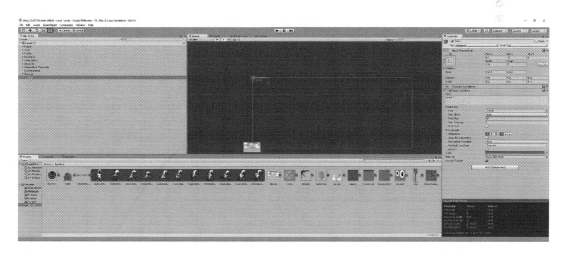

Figure 6-16. *I chose a color that would match Kevin's boots and be readable against a lot of backgrounds*

Rename the text object as Level. Then create another one that will be positioned just below the top one, called Coins. Use the same size and color font and make this one say Coins: 0.

Guess what? It's time to make another script. This one will be called Score and it will be attached to the Coins object we just made. It will read as follows:

```
using UnityEngine;
using System.Collections;
using UnityEngine.UI;
public class Score : MonoBehaviour
{
    Text coins;
    private Player player;

    // Use this for initialization
    void Start()
    {
        coins = GetComponent<Text>();
        player = FindObjectOfType<Player>();
    }

    void Update()
    {
        coins.text = "Coins: " + player.coins;
    }
}
```

Notice the line that says using UnityEngine.UI. This basically tells Unity that we're referring to an additional class in order to gain more options to code with.

The rest of this script is hopefully fairly self-explanatory. All we're doing is repeatedly updating the text (which is a type of String variable) to read Coins: and then the player.coins integer.

Add this as a component to the coins text object and you should now find that the game lets you know how many coins Kevin has collected as he goes about his adventures. Something like you see in Figure 6-17, in fact.

Figure 6-17. *Kevin now has two coins. Way to go, Kevin. Remember to add your coin's sparkle effect, if you haven't already.*

Adding a Sound Effect

As we've done all that, we may as well finish the job and add a little sound effect to play as we're collecting coins. Fortunately, that's rather easy to do.

You will of course need a file that you can use for your sounds (which you can get from the resources included with this book or make yourself) and as you probably expect, you'll want to add this to a new folder called Audio. My audio file is called Bling.wav.

Now add a public Audio Source bling to your CollectCoin script and just above `player.coins++`, add a line that reads `bling.Play()`. This would be *super* simple, except we can't just drop the audio file directly into the box in the Inspector. Instead, we need to use an Audio Source, which is any GameObject that has the audio attached as a component. What I've seen a lot of people do is add the audio file to the empty `Collectibles` GameObject that is the parent of the `Coins` object and then drag *that* into the box in the Inspector. (Make sure to untick Play On Awake).

Unfortunately, you need to do this for the in-game instances of the objects, not the prefab.

There are other ways of doing this, but for now, it should look like Figure 6-18, and this will play a sound every time you pick up a coin.

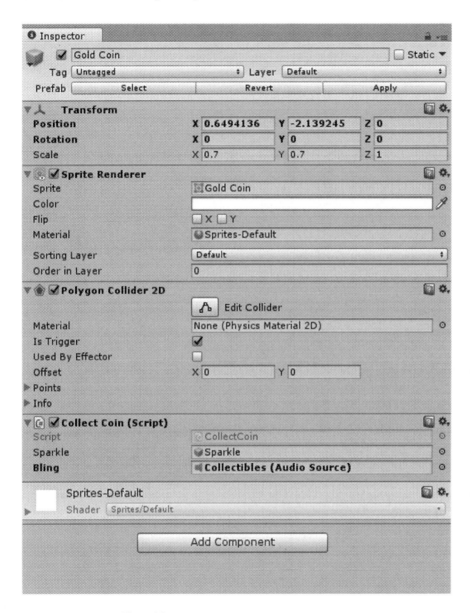

Figure 6-18. *The* Collectibles *object now has Bling as a component*

And with that, we're now ready to try this thing out on an actual mobile device. Unless you're feeling brave, that is.

Some Advanced Theory: Classes, Objects, and Methods, Oh My! Just What Is an Object?

You may have noticed that I refer to pretty much everything in Unity as a GameObject. This terminology is convenient because in a game development environment, most things *are* objects, like trees, enemies, coins, and clouds. But actually there's something a little deeper going on here.

That's because an *object* can also refer to a type of data in a programming language. One of the (other) things that makes Unity so powerful and convenient is the fact that it uses object-oriented programming (OOP). Both C# and Java are OOP, and Unity runs with that fact in an elegant and smart way. You may have heard of OOP before, or this might be your first time encountering it. Either way, OOP is a design philosophy when it comes to programming and it represents something of an evolution that has occurred in coding over the years. Were you to code in an old-school language such as BASIC (as I did on my ZX Spectrum!), you would have programmed in a manner called *imperative* programming.

Objective vs. Imperative vs. Functional

Imperative meant that everything you wrote was sequential, and you would write statements in the order that they were to be executed at runtime. The computer would read your code just as you would read an essay: from top to bottom. The only exception was when you used the command GOTO, which would send the interpreter backwards or forwards to a specific line number in the code. This was very straightforward to understand but it also became *impossible* to manage as programs began to reach millions of lines (which happened a lot). If there was an error in the code, you'd have to scroll through reams and reams of it to find the cause and if you ever wanted to reuse a section, your only option was to copy and paste it.

Then *procedural* programming came along, which solved some of these issues by containing sections of code in discrete sections called *procedures* or *subroutines*. This meant that certain instructions could be called on over and over again and edited separately from the main code—but seeing as you had to *call* the procedures, the code would still be taking a long winding journey and making countless stops along the way. This is what is referred to now as *spaghetti code*.

OOP is simply the next evolution from there. It looks at programming less in terms of the commands and more in terms of the data and objects that those commands describe.

Classes and Objects Explained

In OOP, subroutines are replaced with *classes*, which in turn are used to describe objects. An *object* is a collection of data with properties and with behaviors called *methods*.

All the scripts we've written in our code are really classes because they describe the properties and the behaviors of our objects. Our CollectCoin script (which is really a class called CollectCoin) describes the behavior of the coin (to disappear when collected, to increase the player.coins value) and the properties (the position of the coin, its size, and so on).

The class acts like a blueprint and can create as many coins (objects) as it wants (just as a blueprint for a house can be used to create lots of houses). We call those *instances* of the object. When we destroy our coins, we are destroying *instances* of those coins rather than the class itself. That's why we have one script (class) but lots of copies (instances) of the coins. It's also why we need to destroy our particle effects whenever they finish playing, so that there aren't countless instances of the particle effect object being held in memory at any given time.

And as we've seen by the fact that a method in CollectCoin (onTriggerEnter) can edit a property in Player (coins), classes are able to interact with one another by accessing each other's methods and properties.

A class needn't be attached to a sprite at all either. A class can also be used just for crunching numbers and manipulating *other* classes. You could write a script (class) to control the time limit, for instance, and the object in this case would be *the time limit*—an abstract concept rather than something you could move around. But it's still an object and it's still defined by the class.

This is also what happens when we tell Unity that we're using certain classes at the start of each script—these are classes provided by Unity that provide additional functionality and that we can access the methods and properties of. When we write those lines, we're telling Unity we want to access some methods and properties that it has created for us.

The Benefits of Going OOP in Unity

Therein lies the brilliance of object-oriented programming: it allows us to share elements between programming languages and code in a modular fashion. If you wanted to add collectible coins to a future game, you could simply lift that class and drop it in your new project. Likewise, when we use the Android SDK, we're really giving Unity access to the classes that Google has provided to ensure the code all runs smoothly on Android devices. Using objects allows us to borrow elements from other programmers and implement them in our own code. This also lends itself perfectly to a more open source and collaborative form of development, which is good for the software industry as a whole.

For us, OOP also lets us keep things neatly organized in logical chunks. Rather than having one huge file that determines the behavior of everything in our game world, instead we have GameObjects, all with their own scripts. Unity helps make things even clearer by giving us a visual representation of those GameObjects and by keeping most of the complicated stuff hidden (learning Java, on the other hand, is much more complicated, largely owing to the need to get your head around classes, methods, and objects). In Unity, objects really *are* objects much of the time, and we can literally move them around within our project as tangible units. Unity is a perfect introduction to object-oriented code, then, and when you eventually make the transition to a less visual type of code, it will help to imagine your classes and objects existing in a similar way (hopefully).

If we were being pedantic, it would probably make more sense for us to put our code for dying in the Player script, rather than the Hazards script (which are really classes). Dying is a behavior of the player and so it makes more sense for it to be a method of that class (remember, classes describe objects and behaviors). To do this, we would simply move the code over to a public method (public void dying() {...}) and make the necessary changes. Then we would invoke that method from within Hazards by writing player.dying();. We could also pass information over by placing it inside the brackets. Oh, and private methods and variables are ones that *can't* be accessed by other classes.

Anyway, go ahead and make that change if you like—it will be a good learning opportunity. But if you'd rather not, the code will still work just fine as is.

For our purposes, keeping our code as beautifully organized and efficient as possible is not *super* important. We're making a relatively small game that most devices will be more than capable of running, and at this point it's more important that you follow along and understand everything that's happening. When code gets larger, though—when you're working as a team, or when the game is more resource-intensive—being as elegant as possible in your code starts to pay off. Making code snippets as short and efficient as possible too can actually get quite fun and rewarding. OOP? More like OCD programming.

Don't worry if all that went straight over your head. It took me *multiple* rereads to eventually grasp what OOP really means in a practical sense. Hopefully, though, you at least now have *some* idea what the term means—essentially, to code in a modular fashion—and this will provide a useful foundation as you expand your knowledge over time. That, and it will help you to think more like a programmer, which is always a good thing.

Now, on to the fun part: let's turn this thing into an app.

CHAPTER 7

Making an Android App

Our game is still far from complete at this point, and over the next several chapters you'll learn how to add things like levels, checkpoints, menus, more UI elements, and a host of other features.

But what we *do* have is a basic game that now works as a game and is something that is certainly playable. Our canvas is in place—which is going to be an important point. In short, I feel you've waited long enough. It's time to get this thing up and running on your Android device.

In this chapter, you'll learn how to create an APK, how to test your game on your phone or tablet, and how to add touch controls to your game. By the end, you'll be able to take the game you made with you anywhere and slip it into your pocket. In theory, you could even release it to the world. But I wouldn't recommend doing that just yet....

Adding Touch Controls

Before we begin building an APK, it's a good idea to add touch controls. Right now, you *could* use your app on an Android device with a Bluetooth keyboard, but that's not a terribly convenient way for most people to play. Most people don't even have a Bluetooth keyboard. You want them to be able to play it with just their phone. Fortunately, adding *touch controls* isn't too complicated a process.

If we were making an endless runner, adding touch controls would be incredibly simple. In that case, all we would need would need to do is use the line *Input.GetMouseButtonDown(0)* instead of *Input.GetKey(KeyCode.Space)* or whatever we were using for jump. In Unity, a mouse click and a touched screen are registered as the exact same thing, and because we wouldn't need to know *where* on the screen the user tapped, this would be more than sufficient for controlling our game.

We'll be looking at how to create an endless runner in a future chapter. If that's what you're interested in doing, you can skip ahead to the next section on building an APK. Otherwise, stick with me and we'll look at how to implement proper touch controls.

Designing the Controls

The first thing you're going to want to do is to design some touch controls to look the part when placed on top of your game. They need to be clear and easy to find, but it's also important that they don't distract the player or cover up any important elements of the game. For that reason, choosing something that will look mildly translucent is a good option.

It's also pertinent that the buttons match the aesthetics of your game world. The color you choose needs to stand out against the levels but without clashing in a garish fashion. As your players progress through your game, it's normal to have the color palette of your game world change: perhaps one level is set under water with lots of blues and greens, and another level is set in space with lots of black and white. If you make your buttons red or green, you'll find that they sometimes look ugly against the game world.

© Adam Sinicki 2017
A. Sinicki, *Learn Unity for Android Game Development*, DOI 10.1007/978-1-4842-2704-6_7

For these reasons, I'm making my buttons light grey with a thin, slightly darker grey outline. I also applied a pixelized filter with the image editor GIMP and set the opacity to 80 percent. The result should be something that won't look too distracting and won't feel out of place. You can what I created in Figures 7-1 and 7-2.

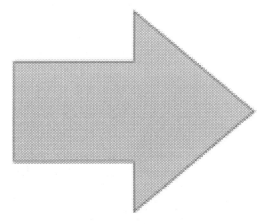

Figure 7-1. *An arrow*

Figure 7-2. *A button*

Note that I only needed to create one directional arrow. That's because I can simply reverse the image in order to create the opposite arrow—no need to spend time drawing two.

Adding Our Controls

Now we need to add these to our game and make them do something. First, add the images to your project's Sprite folder just like you would any other. Now right-click in your Hierarchy somewhere underneath your canvas—you want this new element to be a child of the Canvas GameObject—and select UI ➤ Image. An image will appear in your game that will probably look like a big white square. Select this element and where it says Source Image, drag and drop the arrow sprite you created from your Sprites folder. Where it says

Anchors, choose Bottom Left. Drag and position the arrow so that it's in the lefthand corner of the canvas (which will probably appear massive at this point) and then change the horizontal scale to negative numbers so that the arrow points left instead of right. In other words, change the Width from 1 to –1 so that it will fold back in on itself.

Depending on how large you drew your arrows, you will need to play around to make sure that these images are the right size. You can tweak this later on once the APK is running on your phone, but for now I have mine set to X = –2 and Y = 2 (see Figure 7-3).

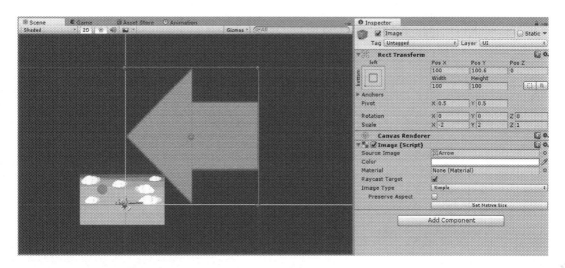

Figure 7-3. *Positioning the first control*

Now do the same thing for the second arrow. This time the position will be slightly to the right, and the anchor will still be bottom left. Of course, the Scale is going to be in positive figures this time. After that, you can add the jump button, which will be our generic "button" image. This one will be anchored to the bottom *right* of the screen. See Figure 7-2. Rename the buttons as appropriate.

What you'll find is that the jump button and the right arrow may overlap at this point or just look very close together (as in Figure 7-4), but you don't need to worry about that. By setting the images to *anchor* to the bottom corners of the screen, you're stating that all positional information is going to be *relative* to that corner. Unity doesn't know what size the phone screen or whatever device you'll be playing on is going to be, and thus the canvas is likely to be a bit of an odd shape. But as long as the jump button is set to be a certain *distance* from the righthand corner and the same goes for the arrows and the lefthand corner, they should be in the correct position once you hit play.

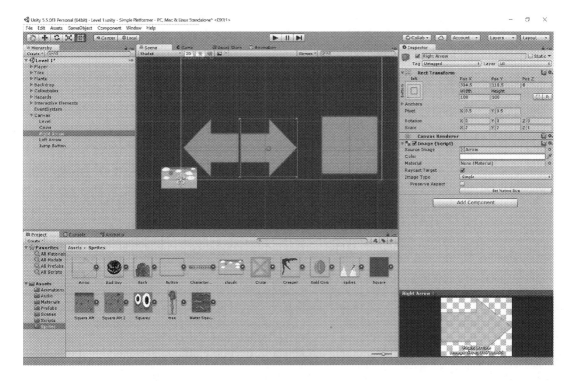

Figure 7-4. *The buttons don't look quite right yet, but have faith*

Of course, for a preview you can hit play and see how it looks on your computer screen (Figure 7-5). When positioning your arrows, it's worth leaving a little space around the edges in order to make sure they aren't too cramped.

Figure 7-5. *See? Our arrows look lovely!!*

Coding the Controls

Now that you have your buttons in place, it's time to make them actually *do* something. With that in mind, we need to create an empty GameObject that will act like a container for these elements. Right-click your canvas, choose Create Empty, and then anchor this new object to the bottom of the screen. Click Stretch so that it becomes as wide as the screen and then drag the elements into here in the Hierarchy. Call your new container TouchController.

Head into your Player script (which, as we learned in Chapter 6, is really a class) and we're going to add two public Booleans. Remember, bools are variables that can be either true or false—1 or 0—and because they're public, they're accessible by other classes (scripts) in our game.

These new variables are going to be called moveRight and moveLeft, and you're going to use them to do this (don't paste this code yet):

```
if (moveright)
{
rb.velocity = new Vector2(movespeed, rb.velocity.y);
}
if (moveleft)
{
rb.velocity = new Vector2(-movespeed, rb.velocity.y);
}
```

Notice that this is doing something very similar to pressing the right and left arrows manually.

The way these touchable image elements work is that they only allow us to register when they get *tapped* and when they get *released*. That means we can't ask Unity whether the button is "being pressed." Instead, we need to set our Booleans to true or false based on when the button is tapped and when it's released.

The reason I told you not to paste that code just yet is that there's an easier way to do this. We already have a bunch of code to handle the player walking left and right, and at the moment it includes things like animations—so we don't want to repeat ourselves.

Instead we're going to use a command called OR. This basically allows us to ask whether one of two things is happening. In this case, we're asking whether the player is pressing an arrow key *or* one of our Booleans is true. In C#, we write OR using the symbol ||.

So, our code should look like this now:

```
if (moveLeft || Input.GetKey(KeyCode.LeftArrow))
    {
        rb.velocity = new Vector2(-movespeed, rb.velocity.y);
        anim.SetBool("Walking", true);
        if (facing == 1)
        {
            transform.localScale = new Vector3(-1f, 1f, 1f);
            facing = 0;
        }

    } else if (moveRight || Input.GetKey(KeyCode.RightArrow))
    {
        rb.velocity = new Vector2(movespeed, rb.velocity.y);
        anim.SetBool("Walking", true);
        if (facing == 0)
        {
            transform.localScale = new Vector3(1f, 1f, 1f);
            facing = 1;
        }

    } else
    {
        anim.SetBool("Walking", false);
    }
```

Now, when you press right and left, your character should still move. But were you to set one of the Booleans to true (remember, all variables equal 0 by default when first created—that is, false), then the player would move automatically.

Likewise, I want you to move the code that is handling the jump action of your player character into a new public method. A *public* method is a method—a snippet of instructional code—that can be executed from other classes (scripts). That means we can now force the player to jump by activating it from external scripts.

We still want to register the button press in our Update method, but instead of including the jump code, we're referencing the new public method that contains said code.

So, you'll be creating the public method like so:

```
public void jump() {

    if (onGround) {
        rb.velocity = new Vector2(rb.velocity.x, jumppower);
    }
}
```

And then from within the Update method, you will simply say this:

```
if (Input.GetKey(KeyCode.Space))
{
    jump();
}
```

The whole thing should look like this:

```
void Update() {

        if (moveLeft || Input.GetKey(KeyCode.LeftArrow))
        {
            rb.velocity = new Vector2(-movespeed, rb.velocity.y);
            anim.SetBool("Walking", true);
            if (facing == 1)
            {
                transform.localScale = new Vector3(-1f, 1f, 1f);
                facing = 0;
            }

        } else if (moveRight || Input.GetKey(KeyCode.RightArrow))
        {
            rb.velocity = new Vector2(movespeed, rb.velocity.y);
            anim.SetBool("Walking", true);
            if (facing == 0)
            {
                transform.localScale = new Vector3(1f, 1f, 1f);
                facing = 1;
            }

        } else
        {
            anim.SetBool("Walking", false);
        }

        if (Input.GetKey(KeyCode.Space))
        {
            jump();
        }
    }
```

```
    public void jump() {

if (onGround) {
rb.velocity = new Vector2(rb.velocity.x, jumppower);
}
        }
```

This is important because we've essentially given ourselves access points that we can use to control the player from *outside* the script. And we're going to be utilizing that from within the script that will control our buttons. If you're struggling to understand what's going on here, consider rereading the section on object oriented programming (OOP) in Chapter 6.

You see? It's always good to learn the theory stuff as you go.

Okay, so now we've done that. It's time to make the buttons responsive. Start by creating another new script, this time called Touch. Touch is going to contain the following code:

```
public class Touch : MonoBehaviour
{
    private Player player;

    void Start()
    {
        player = FindObjectOfType<Player>();
    }

    public void PressLeftArrow()
    {
        player.moveRight = false;
        player.moveLeft = true;
    }
    public void PressRightArrow()
    {
        player.moveRight = true;
        player.moveLeft = false;
    }
    public void ReleaseLeftArrow()
    {
        player.moveLeft = false;
    }
    public void ReleaseRightArrow()
    {
        player.moveRight = false;

    }

    public void Jump()
    {
        player.Jump();

    }
}
```

This is basically a collection of public methods, each of which is going to interact with the Player script (class) in one way or another. As you may have guessed, we're now going to make it so that each onscreen button triggers one of these methods.

Now head back to Unity and add this new Touch script as a component of the TouchController empty GameObject we created earlier (see Figure 7-6).

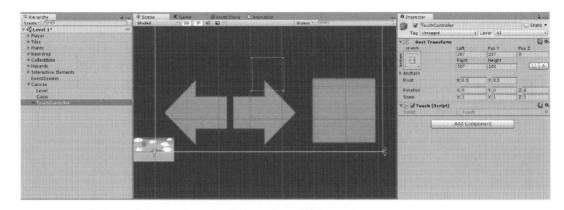

Figure 7-6. *Add the Touch script to the empty GameObject*

Now we're going to add a component to the left arrow—this time a new kind called an Event Trigger. Go to Add Component ➤ Event ➤ Event Trigger. Now click Add New Event Type ➤ Pointer Down. Click the little plus (+) symbol that appears on the right and then take the TouchController GameObject and drag it into the None (Object) box. Then click the dropdown menu on the right and select Touch ➤ PressLeftArrow(). Basically, you're telling Unity that you want the Pointer Down event (the action of pressing the button) to trigger the public method PressLeftArrow that's within the Touch script.

Click Add New Event Type and then choose Pointer Up. This registers the action of the finger being lifted from the arrow. Now select Touch ➤ ReleaseLeftArrow() to go in here. It should look like Figure 7-7 if everything is working properly.

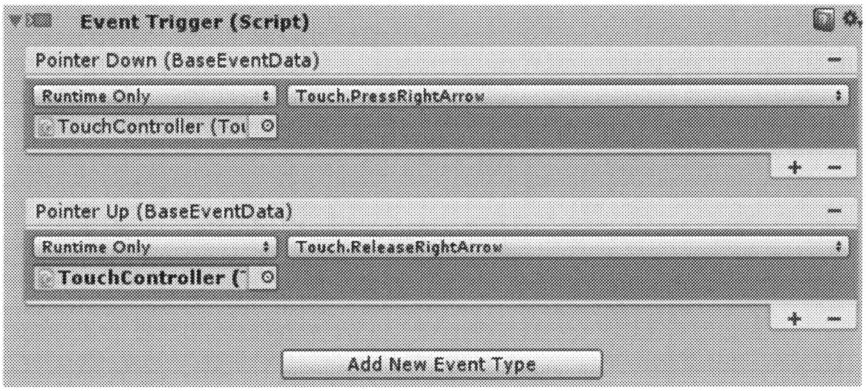

Figure 7-7. *Event triggers added*

As you've probably guessed, you need to do the same thing for the right arrow but using the respective right arrow methods. For the jump button, you're going to do something very slightly different by ignoring the pointer up type of event and choosing the *Jump( )* method for pointer down.

Click play and you should be able to test this. If you don't have a touchscreen laptop to try it on, then just clicking the buttons with your mouse should do the same trick. Don't worry if it doesn't feel like it's very responsive right now—it should be a different story once it's running on an Android device.

Speaking of which....

Creating Your First APK

Now that you have an appropriate form of input, you can finally actually test all your hard work on an Android device.

First, make sure you've saved your scene again by pressing Ctrl+S. Next, head over to File ➤ Build Settings. You'll see a box at the top of this window that says Scenes In Build—this is basically showing you which of the scenes you've created you want to include in the final product. To add your Level 1, just drag it from your Scenes folder in the Project window and drop it into the Scenes in Build area. It should look like Figure 7-8.

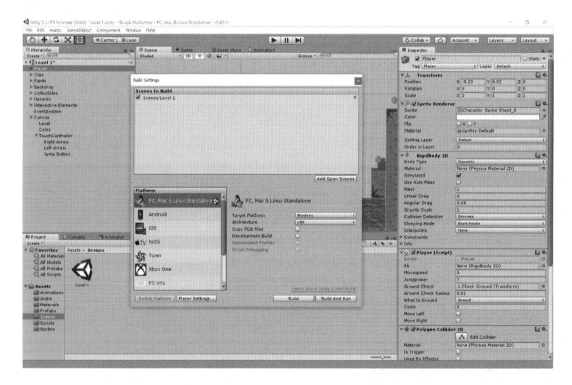

Figure 7-8. *Level 1 is currently the only scene in our build*

When you have more scenes (and you will), you'll need to make sure that the scene at the top is the one you want to run first. That would normally mean a splash screen or menu of some kind (but remember, if you have the free Unity license, your splash screen will be preceded by a Unity one).

For now, don't worry about texture compression. That's useful for creating 3D games and will help you to optimize your apps. For our purposes right now it isn't necessary (our app is pretty small and not very resource-intensive), and not all types of compression are supported by all Android platforms. I discuss texture compression more later in the book.

You'll notice that this window also has the option to select a platform, and right now it likely says PC, Mac & Linux Standalone. You need to change this by clicking the Android option and then clicking Switch Platform.

Player Settings

Next, click the Player Settings button beneath the Platform scroll box and you'll find that some new options open up for you to play with in the Inspector. This is where you can define many of the properties of the APK you're about to build: things like the icon, the package name, and the orientation (see Figure 7-9).

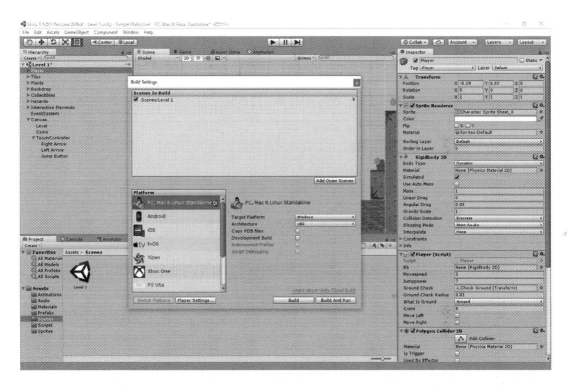

Figure 7-9. *Player Settings is where you set the properties for your new APK*

Before we dive into the settings, fill out the options at the top. Here, you can enter a name for your company and the name of your app. If you leave this as it is, then the company will be DefaultCompany, and the app will be called whatever you called your Project. There's also the option to add an icon here. We're not going to worry about that right now—we'll look at this again when we discuss uploading and marketing your app. For now, we'll stick with the default Unity icon.

Now, what do all the rest of these options do?

Resolution and Presentation

The first thing we're going to look at is Resolution and Presentation. At the moment, the Default Orientation is probably set to Auto Rotation, and beneath that there are tick boxes showing which orientations are permitted—right now, the answer is probably *all of them*.

131

If you want to make a puzzle game (discussed in an upcoming chapter), there's a chance you'll want to support a portrait orientation. There are even a small number of portrait action games like *Fotonica* and *Sonic Jump*. But for the most part, it makes more sense to stick with landscape, which will prevent your players from feeling too cramped and which will show the most screen. Controllers that hold the phone while you play also tend to only support landscape. So, either choose an orientation in the Default Orientation box or untick the two portrait options below.

Icon

The next section is the Icon section. As I said earlier, the icon is something we'll come to later, but as you can see, there is space here to add icons with various different resolutions. If you're keen to put something here, it's fine to just use one image, in which case it's better to use a higher resolution one rather than a lower resolution one. Upscaling results in a better image quality than downscaling. I go into this in more detail later—it's fine to leave this empty for the time being. Figure 7-10 shows what the default icon will look like once installed.

Figure 7-10. *Soon this will be your app*

Splash Image

Next up is Splash Image, which we'll again be leaving blank—especially as you're supposed to leave the default image here on the free license.

Other Settings

Other Settings gives us plenty to play around with. You can change settings relating to the rendering, as well as the minimum API level, write permission, install location, and more. Much of this is rather self-explanatory, and the rest we'll be coming back to later in a later chapter.

You're perfectly fine to skip over this section and leave everything as default again, but one or two things may be worth looking at here. The Bundle Identifier, for example, is where you enter your package name. The correct nomenclature for this is as follows: com.YourCompanyHere.YourAppNameHere. You'll need to set this before your app will build, so go ahead and enter a package name using your own details. It doesn't matter what you choose for now, but do think hard before you publish. Apart from anything else, once the app is uploaded to the Play Store, you won't be able to change this again.

The version and version code are for our sake and Android's sake, respectively. The version is the version as we see it and as our users see it. The version code, though, needs to change each time you update your app in the Play Store. Even if you make the tiniest change and then upload a new APK, you will need to make sure that the new version code is higher than the last one.

The minimum API level meanwhile defines what the lowest version of Android is that you want to support. By default, this is probably set to Android 2.3.1 (Gingerbread). At the time of writing, Google has just unleashed the developer preview for Android O, and the latest version available for users is 7.1 (Nougat).

The lower you make your API level, the more people will be able to download your app. But if you make it too low, you won't be able to access some of the later features of Android. Again, I discuss all this in further detail later in the book.

Preparing Your Phone

One more thing to do before you can try running your game on a phone is to prepare the phone in question. First, that means you need to allow USB debugging. Unfortunately, I can't give you step-by-step instructions, because every Android phone is different (that is the wonder and the frustration of working with Android).

USB debugging lets you install apps over a USB connection and then get feedback about how they're running. See Figure 7-11.

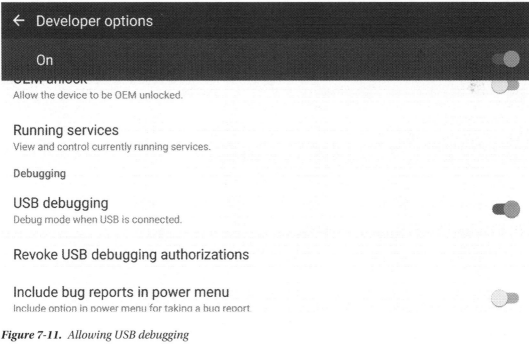

Figure 7-11. *Allowing USB debugging*

Usually, this option can be found under a section within your phone's settings called Developer Options. In some phones this is hidden, so do a Google search to find out how to turn on USB debugging on your particular hardware. Figure 7-11 shows this option on a Samsung Galaxy device.

The other setting you need to change is the one that says "Allow installation of apps from sources other than the Play Store." This normally has the heading Unknown Sources and might be found in the Applications section of your settings, or the Lock Screen and Security section. Again, a quick Google search will help you out. As you might expect, this setting ensures that your phone will accept APKs from other sources—such as your PC—so you need to have it turned on. See Figure 7-12.

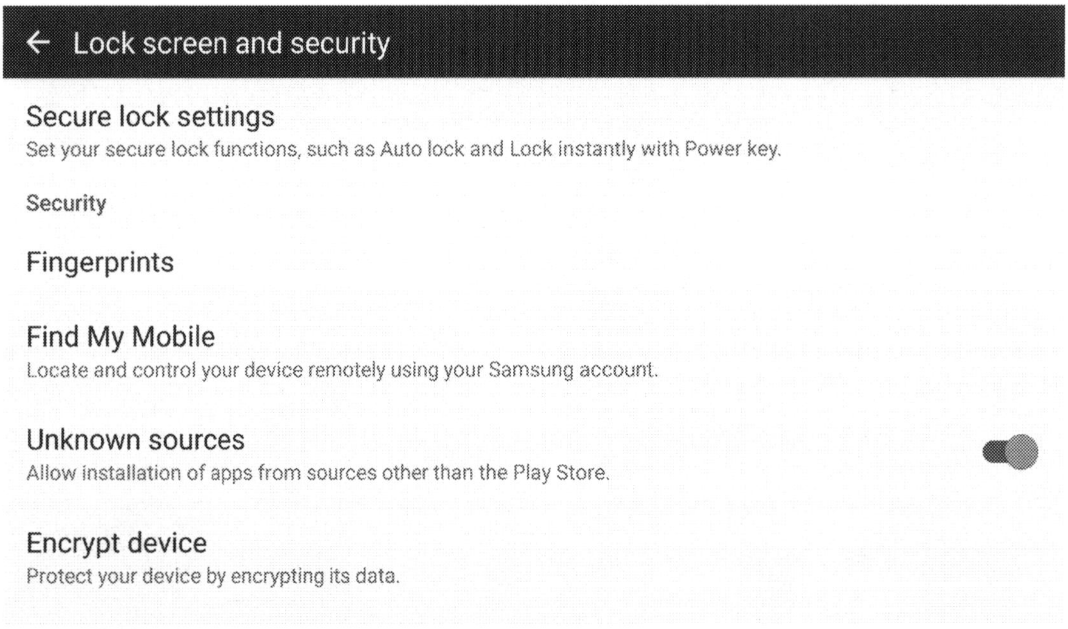

← Lock screen and security

Secure lock settings
Set your secure lock functions, such as Auto lock and Lock instantly with Power key.

Security

Fingerprints

Find My Mobile
Locate and control your device remotely using your Samsung account.

Unknown sources
Allow installation of apps from sources other than the Play Store.

Encrypt device
Protect your device by encrypting its data.

Figure 7-12. You need to tick the Unknown Sources option

Finally, make sure you've set up the drivers on your computer for your phone. This will likely have happened the first time you connected it to transfer photos, but just in case, you may need to do another search and grab those driver files for your phone. But if you can't figure this out, there are other ways you can get the app up and running on your phone.

Pulling the Trigger

Now all that's left to do is to build your app and run it. Go ahead and plug the phone into your PC via the USB port and then hit Build and Run. If everything goes according to plan, Unity will build the APK and then install it on your phone. After showing the splash screen, it should pop straight to life right there before you. Success!

TECHNICAL DIFFICULTIES

Unfortunately, when I did this I ran into some technical difficulties that took a while to figure out. Fortunately for you, it's my job to deal with these things to make your life easier.

After recently upgrading Android SDK Tools, it appears that compatibility has been broken and builds stopped working. That means that if you've only recently installed the Android SDK, things might not work as they should. The solution is to find an older version of Android SDK Tools and replace the folder in the SDK root directory (rename the old one to ToolsXXX or something).

Hopefully, by the time you read this, that little problem will be fixed. If not, you may have to do a little more Googling. Unfortunately, this is the nature of development and especially development on Android. But it does make everything all the more rewarding when it finally does work.

If everything has gone to plan, you should now have a working version of your app on your phone with touch controls. You may find that the UI elements are a little small, so move these around and resize them as you see fit.

Figure 7-13. *That UI is going to need to get a little larger*

Take this moment to bask in your accomplishments. You've just built your first working Android app. Go ahead and show Mom.

But don't get too pleased with yourself—there's still a long way to go. In Chapter 8 we'll be creating multiple levels, menus and save files. We're just getting started.

Figure 7-14. *We did it!*

CHAPTER 8

▨ ▨ ▨

Expanding the Game World with Checkpoints, Levels, and Save Files

A lot of this book is optional. Really, you're already at a point where you can build a nearly-finished game. It now runs on Android, it has animations and sound, and by extrapolating from what you've already learned, you can probably create a bunch of new elements and wrap it up into a "complete" game. Of course, I hope you'll stick with me until the end, because as I think it will result in a better finished product and more coding knowledge for you. (Plus you'll learn how to build virtual reality apps.)

With that said, there are still at least a couple of elements we haven't covered yet that are pretty much *compulsory* if you want your game to feel complete. Those are what this chapter covers.

First, if your levels are going to be more than a couple of platforms long, you're going to need to introduce checkpoints so that your players don't get frustrated by being constantly sent back to the start. Second, you'll probably also want to create more than one level and find a way to transition between them. And if you have more than one level, you're going to need some kind of level select system (menu) *and* a way to save player progress. These are really the only *essential* things you have left to learn before you can finish a challenging and fun game. So let's get to it.

Adding Checkpoints

Before you start adding checkpoints, it makes sense to make your level a little longer. This is the fun bit, so copy and paste some more ground sprites around, add in more spikes and water pools, and let your imagination run wild. In a chapter 10, we'll be going over what makes good level design—so don't put too much time and effort into this just yet. Consider this level design a placeholder that will just give you *something* to run through as you play.

Do make sure that there are some elements along the way that can kill the player, though. That's kind of required for checkpoints to make any sense. You can see what I did in Figure 8-1.

© Adam Sinicki 2017

A. Sinicki, *Learn Unity for Android Game Development*, DOI 10.1007/978-1-4842-2704-6_8

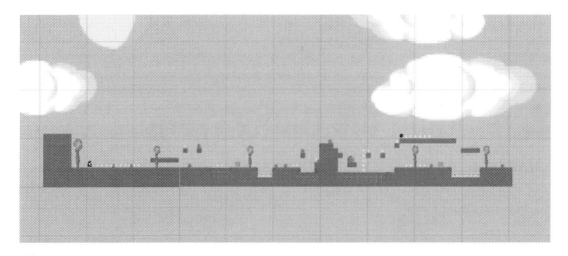

Figure 8-1. *My level 1 is very flat and horizontal, keeping things simple for new players*

Now we're going to create our first checkpoint. This will simply be an empty GameObject that we're going to drop into the game at various locations. And guess what we're going to call the first one? Checkpoint 1.

The most obvious way to handle checkpoint placement is to put them just before the player encounters a significant new challenge or just after. Later in the game, we may try combining multiple hazards in order to create sequences of challenges and thereby increase the difficulty slightly. But for now, let's start with the one new checkpoint to begin with and place it directly before the first pit of spikes.

You want to make this empty object a *trigger*, which, you may recall, means we can detect when someone passes through the collision cage but without it bumping into things. First, give it a circle collider and then tick the IsTrigger box in the Inspector. This means *we* can tell when a user walks over the checkpoint, but *they* won't be any the wiser.

Make this object quite large, because it's important that the player doesn't accidentally *skip* the checkpoint. You can do that using the resize tool or by entering the Radius in the Inspector. Mine is 3, which is more than large enough to prevent it being circumvented. See Figure 8-2.

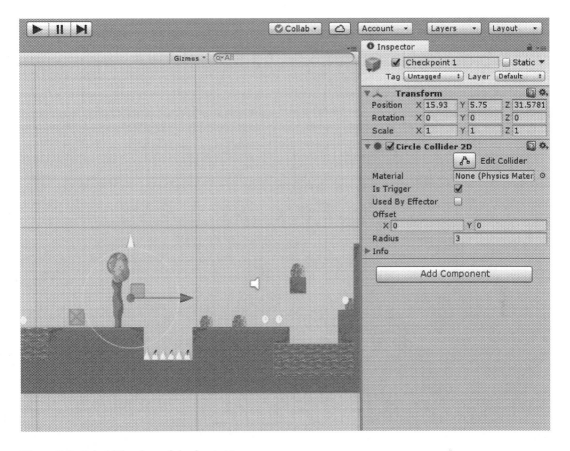

Figure 8-2. *Behold the glory of checkpoint 1*

As you've probably already guessed, it's time for a little more script (class). So create a script and call it Checkpoint. We're also going to be editing our Player script, so open that in Visual Studio as well.

Scripting a More Fitting Death

In fact, we're going to edit the script of Player 1 *first*. If you read the section on object-oriented programming in Chapter 6, then you know that our Player character is really a construct called an object. This object has properties (variables) and methods (behaviors), and it is through these that our *other* objects can interact with it.

If we want to *move* our player, it makes sense to do so by manipulating the variables in the Player script. We start by creating two more public floats: startx and starty. These are going to be the starting points of our player when respawning.

The start of the game is effectively our first checkpoint, so the first thing we should do on spawning our player at the start of the game is to find out where they are in the world so that we can send them back to this exact point each time they die. Currently, we are sending the player back to a specific set of coordinates that we edited, and if we were to move the player in the Scene view, we'd have to update these numbers every time. This would be even more of problem when we start creating multiple levels and were using the same script.

What we'll do instead is check the position of the player when the object is first created and make that the respawn position.

To do this, you simply need to add the following bit of code to the Start method:

```
startx = transform.position.x;
starty = transform.position.y;
```

The preceding code gets the position of the GameObject when it's first created and stores the X and Y coordinates separately.

Now find your Death method. This will either be in your Hazards script or your Player script (if you're one of my top students and you moved it, that is). Either way, you're now going to swap the numbers for your new variables. If the Death method is in the Player script, you can write this simply as follows:

```
transform.position = new Vector2(startx, starty);
```

Otherwise, if it's still in the Hazards script, it will look like so:

```
player.transform.position = new Vector2(player.startx, player.starty);
```

Either way, our player is now respawning to the position that we read at the beginning. I recommend that you move your Death method now so that it's in the Player script. If you haven't already figured out a way to do this and need a little help, just update your scripts as follows.

Player script:

```
public class Player : MonoBehaviour {
    public Rigidbody2D rb;
    public int movespeed;
    public int jumppower;
    public Transform groundCheck;
    public float groundCheckRadius;
    public LayerMask whatIsGround;
    private bool onGround;
    public int coins;
    private Animator anim;
    private int facing;
    public bool moveLeft;
    public bool moveRight;
    public float startx;
    public float starty;
    public GameObject Blood;

    void Start () {
        rb = GetComponent<Rigidbody2D>();
        anim = GetComponent<Animator>();
        facing = 1;
        startx = transform.position.x;
        starty = transform.position.y;

    }
```

```
void FixedUpdate()
{
    onGround = Physics2D.OverlapCircle(groundCheck.position, groundCheckRadius,
    whatIsGround);
}

void Update() {

    if (moveLeft || Input.GetKey(KeyCode.LeftArrow))
    {
        rb.velocity = new Vector2(-movespeed, rb.velocity.y);
        anim.SetBool("Walking", true);
        if (facing == 1)
        {
            transform.localScale = new Vector3(-1f, 1f, 1f);
            facing = 0;
        }

    } else if (moveRight || Input.GetKey(KeyCode.RightArrow))
    {
        rb.velocity = new Vector2(movespeed, rb.velocity.y);
        anim.SetBool("Walking", true);
        if (facing == 0)
        {
            transform.localScale = new Vector3(1f, 1f, 1f);
            facing = 1;
        }

    } else
    {
        anim.SetBool("Walking", false);
    }

    if (Input.GetKey(KeyCode.Space))
    {
        Jump();
    }
}

public void Jump() {

    if (onGround)
    {
        rb.velocity = new Vector2(rb.velocity.x, jumppower);
    }

    }

public void Death()
{
        StartCoroutine("respawndelay");

}
```

```
    public IEnumerator respawndelay()
    {
        Instantiate(Blood, transform.position, transform.rotation);
        enabled = false;
        GetComponent<Rigidbody2D>().velocity = Vector3.zero;
        GetComponent<Renderer>().enabled = false;
        yield return new WaitForSeconds(1);
        transform.position = new Vector2(startx, starty);
        GetComponent<Renderer>().enabled = true;
        enabled = true;

    }
}
```

Hazards script:

```
public class Hazards : MonoBehaviour
{

    private Player player;
    // Use this for initialization
    void Start()
    {
        player = FindObjectOfType<Player>();
    }

    // Update is called once per frame
    void Update()
    {

    }

    void OnTriggerEnter2D(Collider2D other)
    {
        if (other.tag == "Player")
        {
            player.Death();
        }
    }

}
```

Scripting the Checkpoint

You may already have figured out what's coming next. All we need to do with our checkpoint is change the value of startx and starty when they enter the collider.

Our new Checkpoint script is this simple:

```
public class Checkpoint : MonoBehaviour {

    private Player player;
```

```
void Start()
{
    player = FindObjectOfType<Player>();
}

void Update()
{

}

void OnTriggerEnter2D(Collider2D other)
{
    if (other.tag == "Player")
    {
        player.startx = transform.position.x;
        player.starty = transform.position.y;
    }
}
}
```

And don't forget, you also need to attach this script to the checkpoint in question. Then make it a prefab so that you can add more checkpoints around the level easily in future. Give this a try and you should find that you now respawn at the checkpoint rather than at the start of the game.

In fact, you should appear quickly enough to be showered in your own blood (see Figure 8-3). Nice.

Figure 8-3. *Kevin returns!*

Now make a few more checkpoints in smart places and have a little play to see what works best. Organize them in your Hierarchy in a logical fashion too, perhaps by giving them a parent object called Checkpoints. Of course, you could provide some kind of visible indicator to denote your checkpoints—such as the posts found in the *Sonic the Hedgehog* games—but these days it is quite common for players to simply reappear at a different point in the game. We accept this as part of the suspension of disbelief when we load up, and it has become part of the language of video games.

Taking It to the Next Level

We've come a long way, but our game still only has one level. It's time to introduce some form of real progression.

To do that, we're simply going to make another GameObject that will represent the end of the level and make this a trigger. Seeing as Kevin is a spaceman, it would make sense for the end of his level to be some kind of space rocket. Later, we'll animate this; for now, simply reaching the space rocket will end the level. You can see my rocket in Figure 8-4.

Figure 8-4. *This rocket ship signals the end of each level*

Creating a New Level

Before we can add the script, we first need to create another level. And before you do that, be sure to make your Player GameObject a prefab (drag Player into the Prefabs folder and make sure to bring Main Camera and Check Ground along with you). That way, any changes you make will be reflected globally across *all* the levels you make. Do the same thing for your Canvas and all its children.

Once you've done that, try using this easy little trick to make a new level: simply click File ➤ Save Scene As and call it Level 2. Make sure it's going into the same Scenes folder as Level 1 (see Figure 8-5).

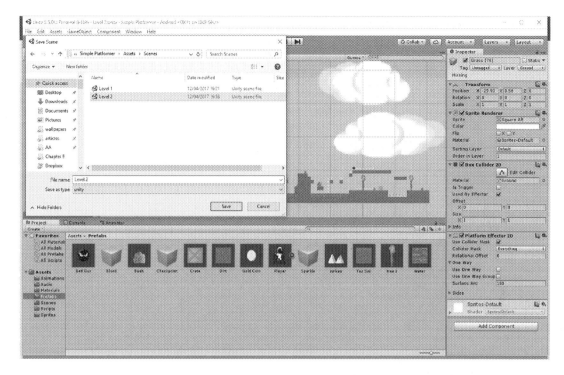

Figure 8-5. *A quick way to make a new level*

This is a great shortcut because it means you have all of your prefabs already in place and you can get things up and running a lot more quickly. Just delete a few elements, move a few things around, and then hit Ctrl+S to save the new layout.

(Alternatively, you could create an entirely new scene by simply right-clicking your Scenes folder and then choosing Create ➤ Scene).

Now if you navigate to the Scenes folder in your Project pane and double-click level one, it should jump between the two layouts. Notice that *everything* is new in the new scene—even the player and the camera. Nevertheless, they are still all *instances* of the same objects that live in your Prefabs folder, so editing scripts or properties will affect everything across all levels.

Escaping the Level

Now that our game has more than one level, we're ready to make it possible to transition between them. Head back to Level 1 and add the sprite to your first level just as you normally would. Make it a GameObject with a polygon collider, tick Is Trigger, create a new script called EndLevel, and add it as a component to the rocket ship.

EndLevel will look like this:

```
using System.Collections;
using System.Collections.Generic;
using UnityEngine;
using UnityEngine.SceneManagement;
```

```
public class EndLevel : MonoBehaviour {
    public string nextLevel;

    void Start()
    {

    }

    void Update()
    {

    }

    void OnTriggerEnter2D(Collider2D other)
    {
        if (other.tag == "Player")
        {
            SceneManager.LoadScene(nextLevel);

        }
    }

}
```

Couldn't be simpler! Note, though, that I included the top of the code with the using commands this time. That's because I'm using an additional class from Unity called SceneManagement. This class lets us use the command that loads up the next scene. The scene in question meanwhile is a public string, which we will name in the Inspector as Level 2. That will make it easier for us to update our level goal for each scene while still using the same script and object.

Before you click play, there's one more thing you need to do: head back into Build Settings and add Scene 2 to your game (just drag it from your Scenes folder and drop it into the window—see Figure 8-6).

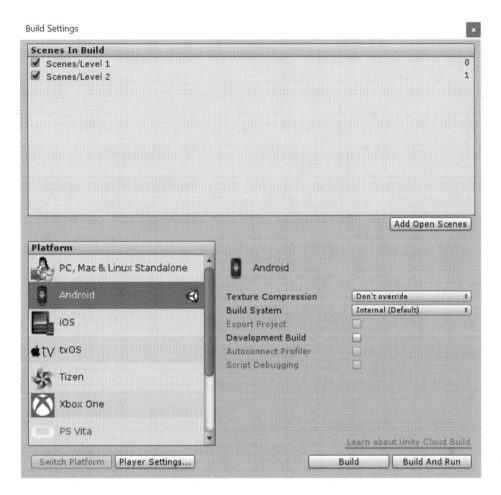

Figure 8-6. *Drag Level 2 into the build settings so you can load it*

Now try completing the level by reaching the rocket. You should find that the next level immediately loads and you're ready to take on the next challenge: creating a level select.

Building a Level Select Screen

In most mobile games—and PC and console games for that matter—players can jump straight into a given level as long as they have previously completed the one before it. This lets them replay their favorite moments, go back to find hidden secrets, and beat their top scores. To allow this, we need to provide some way for our players to view levels and select them. In other words, we need to build a *level select*.

This mean you need to create another scene, but this one will be entirely blank. We'll call it Level Select. Once that's ready, it's time to get reacquainted with Squarey, only this time he has lost a bit of his personality (Figure 8-7).

Figure 8-7. *This will be our selector*

Actually, this isn't Squarey at all, but rather an indicator or selector, meaning we need to have a transparency in the center. This is what will show us which level we're looking to select, so we're also going to need two views, one for each level, that will be the same size. I've made these 500 x 500. You can do this by taking screenshots from your two levels (ignoring the fact that they're essentially the same at this point) and saving them as sprites.

Now, arrange the two level images into the scene so that they're in view of the camera and nicely aligned. Then place your selector on top (with the precise same coordinates) and make sure it has a higher value for Order in Layer. You should have something that looks like Figure 8-8.

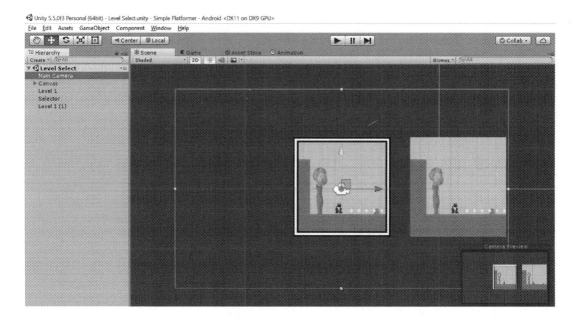

Figure 8-8. *The beginnings of our Level Select scene*

Writing the Control Script

Now we're going to create a new control script that will work much like the Player script. For the most part, we will be controlling the selector just as we would have controlled the player. This *is* our player character for the time being.

Create the script and call it Selector. Then use the following code:

```
public class Selector : MonoBehaviour {

    public bool moveLeft;
    public bool moveRight;

    void Start()
    {

    }

    void Update()
    {

        if (transform.position.x > -5 && (moveLeft || Input.GetKeyDown(KeyCode.LeftArrow)))
        {
            transform.position = new Vector2(transform.position.x - 6, transform.
            position.y);
            moveLeft = false;
        }
        else if (transform.position.x < 1 && (moveRight || Input.GetKeyDown(KeyCode.RightArrow)))
        {
            transform.position = new Vector2(transform.position.x + 6, transform.
            position.y);
            moveRight = false;
        }

        if (Input.GetKey(KeyCode.Space))
        {
            Select();
        }
    }

    public void Select()
    {

    }

}
```

My level images are spaced 6 units apart, so that is how much the selector will move with each step.

As you can see, this is very similar to our usual Player script, although obviously without the Death method or the animations. There are also one or two other differences that you also need to be aware of. We've created a Select method, but for now it's empty. Instead, all that's happening is that the selector is moving 6 units to the left or right when the user taps the arrow key. Notice that we're using GetKeyDown now, so the user has to tap rather than hold down the arrows. I also set moveLeft and moveRight to false immediately after the square moves one step for the same reason.

Finally, I've added a little bit of code to check that the selector isn't going to move off the left or right edge of the screen. You'll need to update this each time you add a new level or potentially use something like numberOfLevels * 6 to calculate how far the selector can move to the right.

If you drag the Main Camera object to make it a child of the selector in the Hierarchy, then the screen will "scroll" as our selector moves. Right now, if you test this, it should work as long as you're using the cursor keys on your computer.

Now you need to create a new Touch script specifically for the Selector. We could add this code to the same Touch script we already created and check the object it's attached to, but making something new is probably simpler.

So create another new script, this time called LevelSelectTouch. This one is effectively a rehash of the previous Touch, making things nice and easy for us:

```
public class LevelSelectTouch : MonoBehaviour {

    private Selector selector;

        void Start()
        {
            selector = FindObjectOfType<Selector>();
        }

        public void PressLeftArrow()
        {
            selector.moveRight = false;
            selector.moveLeft = true;
        }
        public void PressRightArrow()
        {
            selector.moveRight = true;
            selector.moveLeft = false;
        }
        public void ReleaseLeftArrow()
        {
            selector.moveLeft = false;
        }
        public void ReleaseRightArrow()
        {
            selector.moveRight = false;

        }

        public void Select()
        {
            selector.Select();

        }
    }
```

Add this script to the TouchController GameObject in your Hierarchy—*not* to the prefab. Remember, we only want this change to affect this *instance* of the touch controls and not the ones used in Levels 1 and 2.

Now you just need to set up the controls to work with this script. Open Right Arrow, Left Arrow and then Jump in the Inspector and reconfigure the event triggers for each so that they correspond with the correct methods in the new script. If you get stuck, check back and see how we did it last time—the process is the exact same (it's in Chapter 7). Of course, the jump button is going to be tied to the Select method in this case.

And while we're ruining our prefabs, delete the Level and Coins GameObjects from the canvas because they don't make much sense in this context.

Ready to Launch

Give this a try and you should find you can now move the selector around with either the cursors or the on-screen controls. It looks pretty good, although it could probably benefit from a nicer backdrop of some sort (Figure 8-9).

Figure 8-9. *There we go, much better!*

What it *really* needs is the ability to actually *select* the level. A good way to do this would be to give our level images proper names, which will be the same as our scene names (so, Level 1 and Level 2) and make the selector itself a trigger with a box collider. We're also going to add Rigidbodies, which are used for our collisions detection. We obviously don't want our levels to fall off the bottom of the screen, though (darn gravity), so click the little dropdown menu to next to Body Type in order to choose Kinematic (Figure 8-10).

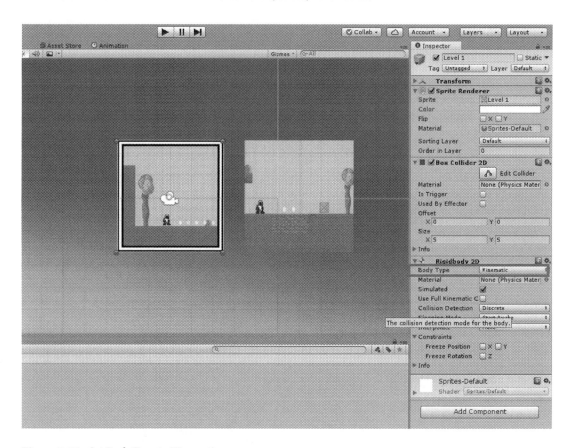

Figure 8-10. *Set Body Type to Kinematic.*

Now update the Selector script like so, remembering to add the new using line up top as well:

```
using System.Collections;
using System.Collections.Generic;
using UnityEngine;
using UnityEngine.SceneManagement;

public class Selector : MonoBehaviour {

    public bool moveLeft;
    public bool moveRight;
    private string levelChoice;

    void Start()
    {

    }
```

```
void Update()
{

    if (transform.position.x > -5 && (moveLeft || Input.GetKeyDown(KeyCode.LeftArrow)))
    {
        transform.position = new Vector2(transform.position.x - 6, transform.
        position.y);
        moveLeft = false;

    }
    else if (transform.position.x < 7 && (moveRight || Input.GetKeyDown(KeyCode.RightArrow)))
    {
        transform.position = new Vector2(transform.position.x + 6, transform.position.y);
        moveRight = false;
    }

    if (Input.GetKey(KeyCode.Space))
    {
        Select();
    }
}

public void Select()
{
    SceneManager.LoadScene(levelChoice);

}

void OnTriggerEnter2D(Collider2D other)
{

    levelChoice = other.name;

}

}
```

That code simply looks for a collision and then gets the name of the offending object to store as a string called levelChoice. When you hit the jump button, levelChoice is then loaded the same way we loaded it earlier. Give this a go and you should find that you can now jump into whichever level you choose. Don't forget to add the Level Select scene to the Build Settings.

Let's take a moment to reflect on what you've accomplished here: you used all the same tricks you've already been using but this time you made a menu rather than a level in a game. This is an early indication of just how versatile the tools that Unity gives us are. It isn't too much of a stretch to imagine creating a puzzle game or even some kind of productivity tool.

Saving Our Progress

A level select isn't much use until we can save our players' progress. We want there to be a sense of accomplishment and progression as they play through the levels, which means that the option to play further should open up as each level is completed. This progress should persist from play session to play session too, because it isn't much fun having to start again from scratch every time.

So we need a way to save our progress, and Unity actually gives us a number of options, from using player preferences to serialization or creating text files.

Technically, what we *should* be using is serialization—it lets you save a lot more information more quickly. Without going into too much detail here, that means converting an object into bytes. It's a little complicated, though, so for now we're going to use PlayerPrefs because it's quick and dirty and much easier to get your head around.

PlayerPrefs is *supposed* to be used for saving preferences like image quality, or whether you want the sound on—settings, in other words. But to be honest, a lot of indie developers use this method exclusively, and if all you need to do is store some top scores and level names, it will do just fine.

It's incredibly simple to save the level as soon as we load it. Just update the EndLevel script attached to the rocket in Level 1 to look like this:

```
public class EndLevel : MonoBehaviour {
    public string nextLevel;
    public int levelValue;

    void Start()
    {

    }

    void Update()
    {

    }

    void OnTriggerEnter2D(Collider2D other)
    {
        if (other.tag == "Player")
        {
            SaveLevel(levelValue);
            SceneManager.LoadScene(nextLevel);

        }
    }

    public void SaveLevel(int level)
    {
        PlayerPrefs.SetInt("farthestLevel", level);
    }
}
```

That one line: PlayerPrefs.SetInt("farthestLevel", level); is all it takes. This creates a new integer with the key farthestLevel and puts it in PlayerPrefs. We just need to add the public variable levelValue in the Inspector (Figure 8-11), and now touching the rocket will load up the next scene *and* update the saved variable.

Figure 8-11. *The rocket has Level 2 value*

To make use of this, we need to make our level select screen a little smarter so that it will be able to show us when a level *isn't* ready to be loaded. Create something that will show in the place of upcoming levels. I'm using a question mark that should match nicely with my backdrop (Figure 8-12).

Figure 8-12. *What's behind door number two?*

Create two of these and place the first one so that it sits behind Level 2 further back in the order (if you get this right, it won't be visible). The second goes along to the right where Level 3 will be later. These shouldn't have colliders; they're just images that will show when the image in front of it is missing. You should have something that looks like Figure 8-13.

Figure 8-13. *There are actually two question marks here—the first one is behind Level 2*

We're now going to create another script called LevelLoader and attach that to the Level 2 image:

```
public class LevelLoader : MonoBehaviour {

    public int thisLevel;
    private Selector selector;

    void Start () {
        selector = FindObjectOfType<Selector>();

    }

        void Update () {
                if (selector.farthestLevel < thisLevel) {
            this.tag = "off";
            GetComponent<Renderer>().enabled = false;
        } else
```

```
    {
        this.tag = "on";
        GetComponent<Renderer>().enabled = true;
    }
    }
}
```

So, these images are now our *level loaders*. When the Level Select scene is created, they'll all appear as they should, and then they'll check to see if the player has gotten far enough yet. If the player hasn't, they'll disappear (*GetComponent<Rendered>().enabled = false*) and set their tag to off.

Attach this to the GameObject and then enter the public integer thisLevel in the Inspector, which should of course be 2.

As you can see, the code we need to check the level is going to be in the Selector script (because we only want to do this once), which has the public property loadLevel. To get this value, all we have to do is add just one line of code to the Start method in that script:

```
PlayerPrefs.GetInt("farthestLevel");
```

Of course, we also need to define the public integer up top.

Now, when the selector is created, it will check the furthest level the player has gotten to by looking at the PlayerPrefs and store this value as a public integer. The LevelLoader images will then disappear if the player hasn't gotten far enough to play them yet. When the player selects the ?, they're still really selecting an "invisible Level 2," but because the tag is set to off, it won't load.

A Few Final Comments

Give it a try and you should find that at first you can only play Level 1. Only after you reach Level 2 via the rocket and then load this screen up again will you be able to choose either. Progress.

This isn't necessarily the most ideal way to handle this. Some of our methods are in unusual places right now in the interests of keeping things simple. What you might do instead is to create a script to act as a kind of "game manager" that stores progress, loads different levels, and so on, and that way keeps your code cleaner. I keep threatening that chapter on optimization and this is something else we'll touch on there.

But for now, I think you've worked hard enough. This was a complicated chapter, so if you've struggled try not to worry. I actually taught you very little that's new (how to load scenes and how save and load variables in PlayerPrefs). Mostly this was just using what you've *already* learned in novel ways. So if you've come this far, you *already* have the tools to make checkpoints and level select screens—it's simply a matter of applying a little ingenuity in order to come up with a system that you like. That's the fun of programming: it's essentially an exercise in resourcefulness.

For the next couple of chapters, things are going to get (a little) less technical again. We'll be introducing some common obstacles, power-ups, and abilities to create more fun gameplay possibilities. Then we'll be discussing what makes good game design. You've done the hard part (for now). It's time to have some fun!

CHAPTER 9

Adding More Game Elements: Springs, Moving Platforms, AI, and More

You've spent the last few chapters working hard to create a working game world. You've developed the engine, created save files, and made your character move and interact with the world the way they should. Hopefully, you've had fun doing it, but it's probably felt a little challenging and quite technical at points along the way.

Well, now it's time to bask in your achievements for a bit. You've created this world. Let's have some fun in it.

After all, a typical game will involve plenty of different obstacles, hazards, and power-ups, each of which will normally create unique gameplay challenges and fun encounters. *Sonic* has springs, rings, posts, Badniks, spike pits, chaos emeralds, and loop-de-loops. *Mario* has mushrooms, Bullet Bills, ghosts, question mark boxes, and Yoshi(s). *Super Meat Boy* has portals, giant saws, missiles, and piles of used needles.

It's time for you to get creative and to start introducing more elements into your *own* game. And the best part? Creating these challenges is almost as much fun as getting to play through them later on.

In this chapter, you'll learn how to create all kinds of environmental hazards and enemies and you'll be able to dip back in any time you want to add another element to your own game world. I hope it will also serve as a source of inspiration to help you come up with your own obstacles and challenges. Of course, we'll learn a few new concepts along the way as well.

By the end, you'll also learn how to plunder the Asset Store so that you can access particle effects, scripts, and sprites that others have lovingly created and use them in your own games.

Ready? Let's have some fun!

Some Common Game Objects and Their Behavior

Although every platformer is different and you should do what you can to differentiate yourself and stand out from the crowd, it's also true that certain tropes crop up time and again. This is normal in any genre in any form of media, so don't worry if you find yourself falling back on "old favorites."

So, under the assumption you'll be using some of the more common assets and objects in your game design, this section will show you how to build basic elements like springs and moving blocks.

Springs

The first game object we're going to create is the *spring*, or "bounce pad." Arguably popularized by *Sonic the Hedgehog*, the spring is now a common trope in platformers used as a means of propelling the player up a level.

Take a look around the Unity IDE and you may find something that *looks* like it will do the job: you can add a "bounciness" property to a Physics Material 2D. Unfortunately, that's not what we're looking for because this will make the ground act a lot more like an *actual* bouncy surface. That is to say that it will propel the character higher the further they fall and eventually return less and less energy. You can do some fun stuff with that, but it won't act quite the way we want it to.

Instead we're going to create a spring sprite (Figure 9-1) and add it to your level, as you're accustomed to doing by now (Figure 9-2). Notice that we're using an edge collider along the top edge (rather than the usual box collider).

Figure 9-1. A spring

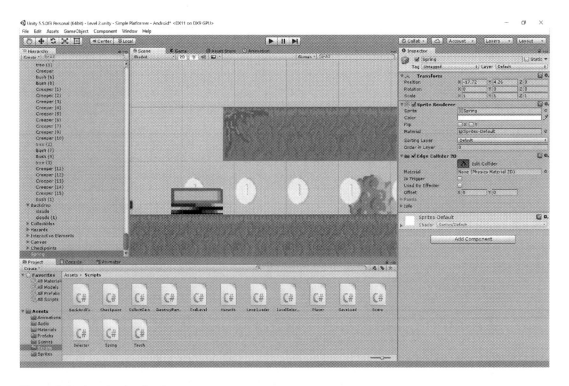

Figure 9-2. A spring in a level

Next, you're going to create a `Spring` script and add the following code:

```
public class Spring : MonoBehaviour {

    private Player player;
    // Use this for initialization
    void Start()
    {
        player = FindObjectOfType<Player>();
    }

    // Update is called once per frame
    void Update()
    {

    }

    void OnCollisionEnter2D(Collision2D other)
    {
        if (other.gameObject.tag == "Player")
        {
            player.SuperJump();
        }
    }

}
```

As you have maybe already guessed, you're also going to add the `SuperJump` method to your `Player` script:

```
public void SuperJump()
{
    rb.velocity = new Vector2(rb.velocity.x, jumpPower * 2);

}
```

Of course, remember to add the new `Spring` script to your GameObject and make it a prefab—the usual stuff.

Now when you touch the spring, Kevin is going to be launched up into the air at twice the height he can normally jump. I've kept the height proportional to his jumping height just in case we ever decide to change the scale of the level. If you want to, you can add animations and sounds to the spring as well.

Moving Platforms

A common trope in any platform game is the moving platform. You have platforms that move left and right and carry you over chasms and you have platforms that move up and down and act like elevators.

We can already make things move left and right—we've done that with our enemies already. The problem is that if you attach this movement script to a piece of ground, Kevin won't move *with it*. Instead, the ground will move out from under him, and he'll drop off of it. Not good.

Meanwhile, if the platform moves up and down and your player is on it, he will judder and freak out and possibly fall through the floor. We essentially need to modify this script so that we can *stick* to the top surface and travel with it.

How might we do this?

I'll give you a second to think … what have we used previously in this book that allows a GameObject to move in relation to *another* GameObject?

Got it?

The answer is that we need to make Kevin a *child* of the GameObject he's standing on. To do that, open up your movement script (we called this BackAndForth) and get ready to make some changes. We're not only changing the script so that our character becomes a child of the platform when they come into contact with it, we're also adding another dimension of movement so that it can also move upward and downward. The direction integer variable is now public, meaning we can edit it from the Inspector. It's no longer set to 0 in the onStart() method either, but remember that an integer always begins life as 0 if it is unset.

That means that our enemy behavior won't have changed—they will continue to move left and right because the direction variable will default to 0. For the platform, though, we have the option to set it to 2 or 3, which will make it move up then down, or down then up.

After all that, BackAndForth should now look like this:

```
public class BackAndForth : MonoBehaviour
{

    public double amounttomove;
    public float speed;
    private float startx;
    private float starty;
    public int direction;
    private Player player;

    // Use this for initialization
    void Start()
    {

        startx = gameObject.transform.position.x;
        starty = gameObject.transform.position.y;
        player = FindObjectOfType<Player>();

    }

    // Update is called once per frame

    void Update()
    {
        if (gameObject.transform.position.x < startx + amounttomove && direction == 0)
        {
            gameObject.transform.position = new Vector2(gameObject.transform.position.x
            + speed, gameObject.transform.position.y);

        }
        else if (gameObject.transform.position.x >= startx + amounttomove && direction == 0)
```

```
        {
            direction = 1;
        }
        else if (gameObject.transform.position.x > startx && direction == 1)
        {
            gameObject.transform.position = new Vector2(gameObject.transform.position.
            x - speed, gameObject.transform.position.y);
        }
        else if (gameObject.transform.position.x <= startx && direction == 1)
        {
            direction = 0;
        }

        if (gameObject.transform.position.y < starty + amounttomove && direction == 3)
        {
            gameObject.transform.position = new Vector2(gameObject.transform.position.x,
            gameObject.transform.position.y + speed);

        }
        else if (gameObject.transform.position.y >= starty + amounttomove && direction == 3)
        {
            direction = 2;
        }
        else if (gameObject.transform.position.y > starty && direction == 2)
        {
            gameObject.transform.position = new Vector2(gameObject.transform.position.x,
            gameObject.transform.position.y - speed);
        }
        else if (gameObject.transform.position.y <= starty && direction == 2)
        {
            direction = 3;
        }

    }

    void OnCollisionEnter2D(Collision2D other)
    {
        if (other.gameObject.tag == "Player")
        {
            player.transform.parent = gameObject.transform;
        }
    }

    private void OnCollisionExit2D(Collision2D other)
    {
        if (other.gameObject.tag == "Player")
        {
            player.transform.parent = null;
        }
    }
}
```

I also recommend that you create a new Physics Material 2D for the platform and set the friction to something high. This is to prevent Kevin from sliding too much on the platform, which looks a little odd in conjunction with the movement.

It's also a good idea to use an edge collider and add a platform effector. Tick Used by Effector and Use One Way, and this will prevent our player from getting crushed by the platform or sticking to the side and moving as a child of the platform. If this prevents the player from being able to jump off the platform, you may want to increase the radius of your Ground Check slightly. There are other ways to accomplish the same thing that may be a little more elegant, but this is an easy "fix" that will get your moving platforms up and running.

If everything has worked, Kevin should now move with the platform whether it's going left and right or up and down (Figure 9-3). This creates tons of platform challenge opportunities, so have some fun with it.

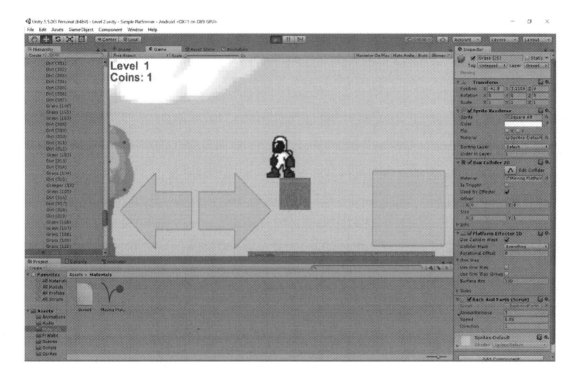

Figure 9-3. *Kevin going for a ride*

Collapsing Platforms

You know what else is great? *Collapsing* platforms. These are the platforms that crumble underfoot when you land on them and thereby encourage you to run and jump quickly in order to avoid falling to your doom.

With this kind of thing, it's important that you communicate to the player the nature of the challenge that they're about to face. It's not fair to sucker punch your player by having a platform drop out from underneath them without warning, and for that reason it's normally advisable to have a visual indicator that the ground isn't quite stable.

For that reason, I created a design for a crumbling platform you can see in Figure 9-4.

Figure 9-4. *A crumbling platform tile*

We want this platform tile to begin to crumble once we land on it, so we're going to create a new script called Crumble. This script will simply start a timer as soon as the player touches the object and then cause the object to fall and disappear once that timer is complete.

The code looks like this:

```
public class Crumble : MonoBehaviour {
    private Player player;
    private Rigidbody2D rb;
    public int timeToCollapse;
    private int timeLeft;
    public int timeToRestore;
    private int restoreTime;
    private float startY;
    private float startX;
    // Use this for initialization
    void Start () {
        rb = GetComponent<Rigidbody2D>();
        player = FindObjectOfType<Player>();
        startX = transform.position.x;
        startY = transform.position.y;
        timeLeft = -70;
    }

    // Update is called once per frame
    void Update () {
        if (timeLeft > -70)
        {
            timeLeft = timeLeft - 1;
        }
        if (timeLeft == 0)
        {
            rb.constraints = RigidbodyConstraints2D.None;
        }
        if (timeLeft == -62)
        {
            GetComponent<Renderer>().enabled = false;
            restoreTime = timeToRestore;
        }
        if (restoreTime > 0)
        {
            restoreTime = restoreTime - 1;
        }
```

```
        if (restoreTime == 2)
        {
            transform.position = new Vector3(startX, startY);
            transform.rotation = Quaternion.identity;
            GetComponent<Rigidbody2D>().velocity = Vector3.zero;
            rb.constraints = RigidbodyConstraints2D.FreezeAll;
            GetComponent<Renderer>().enabled = true;
        }

    }

    void OnCollisionEnter2D(Collision2D other)
    {
        if (other.gameObject.tag == "Player")
        {
            timeLeft = timeToCollapse;
        }
    }

}
```

When the player touches the collider, that begins the countdown, which will be a value chosen in the Inspector. When the countdown passes zero, the constraints are removed from the Rigidbody, allowing it to fall and to rotate through the air. The timer carries on counting down *past* zero to –70 so that we have time to see the platform fall and disappear. Just before the time reaches that point, the object will stop being rendered and become invisible. This will then begin a new countdown: a *restore* timer. This is also set in the Inspector, and when this counts down to zero, the object is returned to its original position, with the constraints newly frozen, rotation set to zero, and the rendering back.

From the player's perspective, this then creates a tile that can be stood on for a limited period of time before it drops off of the screen and eventually disappears. You may want to add a "rumble" animation and a sound effect for added drama, and from there you can introduce some cool reflexive platforming. It should all look something like Figure 9-5.

Figure 9-5. *Running along collapsing blocks … action!*

Better AI

Another thing you may want to add to your game at this point is a better enemy AI. Right now, our enemies just move left and right and are literally no more intelligent than our moving platforms. Something more challenging for the player would be an enemy that would actually seek the player out and chase them down.

I think something ground based would be more interesting here, so I've created another enemy. This time I'm going with a kind of mean-looking mechanical rat (see Figure 9-6). Why? Probably because it is late and I've lost it.

Figure 9-6. *Look, it's an alien planet. It doesn't need to make sense*

This little guy is going to use a new script, which will be called GroundEnemy. The basic behavior of this character is going to be to follow the player along the ground. So, if our horizontal position is bigger than the player's, we reduce the value of X. If it's smaller, we increase that value. We also need the rat to flip around when he changes direction, just like the player.

This simple script looks like so:

```
public class GoundEnemy : MonoBehaviour {
    private Player player;
    private int facing;
    public float enemySpeed;

void Start () {
        player = FindObjectOfType<Player>();

    }

void Update () {

        if (gameObject.transform.position.x > player.transform.position.x)
            {
                gameObject.transform.position = new Vector2(gameObject.transform.position.x
                - enemySpeed, gameObject.transform.position.y);
                if (facing == 0)
                {
                    facing = 1;
                    transform.localScale = new Vector3(.2f, .2f, 1f);
                }
            }

        if (gameObject.transform.position.x < player.transform.position.x)
            {
                gameObject.transform.position = new Vector2(gameObject.transform.position.x
                + enemySpeed, gameObject.transform.position.y);
                if (facing == 1)
                {
                    facing = 0;
                    transform.localScale = new Vector3(-.2f, .2f, 1f);
                }
            }
        }

}
```

Fun fact: the first game I ever made was based around this script (except in BASIC for the ZX Spectrum). This was the point at which I "got" programming. I made a dot that could move around the screen and would be chased by a second dot. The player's objective was to trick the enemy into landing on a small mine (a red dot). Maybe that's not a fun fact … sometimes I get confused.

Ahem. Of course, you should also add the Hazards script if you want the bad guy to actually be lethal (and you'll need to add an onCollissionEnter2D method so that both colliders *and* triggers will kill the player). You can see the enemy giving chase in Figure 9-7.

Figure 9-7. *Run Kevin, it's some kind of robot rat*

Anyway, this script is a little *too* simple at the moment. As it is, the enemy will start chasing the player as soon as the game begins and probably end up stranded in a pit somewhere. Not only that but he is very easily fooled and will be stymied by pretty much any obstacle.

To solve this problem, we're first going to get him to spring into action once the player reaches a certain proximity and then stop following after the player gets away. The proximity will be a public integer that we can set in the Inspector. A useful tip is to make sure that you play around with different ranges and different speeds. Ideally, you don't want the enemy to start moving until the player can *see* them on the screen. Likewise, the ideal speed will be one that allows the player to escape but only after a tense chase.

Notice how tweaking these numbers even just slightly alters the pace and the tension of your game considerably. This is similar to being a film director, and we'll be discussing these kinds of aspects much more in the next chapter.

While we're at it, why don't we get a little more creative and give our enemy the ability to traverse the environment a little more? For example, it would be great if Roborat (yes, I shall call him *Roborat*) would jump over blocks to try and reach the player and if it could get itself out of pits. To do this, we'll be using a new feature: raycasts.

Using Raycasts

Raycasts are a little like the reverse sensor in your car; they send out a beam that checks for collisions and then return "true" if there's a hit. What we want to do is give our enemy the ability to look to see if something is blocking its path and then jump over it. That means it will also need its own groundCheck too (so it doesn't keep jumping and fly through the air). Handle this the exact same way you did for the player: create an empty GameObject with a small radius and then get it to check for ground to set a Boolean. You can copy and paste the code directly, and it should then look something like this once it's in place:

```
public class GoundEnemy : MonoBehaviour {
    private Player player;
    private int facing;
    public float enemySpeed;
    private bool chaseIsOn;
    public int attackRange;
    public Transform groundCheck;
    public float groundCheckRadius;
    public LayerMask whatIsGround;
    private bool onGround;

    void Start () {
        player = FindObjectOfType<Player>();

    }

    void FixedUpdate()
    {
        onGround = Physics2D.OverlapCircle(groundCheck.position, groundCheckRadius,
        whatIsGround);

    }
```

You should also have something that looks like Figure 9-8 in the Inspector.

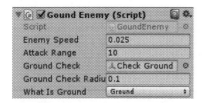

Figure 9-8. *Remember, you're creating an empty GameObject just below the character to use as a transform and then adding it to the Inspector*

The raycast is an invisible line, and we're going to use more transforms and empty GameObjects in order to define its position. To check that this is working, we're going to use a debug function to draw a straight line between two points. This is a handy feature of Unity that lets you draw directly onto the screen in a way that is only visible in the Scene view. The players won't see it, but we can use it to test our game.

So, create two new empty GameObjects that are children of the rat (which sounds like a strange book title: *Children of the Rat*). The first one should be dead center, which we will call Sight Start. The second will be two units in front of the rat and will be called Sight End.

Now we're going to create two new public transforms, which will be enemySightStart and enemySightEnd. Once again, we'll use the Inspector to drop the two empty objects we just created into there. If you've done this right, you should be able to add this line:

```
Debug.DrawLine(enemySightStart.position, enemySightEnd.position, Color.red);
```

And then see a red line appear in the Scene view between two points (see Figure 9-9). Now we're just going to swap this line for a raycast.

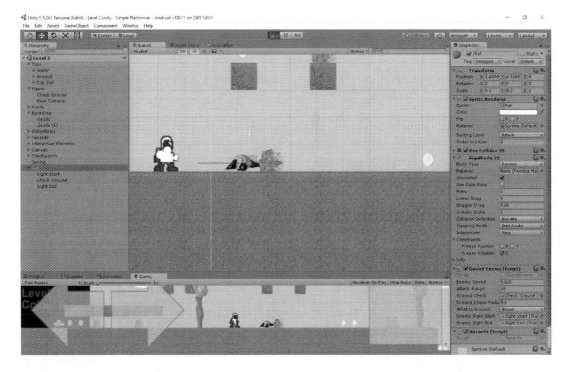

Figure 9-9. *Once the transforms are set, your rat should look like he's jousting*

Our raycast is going to go precisely where the line is currently, but it can be useful to *keep* the line anyway, seeing as the raycasts are completely invisible and can otherwise be difficult to visualize.

Fortunately, using our raycast is pretty simple—especially since you're familiar with using the overlap circle.

We're going to use Physics2D.Linecast for this job. There are other kinds of raycast, such as Circlecast, but for a 2D game with simple rules, a line is the most efficient option. We need to give this function a start point and end point (as we did with our line) and then we're also going to provide a layer mask. We don't want the enemy to jump over the player, so the layer it's looking for is Ground.

This will go inside the update and will only operate if chaseIsOn Boolean is true (that is, if the player has been sighted):

```
if (Physics2D.Linecast(enemySightStart.position, enemySightEnd.position, whatIsGround)) {
        Jump();
    }
```

171

As you can see, I've also created a Jump method just as we did for the player. This should be familiar:

```
private void Jump()
    {

        if (onGround)
        {
            rb.velocity = new Vector2(rb.velocity.x, jumpHeight);
        }


    }
```

This is actually all it takes for our enemy to now be able to leap over obstacles (see Figure 9-10). Nothing can stop him now—he's like a Terminator.

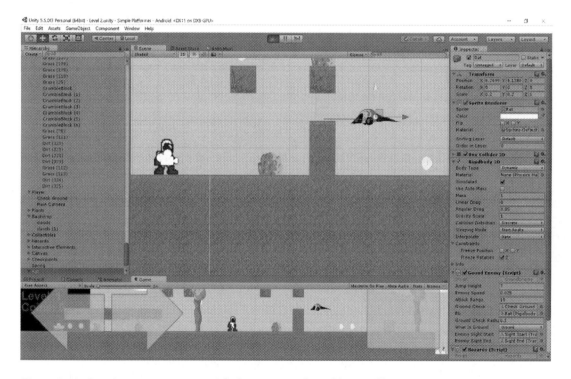

Figure 9-10. *Leaping rats—a common sight for an ex-Londoner like myself*

The good news is that when the rat turns around, the Sight End object will flip as well because it's a child of the rat. It wouldn't take much more code to make the rat attempt to jump chasms as well; we'd just need a second raycast that looks at the ground just below the first one. Add that and make sure that the enemy jumps when that point *doesn't* overlap ground (Figure 9-11).

Figure 9-11. *Our rat friend looking for the floor*

Coding Enemy Behavior

I've also added something else, which is essentially the same code from the BackAndForth script. I want the rat to move left and right so that it's "on patrol" until it begins chasing the player. It isn't particularly natural-looking to have an enemy that stays perfect still until the player is sighted ... although that would be creepy, I grant you. We're going to make this code a *little* smarter, though, by getting the enemy to change direction on patrol if it gets close to the edge so that it doesn't patrol off of platforms or into walls.

I'm also going to move the code around slightly so that it isn't all sitting in the Update function—that looks a little ugly. If you want to take the easy route, you can just copy and paste this code to create your own ground enemy:

```
public class GoundEnemy : MonoBehaviour {
    private Player player;
    private int facing;
    public int jumpHeight;
    public float enemySpeed;
    private bool chaseIsOn;
    public int attackRange;
    public Transform groundCheck;
    public Rigidbody2D rb;
    public float groundCheckRadius;
    public LayerMask whatIsGround;
    private bool onGround;
    public Transform enemySightStart;
    public Transform enemySightEnd;
    public Transform enemySightEnd2;
    private float startX;
    public double amountToMove;
```

```
void Start () {
    player = FindObjectOfType<Player>();
    rb = GetComponent<Rigidbody2D>();
    startX = gameObject.transform.position.x;
    facing = 3;
}

void FixedUpdate()
{
    onGround = Physics2D.OverlapCircle(groundCheck.position, groundCheckRadius,
    whatIsGround);
    Debug.DrawLine(enemySightStart.position, enemySightEnd.position, Color.red);
    Debug.DrawLine(enemySightStart.position, enemySightEnd2.position, Color.green);
}

void Update()
{

    if (gameObject.transform.position.x - player.transform.position.x < attackRange &&
    gameObject.transform.position.x - player.transform.position.x > -attackRange &&
    chaseIsOn == false)
    {
        chaseIsOn = true;
    }
    if (gameObject.transform.position.x - player.transform.position.x > attackRange ||
    gameObject.transform.position.x - player.transform.position.x < -attackRange &&
    chaseIsOn == true)
    {
        if (chaseIsOn)
        {
            startX = gameObject.transform.position.x;
        }
        chaseIsOn = false;
    }

    if (chaseIsOn)
    {
        Pursuit();
    } else
    {
        Patrol();
    }
}

private void Patrol()
{
    if (facing == 3)
    {
        facing = 0;
        transform.localScale = new Vector3(-.2f, .2f, 1f);
    }
```

```
    if (gameObject.transform.position.x < startX + amountToMove && facing == 0)
    {
        gameObject.transform.position = new Vector2(gameObject.transform.position.x
        + enemySpeed / 2, gameObject.transform.position.y);

    }
    else if (gameObject.transform.position.x >= startX + amountToMove && facing == 0)
    {
        facing = 1;
        transform.localScale = new Vector3(.2f, .2f, 1f);
    }
    else if (gameObject.transform.position.x > startX && facing == 1)
    {
        gameObject.transform.position = new Vector2(gameObject.transform.position.x
        - enemySpeed / 2, gameObject.transform.position.y);
    }
    else if (gameObject.transform.position.x <= startX && facing == 1)
    {
        facing = 0;
        transform.localScale = new Vector3(-.2f, .2f, 1f);
    }

    if (Physics2D.Linecast(enemySightStart.position, enemySightEnd2.position,
    whatIsGround) == false || Physics2D.Linecast(enemySightStart.position,
    enemySightEnd.position, whatIsGround))
    {
        if (facing == 1)
        {
            facing = 0;
            transform.localScale = new Vector3(-.2f, .2f, 1f);

        }
        else
        {
            facing = 1;
            transform.localScale = new Vector3(.2f, .2f, 1f);

        }
    }
}

private void Pursuit()
{

    if (Physics2D.Linecast(enemySightStart.position, enemySightEnd.position,
    whatIsGround) || Physics2D.Linecast(enemySightStart.position, enemySightEnd2.
    position, whatIsGround) == false)
    {
        Jump();
    }
```

```csharp
        if (gameObject.transform.position.x > player.transform.position.x)
        {
            gameObject.transform.position = new Vector2(gameObject.transform.position.x
            - enemySpeed, gameObject.transform.position.y);
            if (facing == 0 || facing == 3)
            {
                facing = 1;
                transform.localScale = new Vector3(.2f, .2f, 1f);
            }
        }

        if (gameObject.transform.position.x < player.transform.position.x)
        {
            gameObject.transform.position = new Vector2(gameObject.transform.position.x
            + enemySpeed, gameObject.transform.position.y);
            if (facing == 1 || facing == 3)
            {
                facing = 0;
                transform.localScale = new Vector3(-.2f, .2f, 1f);
            }
        }
    }

    private void Jump()
    {

        if (onGround)
        {
            rb.velocity = new Vector2(rb.velocity.x, jumpHeight);
        }

    }

void OnCollisionEnter2D(Collision2D collision)
    {
        if (collision.gameObject.tag == "Enemy")
        {
            Physics2D.IgnoreCollision(collision.collider, GetComponent<Collider2D>());
        }
    }
}
```

This is still fairly simple as enemy AI goes, but it results in some quite enjoyable behavior. Our bad guy will now slowly patrol (I set this to half speed) until the player gets in proximity. Being a rat, he can smell Kevin, and so once Kevin gets too close the rat gives chase and leaps over obstacles and pits in hot pursuit. If he touches Kevin, we die. If Kevin makes it away in time, the rat loses interest and patrols whatever space he's in.

That last method—the onCollission2D method—is there to prevent rats from bumping into each other. I included this so that you could make a "pit" of rats for the gross-out factor. You will need to tag the rats as Enemy for it to work, though.

If Roborat finds himself stranded on a platform (see Figure 9-12), he'll often just freeze. So, he's not perfect. But he's still pretty interesting and certainly dynamic enough to create lots of gameplay opportunities.

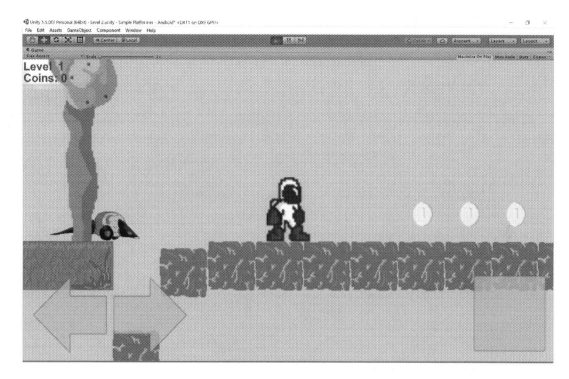

Figure 9-12. *So long, sucker!*

And feel proud: you just created your first artificial intelligence. All in a day's work.

Arming the Player

Our rat has turned out to be a pretty mean threat and certainly enough of a challenge to give our players a hard time. It's time that we gave our players a way to fight back.

Creating a bullet that the player can fire is relatively easy, though we will need to do a little juggling to make sure we're referencing the right instance of our Bullet object. Allow me to explain. First, we need to create a new GameObject, called Bullet. This is our bullet, which will have public variables for its direction and speed. It will also have a collider. The script looks like this:

```
public class Bullet : MonoBehaviour {

    public float speed;
    public int direction;
    private int timeLeft;
    public GameObject Blood;
```

```
    void Start () {
        timeLeft = 100;
        }

    void Update () {
        timeLeft = timeLeft - 1;
        if (timeLeft < 1)
        {
            Destroy(gameObject);
        }
        if (direction == 0)
        {
            gameObject.transform.position = new Vector2(gameObject.transform.position.x
            - speed, gameObject.transform.position.y);
        } else if (direction == 1)
        {
            gameObject.transform.position = new Vector2(gameObject.transform.position.x
            + speed, gameObject.transform.position.y);
        }
    }

    void OnCollisionEnter2D(Collision2D other)
    {
        if (other.gameObject.tag == "Enemy")
        {
            Destroy(other.gameObject);
            Instantiate(Blood, transform.position, transform.rotation);
        }
        else if (other.gameObject.tag == "Player")
        {
            Physics2D.IgnoreCollision(other.collider, GetComponent<Collider2D>());
        }
        else
        {
            Destroy(gameObject);
        }
    }
}
```

Notice that killing a rat will cause the same bloody particle effect that occurs when the player dies. That means you need to add that public GameObject in the Inspector just the same as before. Notice too that our onCollision method checks the object tag, so that rats get destroyed with the blood, players get ignored, and anything else destroys the bullet. The bullet also times out after a set duration and self-destructs to remove itself from memory, just like the particle effects did before.

Likewise, we're also going to want to create a new public object called Bullet in the Player script. You need to place the bullet prefab in there through the Inspector.

You'll then add the following bit of code:

```
if (Input.GetKeyDown(KeyCode.LeftControl)) {
                var newBullet = Instantiate(bullet, transform.position, transform.rotation);
                var bulletScript = newBullet.GetComponent<Bullet>();
                bulletScript.direction = facing;
        }
```

This is the new part. Here, we want to not only instantiate a new object but also set some of the properties for that object *as* it's created. To do that, we need to use GetComponent in order to get the reference to the script from this instance. From there, we can then access the public variable and change it.

Ultimately, you should end up with a bullet that can plough through enemies, as seen in Figure 9-13.

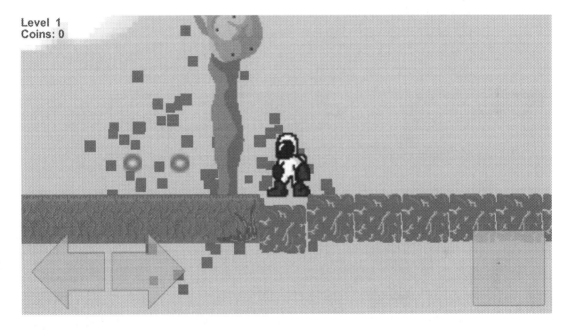

Figure 9-13. *Alas, poor Roborat*

(Of course, later on you'll want to go into your canvas and add a "fire" button. I'm leaving this out as I think that the bullet makes our player a bit overpowered. This section is here simply for your own reference and so that you can add bullets and guns to your game if you want to. Likewise, you're also going to need to add a gun of some sort to your player sprite and possibly a new animation.)

Using Assets from the Asset Store

I could carry on talking you through how to create different objects and behaviors until I'm blue in the face but I'd never show you how to make *everything* you could possibly need. How about portals to teleport the player? What about switches that open doors? What about flying enemies? Or double jumping? Or power-ups?

Hopefully, you'll be able to figure some of this stuff out yourself now. This chapter has introduced raycasts, gone into more detail regarding instantiating, and generally added to your knowledge. Using that new information and building on what you already knew, you should be able to come up with creative solutions to nearly any problem you can dream up. Remember, there's no such thing as a lack of resources, only a lack of resourcefulness.

But if you *can't* figure it out on your own, or you just don't have the time or inclination, you can find prefabs that have already been made by others (including Unity Technologies) and add them to your own projects. This is where the Asset Store comes in (Figure 9-14).

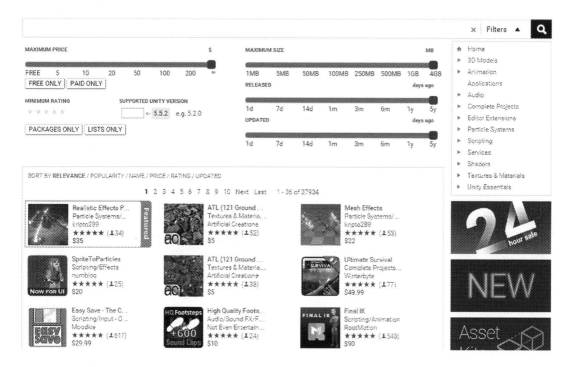

Figure 9-14. *The Asset Store in all its glory*

To start browsing here, just select the Asset Store tab and take a look around. You'll see all kinds of things—from particle effects, to scripts, to sprite packages, to entire game demos. You'll notice that there are sliders to let you set the price (many assets are free) and the file size and you can pick from categories on the righthand side. If you click the name of a publisher—say, Unity Technologies—you can see all of their assets and packages.

I want you to find the selection of assets called 2D Platformer from Unity Technologies (Figure 9-15). This is basically a full 2D game, but rather than use the whole thing, for now let's try selecting just one element that we want to bring over. Specifically, let's grab a sound effect file: Player-jump1.wav.

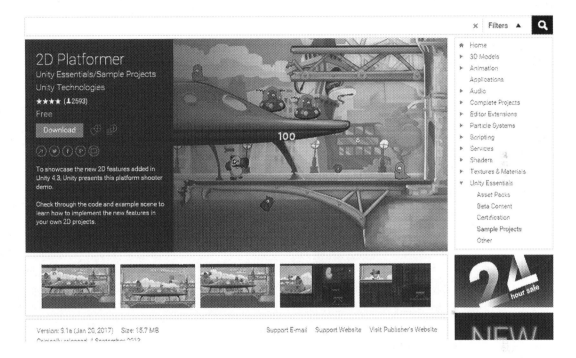

Figure 9-15. *This will do just nicely*

Click Download in the store and then click Import. Unity will warn you that you're at risk of overwriting your hard work, but don't worry about that—you'll be able to choose precisely what you want to add on the next screen. So click OK, deselect everything from the list in the window that opens up (click None), and then manually reselect just the sound effect (Figure 9-16).

Figure 9-16. *Only select what you want*

Now click Import and after a second you'll find new subfolders in your Audio folder. Click through these and you'll eventually get to the sound effect you wanted.

You can now create an audio source as before and get it to play when Kevin jumps. This voice is definitely all wrong for him, but hopefully you see the possibilities here—you can find pretty much anything you could want in the Assets Store, and though you might need to pay for some, you'll find it isn't usually too expensive. Often the quality and professionalism of the resources here will outstrip what you can do yourself, and this will speed up development while resulting in an end product with higher production values and more "sheen." I don't want to recommend anything specific, seeing as the contents of the store change all the time and that might date this book. Right now, however, there is a 2D Essentials–curated selection which includes some cool things like weather particle effects, dynamic lighting, reflective 2D water, and a "Pro Camera 2D."

Hopefully, your mind is now reeling at the possibilities, but the most important thing is that you *don't get carried away*. Good game design doesn't just mean throwing every cool thing you can at the player—it's as much about restraint as anything else. With great power comes great responsibility.

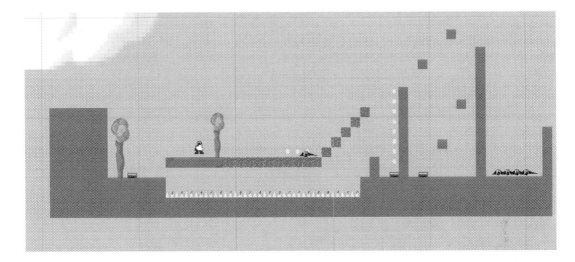

Figure 9-17. *My Level 2 looks like this right now, which is all wrong. Find out why in the next chapter.*

That's why Chapter 10 provides you with a basic introduction to good game design, finesse, and style. You have the raw skills—now it's time you learn what to do with them.

▉ ▉ ▉ ▉

CHAPTER 10

Making the Game Fun and Optimized

Congratulations, you can now make games with Unity!

No, seriously, if you were to stop reading right now, I'm fairly confident you could build a complete game with levels and everything. And you'd probably even be able to figure out how to release it on the Play Store after a little reading around (though I'll be explaining that in Chapter 12).

Yes, you can build a game. But can you build a *good* game? Because those are two very different things. Remember: with great power comes great responsibility. I feel I'd be doing a disservice to the world if I were teach you how to make games and then set you free with zero guidance on what makes a game *fun*.

That's what we'll be looking at in this chapter. We'll also be discussing a little bit about optimization (to get your game to run more smoothly and take up less space) and even how to make your levels a bit prettier. This is the cherry to go on top of your programming cake. Let's go!

Onboarding and Tutorials

Remember the days when you'd buy a computer game from a store and then wait in clothes shops while your mom finished her shopping? You were probably happy sitting there because you had the manual to read, which was filled with backstory, tips, and explanations about how everything in the game worked. It filled you with anticipation for the game and ensured you had a good idea of how to get started once the cartridge/disk was inserted.

These days, games rarely come with a manual, and that's especially true for mobile games. But that doesn't mean you can assume your player knows how to play right away. In fact, you shouldn't even assume they've ever played a *video game* before. Because some of your players probably *won't* have, and those are still customers that you want to stick around. Every game is someone's first. So it becomes your job to teach the player "on the job," as it were, and that means you need a tutorial level.

Actually, the tutorial level is almost as much of an anachronism as the instruction manual itself. Put your hand up if you can remember the last tutorial level you actually *enjoyed*. No, didn't think so!

A good first level then should instruct the player on how everything operates without explicitly telling them a single thing. This means you're going to need to use visual cues, as well as gameplay tropes that create a foundation of knowledge and then build on that.

© Adam Sinicki 2017

185

A. Sinicki, *Learn Unity for Android Game Development*, DOI 10.1007/978-1-4842-2704-6_10

Dissecting the Perfect Opening Level

Though the lack of manual might be a modern problem, the perfect example of an opening level that implicitly teaches the player how to play can be found in one of the all-time classics: *Super Mario Bros.* This game's opening level, called World 1-1, is one of the most analyzed and highly praised levels in all of gaming history—and for good reason. Let's look at how it works.

For your convenience, I've recreated that first level layout using the assets from our simple platformer (Figure 10-1). This may or may not be sacrilege.

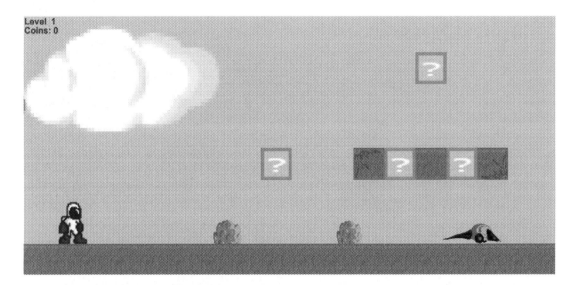

Figure 10-1. *Hmm, this is oddly familiar...*

Right from the very first screen, the player begins to learn how to play. Here, they're greeted by their protagonist, Mario (or in our case, Kevin). Mario has been positioned at the far left of the screen with the camera pushing forward to the right. This immediately and wordlessly tells the player: *go right.*

As Mario goes right, he will see an angry Goomba heading towards him (which we've replaced with our RoboRat). Did you know that we are evolutionarily programmed to feel stress whenever something moves directly towards us? That's why commuting is such a nightmare. This movement pattern combined with the Goomba's angry eyebrows should be enough to tell us that we need to avoid the enemy. The only way we can do that is to jump—otherwise, we die (Figure 10-2).

Figure 10-2. *Jump or die*

Jumping is *the* main mechanic in Mario, and this opening ensures that the player understands how this works before they get any further. If they lose all their lives and go back to the start, then they've lost nothing because they haven't made any progress yet. So this is a fine place to experiment.

The next thing Mario will encounter is a question mark box. This box is *begging* to be touched by the strong visual cue that is the question mark. This universal symbol is saying, "Ooh, what's in here?" (The "Ooh" is optional).

When Mario touches the question mark by bouncing into it, he'll find that it produces a mushroom. The design of the next bit of level is such that Mario is almost *forced* to then collect said mushroom. It will emerge from the box, travel to the right above Mario, and then bounce back off the pipe to head left. Mario is likely to be underneath the next platform at this point and so even if he tries to jump and avoid the mushroom, it will still probably hit him. Figure 10-3 approximates this in our game.

Figure 10-3. *Were this Mario, a mushroom would now be appearing*

Thus, the player learns how they can become "Super Mario."

The level continues in this vein, teaching the player every skill they need in a simple, wordless manner. The next few levels are concerned with giving the player plenty of time to practice those skills before chaining a few obstacles together in order to make real challenges. As the game progresses, the number of obstacles that must be circumvented in sequence will increase, and eventually new quirks and twists will start to be introduced.

Making Sure Your Players Understand Your Game

This may all sound like common sense to you (aren't you clever), but it's surprisingly easy to lose sight of these points when you're in the throes of level design.

Take a look at what you've created already. I know you're only playing around at this point, but I'd be willing to bet that you've laid out some pretty fiendish traps. It's easy to get carried away with this and to mistakenly think that hard = fun. This philosophy is going to lead to a lot of people giving up on your game before they've given it a proper chance. This is e*specially* true if the player doesn't have much prior experience with gaming.

Something that you must *always* do, then, is give your game to people to try out. The advantage of developing for Android is that you can take your phone down to the pub and pass it around to see how your friends manage. What you may find is that things that seem obvious to you are obtuse or unfair for first-time players. You'll see where your players get stuck and at what point they consider giving up. If you've done this right, they should be able to get through at least the first few levels without getting overly frustrated. It will take at least that long for them to get hooked.

A tip from Shigeru Miyamotu, the genius mind behind Mario and World 1-1, is to design your first level *last*. This makes it much easier to take a step back and avoid the temptation to become sadistic with your level design.

The Difficulty Curve

You do need to start introducing significant challenges at some point in your game, though, because otherwise it will become boring. Fun lies at the sweet spot between *impossible* and *too easy*.

Why? Because from a neurological standpoint, games are fun as long as we are *learning*. Yes, I'm about to get deep.

Your brain evolved to help you survive. And what is it that makes humans so incredibly adept at survival? Our ability to adapt and to learn. We thrive because we learn how to utilize the environment around us and cope with changing climates and circumstances. Our reactions get better with practice, and set movement patterns become deeply ingrained through repetition.

The brain wants to *keep* learning, so it rewards that learning by releasing certain neurotransmitters and hormones. When you are working toward a goal, the brain releases dopamine to keep you focused. When you *accomplish* that goal, it releases endorphins—which feel *great*. This encourages the brain to rewire itself, so that you stand a better chance of accomplishing that same thing again. Games use sound effects to signal reward, which strengthens that response.

If you present the brain with too little stimulation or challenge, it becomes bored. Boredom is bad for us because it can literally cause the brain to atrophy. When bored, we'll quickly look for something else to do.

Likewise, though, when you present the brain with an impossible challenge, it quickly becomes deflated and gives up.

But if you're given a challenge that's *just* hard enough to require a lot of work but not *so* hard as to be impossible, then this can stimulate and engage you as the brain learns, adapts, and grows. If a game gets this *just right*, then the player will enter what is referred to in neuroscience as a *flow state*—a state of mind where we are completely focused on the task in hand to the point that time around us almost seems to dilate and slow down. Brain imaging studies show some fascinating changes in the way the brain works at this point; it enters a state called *hypofrontality* in which the frontal regions of the brain become suppressed, and we begin to act *purely on instinct*. This balance is demonstrated in Figure 10-4.

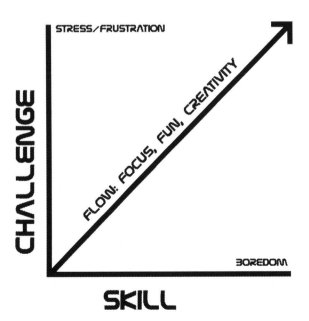

Figure 10-4. *For your players to be engaged and have fun, your difficulty curve must perfectly match their level of ability*

You've probably experienced this at some point during a bullet hell shooter where you've danced around hundreds of bullets on the screen in a trance, or during an intense, boss battle where you only have one life remaining.

The brain is engaged because it's learning and growing, and you can feel the fruits of this labor when you return to an earlier level and find that your new muscle memory now makes previously seemingly impossible challenges easy.

As a game designer, it's your job to ensure that the intensity of the challenge ramps up perfectly as the player improves in skill and experience, with the end goal being to keep them in that sweet spot. Better yet, you should give your game depth so that they can return to earlier levels and use their new skills to get better times or find hidden collectibles.

(That said, pacing is also important, and you *do* need to provide the player with occasional space to breathe so that they can recover.)

Other Ways to Make Your Game Fun

So, it's so important that you keep teaching the player as they progress through the game and keep the challenge fair but rewarding.

But that's not the only way to make your game enjoyable. Another useful tool is variety. One way to stimulate a flow state in the real world is to put a person in a novel environment, and this is something we can use to our advantage. The brain wakes up and pays attention when the surroundings are unfamiliar because this once again represents a learning opportunity.

That's why you should keep introducing new mechanics *and* switching up your environments. This is why it is so common to see "snow levels" and "volcano levels" in games. You can be more inventive than that, of course, but the most important thing is that you keep changing the palette and the tone. That creates a sense of discovery and encourages your player to want to keep pushing forward.

Puzzle solving is another trope that players enjoy in games. Once again, there is a neurological reward that comes from that "eureka" moment and from letting everything click into place.

So how do you design a good puzzle? The answer is to introduce elements to your game and then ask the player to look for new ways to combine and use those elements. So, the box you used to climb a ledge becomes a weapon you can drop on an enemy (see Figure 10-5). This requires *lateral thinking* and challenges the brain to overcome *functional fixedness*—the temptation to view objects and elements only within the context that they were originally introduced.

Figure 10-5. *Tee hee!*

The best way to increase the challenge with your puzzles is to gradually increase the number of steps that the player needs to take in order to solve them.

Finally, a great way to reward your players and engage them further is to empower them to somehow have an impact on the world around them. This often relates to the central *hook* of your gameplay—the mechanic that sets your game apart and allows your character to navigate the world in a unique manner. If this mechanic also happens to let the player see the effect they're having on their surroundings, then it will help to make them feel more powerful, which a lot of fun can be derived from. That's why games like *Angry Birds* or even *Just Cause* essentially revolve around causing large amounts of destruction. It makes the player feel *powerful*. Other games like *Godus* take this one step further by letting the player play as a god.

That said, *depowering* the player to create a sense of tension, isolation, and danger can be a good way to increase their focus and attention and make their victories even *more* rewarding. This is perfectly illustrated in games like *Limbo*.

Emergent Gameplay

Other things to consider are the aspects of your game that you *can't* design. Your world will be an ever-changing series of permutations, which will be based on random events and the actions of your player. You can't anticipate every single scenario, then—meaning some gameplay possibilities will be out of your hands. But this isn't a bad thing. It's actually a *great* thing. This is how emergent gameplay is born: when elements you created interact in unexpected ways, creating new challenges and unique situations for the players. For example, if Roborat were able to trigger the falling blocks, under the right circumstances that could result in both the player and the rat jumping across falling debris. Emergent gameplay is amazing because it gives each player their own unique stories to tell and ensures that every game session is different. You just create the elements, stir them together in a big pot, and then wait for the magic to happen.

Interactions Between Hardware, Game Engines, Format, and Gameplay

In a chapter 5, I mentioned that the game physics and elements you create would be inseparable from the gameplay and the challenge. What I meant by that is that there's a two-way interaction here that must be considered during your design. Decisions you make regarding the functioning of the game world will have direct consequences regarding the way your game is played and the challenges that are possible. For example, the amount of friction you add to a surface will change the difficulty that's presented by a series of moving platforms, as we saw before. Likewise, so will the size of the directional buttons on the screen and the players' own fingers. All this needs to be taken into account when creating a challenging sequence and when designing the game physics in the first place.

As we'll see, this two-way relationship goes much deeper....

Creating a Great Camera

One of the best examples of how gameplay mechanics and the programming of your game engine intersect can be seen with the camera.

Right now, your Camera is incredibly simple: it's a child of the Player and so moves at the exact same speed the player does. You may not have given this much thought, but if you now go back to your favorite platform games, you may notice that this is *not* how the majority of games behave.

For example, we saw in that early example of Mario that the camera begins far to the right of the player, indicating the direction that they should move. This is also the position you'll see the camera in in any "endless runner game," and in this case the camera takes that position so as to make sure the player has lots of opportunity to see upcoming obstacles and therefore more time to react. The player *can't* run backwards in these types of games, so what use is there in having lots of useless space to the left of them?

The faster paced a game is, the more drawn back the camera should likely be with a wider FOV (field of view) in order to show more of what's coming up.

In games with lots of platforming, it's important to prevent nausea. In that case, the camera will sometimes have a neutral zone in the center that the player can move around in and then scroll only once they move out of this center. Other platformers solve this issue by having the camera "snap" to whichever platform the character is touching at any given time.

In Figure 10-6, the black box denotes our neutral zone. There's a lot of space up and down, but not so much room left and right. So if the player moves left or right, the camera will track pretty soon after with only a slight delay (meaning they'll feel quicker when dodging obstacles). However, there will be more space for the player to jump up and down without the camera bobbing up and down madly. This would lend itself best to a less vertical level design with lots of jumping across gaps. See how the camera behavior reflects the level layout and vice versa? This is the same kind of camera behavior seen in the 2D *Sonic the Hedgehog* games, which is actually crucial owing to the many hills and gradients in those games. If the camera simply followed Sonic, it would be *constantly* moving up and down to a nauseating degree—especially at those speeds.

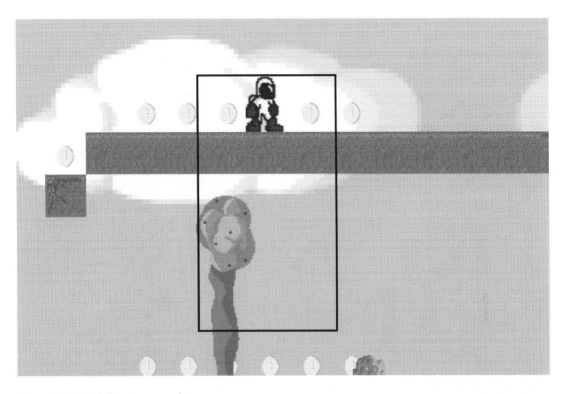

Figure 10-6. *A different approach to our camera*

In other cases, the camera can be used to dramatic effect—hinting at dangers that lie ahead or slowing down as the player approaches a large challenge. If the camera stops moving forward, the player will instantly wonder whether they should continue and start to wonder what lies beyond their field of vision (FOV).

So, if your game design isn't working quite as you think it should, consider whether there is the right amount of synergy between the worlds you're dreaming up and the movement of the camera. Could the game be made more fun by coding some more advanced behavior into your camera or even just moving it backwards slightly?

Hardware and Business Models

It's not just the physics and code that will define what's possible and what's fun in your game design. It's also the hardware you're targeting and the business model you want to use.

For an example of how hardware and monetization can directly impact on the way a game is played, look no further than your local video arcade machine. Arcade games were conventionally very difficult and had lives systems because they wanted players to insert more coins. Likewise, they had to be easy to learn and challenging to master so people would keep coming back to top the high-scores charts.

When games migrated to PCs, they started to become a lot more complex and intricate. They became even more elaborate with the introduction of save files and more powerful hardware.

Interestingly, mobile games have taken things back a little bit. Mobile gaming on small screens lends itself to more "bite-sized" chunks of gameplay (see Figure 10-7), whereas the introduction of alternative monetization options like "free to play" mean that games once again need to give us incentives to keep spending.

Figure 10-7. *Breath of the Wild works well as a portable game due to the ability to so easily dip in and out*

Online functionality meanwhile means that "high score" lists have once again become more important. The point here is that nothing should be included in your game because "that's what games do." Everything should have a purpose, and that purpose will be defined by *multiple* different factors.

Whether you want to create a "sit-down" game with a one-off payment aimed at tablet devices or a free-to-play endless runner for casual gamers is going to completely change the way you go about your level design. This means you need some concept of your entire end game before you go about designing that first level.

And to think you were just going to start *dropping things in places.*

Making Your Game Look Awesome

Although gameplay is arguably more important than looks, it's still very important that your game has both. We've already seen that the graphics in your game will have an impact on the way your game works; graphics can convey a sense of place and can provide cues for interactions. At the same time, though, it's going to be the screenshots and gameplay footage more than anything that helps you to sell your game.

In other words, it's time we looked at adding a lick of paint to the game we've built. What are some ways we can improve the way it comes across in photos?

Easy Ways to Make Your Game More Attractive

If you were to take a look at what we've created, it would be fair to say that *at the moment* it's not all that attractive. It doesn't quite look like a professional game yet, and that's what we're looking to fix here (see Figure 10-8).

Figure 10-8. *The current look*

But what precisely is wrong? What's missing?

The first issue is that everything is very inorganic. The platforms are made from straight lines and are all uniformly the same. A quick way to change this is to rotate some of them by 90 or 180 degrees. That's an efficient way to reuse the same assets and keep file sizes low, but it still adds some variation to the way things look. Likewise, we should consider using some more detailed sprites for the edges of our platforms. That will give the effect of natural decay and quickly make things look a lot more *real*.

We can add more details, like the vines we used earlier, to make every piece of land look a little different. Basically, we want everything to look as random as possible, and we can accomplish that with a little code.

Figure 10-9 looks much better.

Figure 10-9. *Not much has changed, but it looks slightly more organic*

As it is, another issue with our game world is that it's static. Look outside your window, and you'll see that something is *always* moving, whether it's a tree branch blowing in the wind or rainwater dripping from a pipe. The same is true of the best games, and that's why nearly everything is animated, from the flowers to the stars in the background. That not only makes your world feel *alive*, it also brings a lot more character and personality to your game and makes it more interesting to look at.

There is a cut-off point, though. We don't want to distract our players from the important elements.

Of course, we're missing animations *throughout* the game at the moment. You'll want to give your bad guys animations and your player animations for doing things like jumping or shooting. This is another way to help the player feel that they're interacting with the world. The spring should *wobble* when they bounce off it.

A final problem is that the game lacks depth. The background we designed is pretty flat and lacks interest until we reach the clouds or the sun. This worsens the feeling that everything has been cut out of pieces of cardboard, so you should look to improve it by adding in a few more layers.

In Figure 10-10 I've added clouds at the foreground with some transparency that will move faster than the middle ground as the level scrolls. I've also added a few more in the background and introduced a layer of mountains. Those mountains move at yet another speed and they help to ensure that our game world never looks completely blank in the background.

Figure 10-10. *With these few changes, our game is starting to look more interesting*

How to Create Great-Looking Sprites and Choose a Design Language for Your Game

Although adding these elements can do a lot to improve the look and feel of your game, they all require you to have some basic skill when it comes to creating your own sprites. What do you do if you don't have an artistic bone in your body?

One option is to outsource your artwork. Sites like Fiverr, Freelancer, and UpWork allow you to connect with freelancers offering a wide range of services including art and design. These are also great places to get background music and sound effects.

Option two is to make a stylized game that uses a unique art style that greatly reduces the amount of work you need to do. A lot of games these days use a black and white art style, silhouettes (like the aforementioned *Limbo*), or various retro-looks (as seen in *VVVVVV*, which looks like it was designed on a ZX Spectrum). Figure 10-11 shows us what our game might look like were it designed for a Game Boy.

Figure 10-11. *Retro-style Kevin*

Using a specific art style like this can allow your game to stand out and grab attention in the Play Store, while also giving it a strong identity. If you choose something somewhat minimal, you'll save yourself a lot of time as well and remove the need to get great at design.

For our game, we've gone with a pixel art style. This is another retro-inspired look that gives our game a sense of nostalgia and frees us from needing to create photorealistic sprites.

So how do you achieve this style? The answer is simple: just use *any* image-editing software such as GIMP or even MSPaint and then zoom in as close as you can. If possible, select Show Grid Lines in the settings. Now, using a pencil tool that has 100% opacity, you can go about drawing the outline for your sprite. You should be able to see the individual pixels as you are drawing.

Take time and care as you draw your sprite and make sure to keep an eye on any patterns that form. For instance, if you're drawing a gradient, you may notice that the pixels move one up, three across each time. This will result in something that looks more consistent and controlled. Luckily, you can just hit Ctrl+Z if you make any mistakes. Another tip is to consider using layers where available (GIMP and Photoshop offer this feature, but MSPaint doesn't) and that way trace around the images you want to turn into pixel art.

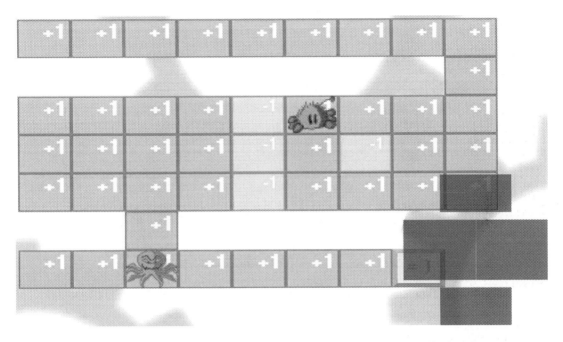

Figure 10-12. *An early app I made used a pastel color palette and a Sudoku-inspired look: Debugger: Brain Untraining*

You can outline your sprites or you can use block colors. I also recommend adding shading. That normally means you'll use three colors: one for the main fill, one for shadows, and one for highlights. Make sure the shadows are consistently on the same side in *all* your sprites that are going to be in the same scene—otherwise it will look confusing because it will be unclear where the light source is.

Finally, export your image. Now, you may find that it looks *tiny* when you do this, but that can be fixed when you import it into Unity and set the Pixels Per Unit and the Scale. Make a small image bigger and the pixels will really pop.

Optimization

This chapter has been all about taking your functional game and turning it into an *awesome* game. To this end, we have one left item left on our agenda: optimization. We've looked at the surface details—now we need to take another look at what's on the inside.

First, what do I mean by *optimization* anyway? Essentially, I'm talking about making your game run smoothly *and* be easy to edit, improve, and update going forward. Good code should use as few lines as possible, with everything organized neatly so that it's easy for you to find whichever element you need.

tipsForBetterCode

Whenever you write code, you need to have your eye on the future. One day, you're going to want to update your game to fix a bug or add a new feature (again, this is especially common on mobile) and will come back to it after being away for a while. In an ideal world, this should be a painless experience. Everything is simple to understand and you don't need to spend ages squinting at the screen. You should know where everything is and what you need to change to achieve your desired results. This becomes *even more* important if you're working in a team.

As mentioned, better code also means *less code*. The more code there is on the page, the harder it's going to be to find whatever it is you're looking for, and the more steps each process will likely take. More steps = slower execution.

So how can you start making more elegant programs? Here are some tips to get you started:

1. Place multiple variables on a single line:

    ```
    public float startX;
    public float startY;
    ```

    becomes

    ```
    public float startX, startY;
    ```

2. Always make sure to use variables with sensible names that describe their function. This may sound obvious, but you'd be surprised how often programmers use completely random labels. If your variable tells the character how high they should jump, it should be called something like `jumpHeight`. This also means avoiding abbreviations (`jh`), which will quickly become obtuse and confusing.

    In fact, the ideal situation is that your variables allow your code to read like English. When using a Boolean in particular, this can be either true or false, which means you can create lines like this:

    ```
    if (playerIsGrounded) {
    ```

    This tells us everything we need to know, even if we don't know a line of programming.

3. Use *camel case*. This means that each new word in a variable begins with a capital letter in order to help the reader break it up (sometimes this excludes the first word). For example: `jumpheight` should be written as either `jumpHeight` or `JumpHeight`. Not only does this further aid readability, but you'll also see that Unity breaks these variables up into individual words when you view the variables in the Inspector.

4. Avoid using "magic numbers." In other words, don't assign random significance to a number as a way to get around a coding challenge. I did this in Chapter 9 when I used the timer that went *beyond* zero for the falling blocks. The timer stopped when it reached –70. Why minus seventy?

    One way to avoid this would be to use constants. A *constant* is a type of variable that has a fixed value and can't be changed once it's been defined. This has no memory overhead, and its main purpose is usually for legibility. We could create a constant integer for instance with the value of –70 and call that `endOfFallAnimation`. Now our falling block would stop at the `endOfFallAnimation` rather than at –70. Makes a lot more sense!

Remember our `Player` script and its use of 1 to represent "right" and 0 to represent "left"? If you take a hiatus from your code and then come back to it, this can be pretty confusing too. So instead why not use this:

```
const int left = 0, right = 1;
```

Now we can say

```
if (facing == right)
```

which is far easier for us to read back. (This still shows as 0 and 1 in the Inspector, however.)

Another advantage of using constants is that it's far easier to search and replace values later on should you want to make changes.

5. Describe *why* not *what*. When writing comments, describing *the purpose* of a method is much more important than describing what it does. What is the relevance of this function? How does it relate to the rest of the script?

6. Avoid writing the same code twice wherever possible. The more of your code you can place in distinct methods, the easier it will be to quickly locate what you're looking for and the less you'll need to type in total. Using methods also allows you to copy and paste whole chunks of code from one script to the next.

7. Use loops! A *loop* is piece of code that repeats itself until a certain condition is met or broken. For example, a `while` loop looks like this:

```
int count = 1;
        while (count <= 4)
        {
            count = count + 1;
        }
```

This just counts to four and then stops, but we can use this structure to execute the same command four times.

Actually, though, for loops that use an incrementing variable, it often makes sense to use `"for"`. This is an example of accomplishing the same thing with fewer lines of code. A `for` loop looks like so:

```
for ( init; condition; increment )
{
   statement(s);
}
```

Whatever type of loop you go for, they serve a similar purpose to methods in that they help you to segment your code and prevent you from writing out lots of functions repeatedly.

8. Use smart tags and layers. Just as you need to be sensible with variable naming conventions, the same goes for the names you assign while inside the Unity IDE. By now, you know to use correct parenting and to create prefabs rather than dealing with instances as well.

Performance and Compatibility

The preceding tips will help make your code logical and readable and in some cases a little speedier too. Really, though, the main bottlenecks in terms of speed will lie outside your scripts.

Smaller Images

For instance, you need to make sure that you use images that aren't *too* large. The larger an image, the bigger the file size of your app and the longer it will take to load. I'd like to tell you that the size of your app doesn't really matter, but that would be a lie: I've personally had multiple negative comments from my own users when APK sizes have gotten too big, so this is something people really care about.

Note that you can show a load screen if necessary by loading scenes from a co-routine (like we used for our `Player.Death` method) and then showing a loading UI over the old scene. However, we still want load times to be as short as possible, so you should avoid sticking huge images in your scenes unnecessarily. This is another reason that choosing a pixel art style makes a lot of sense: it lets you keep smaller file sizes and then scale them up without having to worrying about pixelation. Choosing the right kind of image compression (JPG image format rather than PNG when it's okay to lose a little quality) will also help with this. So too can reusing assets, which is why rotating tiles was a good move earlier.

Unity will add additional compression for your images when you build your APK, and you can set the type of texture compression you want to use in build settings. This additional compression will affect the speed and size of your app but also its compatibility and whether or not it supports alpha (transparency). From Unity's own documentation:

Texture Format	What internal representation is used for the texture. This is a tradeoff between size and quality.
RGB Compressed DXT1	Compressed RGB texture. Supported by Nvidia Tegra. 4 bits per pixel (32 KB for a 256 x 256 texture).
RGBA Compressed DXT5	Compressed RGBA texture. Supported by Nvidia Tegra. 6 bits per pixel (64 KB for a 256 x 256 texture).
RGB Compressed ETC 4 bits	Compressed RGB texture. This is the default texture format for Android projects. ETC1 is part of OpenGL ES 2.0 and is supported by all OpenGL ES 2.0 GPUs. It does not support alpha. 4 bits per pixel (32 KB for a 256 x 256 texture)
RGB Compressed PVRTC 2 bits	Compressed RGB texture. Supported by Imagination PowerVR GPUs. 2 bits per pixel (16 KB for a 256 x 256 texture)
RGBA Compressed PVRTC 2 bits	Compressed RGBA texture. Supported by Imagination PowerVR GPUs. 2 bits per pixel (16 KB for a 256 x 256 texture)
RGB Compressed PVRTC 4 bits	Compressed RGB texture. Supported by Imagination PowerVR GPUs. 4 bits per pixel (32 KB for a 256 x 256 texture)
RGBA Compressed PVRTC 4 bits	Compressed RGBA texture. Supported by Imagination PowerVR GPUs. 4 bits per pixel (32 KB for a 256 x 256 texture)
RGB Compressed ATC 4 bits	Compressed RGB texture. Supported by Qualcomm Snapdragon. 4 bits per pixel (32 KB for a 256 x 256 texture).
RGBA Compressed ATC 8 bits	Compressed RGBA texture. Supported by Qualcomm Snapdragon. 6 bits per pixel (64 KB for a 256x256 texture).

RGB 16 bit	65 thousand colors with no alpha. Uses more memory than the compressed formats, but could be more suitable for UI or crisp textures without gradients. 128 KB for a 256 x 256 texture.
RGB 24 bit	Truecolor but without alpha. 192 KB for a 256 x 256 texture.
Alpha 8 bit	High-quality alpha channel but without any color. 64 KB for a 256 x 256 texture.
RGBA 16 bit	Low-quality truecolor. The default compression for the textures with alpha channel. 128 KB for a 256 x 256 texture.
RGBA 32 bit	Truecolor with alpha—this is the highest-quality compression for the textures with alpha. 256 KB for a 256 x 256 texture.
Compression quality	Choose Fast for quickest performance, Best for the best image quality, and Normal for a balance between the two.

Collisions

Performance shouldn't be much of a concern if you're making a 2D game in Unity. Unless you have countless elements on the screen, all running complex animations and scripts, the majority of Android phones will be able to handle most things you throw at them.

But that's not to say there isn't a benefit to keeping the demands of your app as low as possible (consider battery drain and keeping other apps in memory, for instance), and you certainly want to avoid any chance of your app becoming unresponsive.

At runtime, then, one of the biggest things to consider is how many colliders you have. The size of a collider doesn't matter, but what *is* an issue is the *number* of colliders and the complexity of said colliders. Our tiles use individual colliders, for example, which makes development *much* easier and allows us to use prefabs. This is the best practice for our purposes for the most part because the cost in performance is by far outweighed by the flexibility and ease with which we can add future updates. See Figure 10-13.

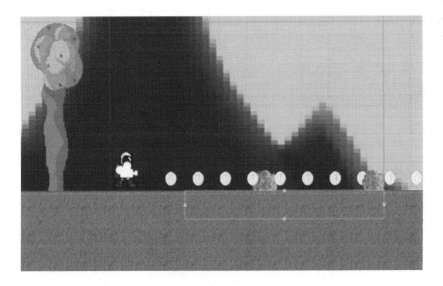

Figure 10-13. *I have drawn a single box collider around a bunch of tiles here*

You can make the blocks children of the one with the collider and save them as a prefab to rapidly implement them into your game. Alternatively, you can simply draw larger platform boxes with their own larger colliders.

Bear in mind as well that the tiles beneath the surface actually don't *need* colliders. Removing the colliders from here is probably one of the quickest and easiest ways to get our app to perform better.

Even worse than having lots of small colliders is to use complex polygon colliders with lots of different points and angles (see Figure 10-14). This creates more math for Unity, because it needs to work out how each point will interact with surfaces it bumps into. This is why it makes sense to use a box collider for your character (or a polygon collider that is a slightly deformed box) *rather* than using a polygon collider that perfect adheres to the contours of the character.

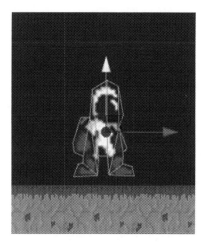

Figure 10-14. *An overly complex collider*

Even the overly complex collider in Figure 10-14 would be unlikely to cause any noticeable slow-down, but if you had *lots* of objects with colliders like this, things could start to get a little choppy. At the end of the day, this is wasteful because it won't have any meaningful impact on the way the player actually plays the game.

Making Other Types of Games

During this chapter, we've discussed a lot about the interplay between gameplay mechanics, design, and hardware. But so far, we've yet to *truly* consider the nature of the platform we're developing for.

After all, the platformer dates back to the NES and other early computers and doesn't *naturally* lend itself to the touchscreen input of mobile devices. There is definitely still a market for platform games on Android, and this was a particularly good choice for a tutorial because it allowed us to experiment with lots of different concepts.

But if you wanted to dabble in a genre that was more ideally suited to mobile, you might opt instead to develop an *infinite runner*. This looks and acts like a platformer except for one key difference: the player continually runs forward. Great examples include *Canabalt, Sonic Runners, Super Mario Run, Temple Run,* and *Jetpack Joyride*. Here, the player only needs one input—jump—which declutters the screen (no more arrow keys obscuring the play space) and provides gameplay that is perfect for quickly dipping in and out of.

To make what you've built an infinite runner, you can just modify the Player script to run forward automatically. You could then design levels with this in mind *or* if you want it to be truly "infinite", have your levels generate themselves on the fly (called *procedural generation*). This means you're going to need to introduce an algorithm that instantiates new platforms randomly (and probably destroys old ones) while ensuring there is always a route across for the player. Using larger platform tiles is often a good idea here, and of course you need the difficulty and speed to ramp up gradually.

You could likewise remove the gravity from the physics engine to turn it into a space shooter of some sort, or even a top-down game.

Puzzle Games and More

The potential problem with platformers, first-person shooters, and racing games on Android is that they essentially involve *retrofitting* an old game genre onto new hardware. Conversely, arguably the most inventive and interesting Android games are those that find new ways to take advantage of the hardware.

Angry Birds is a good example of this because it utilizes the touchscreen in a very natural way to open up new gameplay possibilities. *The Room* and *Monument Valley* take this even further by letting the player interact *directly* with the game world by reaching out and touching, twisting, and dragging various elements and even including tilt controls at times. Remember how we said the player likes to feel that they are impacting the game world?

You can get your game to use the phone's accelerometer as simply as this:

```
rb.velocity = new Vector2(Input.acceleration.x, rb.velocity.y);
```

What if tipping the phone could cause enemies and collectibles to slide across the screen?

Likewise, you can use multitouch very easily too, opening up a range of other possibilities:

```
void Update ()
    {
        Touch myTouch = Input.GetTouch(0);

        Touch[] myTouches = Input.touches;
        for(int i = 0; i < Input.touchCount; i++)
        {
            //Do something with the touches
        }
    }
```

Don't be limited by old notions of what a "game" has to be. You can set any condition to end the level, whether it's getting a ball to roll onto a target that acts like a trigger or counting when the player has collected every coin on the screen. There doesn't even need to be a "player" object at all—just look at *Tetris*, the original mobile hit.

Oh, and speaking of different kinds of mobile games, I've got something exciting in store for you in the next chapter. First, we'll be discussing how you would go about creating a 3D game for Android with realistic graphics (yes, you can do that). Then we're going to discuss how you can actually *enter* that world using a Samsung Galaxy Gear or Google's Daydream View headset.

It's an exciting new frontier for mobile developers, and we're going to make sure you're right on the crest of that wave.

Figure 10-15. *Now that's starting to look like a game I want to play!*

■ ■ ■ ■

CHAPTER 11

An Introduction to 3D Game Development and Virtual Reality

Chapter 10 ended by discussing how Unity could be used to create other types of games such as puzzlers, infinite runners, and more. All that would require is to tweak some of the scripts and GameObjects from our simple platformer. You could change the objectives, the input method, and the whole experience. You can even make utilities this way.

But there's an entire additional category of game that we have yet to address and that would require a rather different approach: 3D games. Although 3D controls can sometimes be difficult with a small touchscreen, there are plenty of examples of games out there that have managed to get around this limitation; some have gone on to become highly popular. Hit 3D titles include the likes of the *N.O.V.A.* series, *Asphalt 8: Airborne, Geometry Wars 3,* and *Minecraft: Pocket Edition* to name just a few.

What's even more exciting is that once you learn the skills necessary to create 3D games, you'll be in position to start creating your own virtual reality experiences for the Galaxy Gear VR and Google Daydream Headset.

Creating a 3D World

To get started, the first thing you'll need to do is to create a 3D environment for your character to begin exploring. It may feel weird saying goodbye to Kevin, but it's time to move on.

Click File ➤ New Project but this time choose to start a 3D project (Figure 11-1). You'll then be presented with a similar setup to what you're used to, except the perspective is going to be 3D. That change in perspective also affects the grid, which will now be viewed from above at an angle (Figure 11-2).

© Adam Sinicki 2017
A. Sinicki, *Learn Unity for Android Game Development*, DOI 10.1007/978-1-4842-2704-6_11

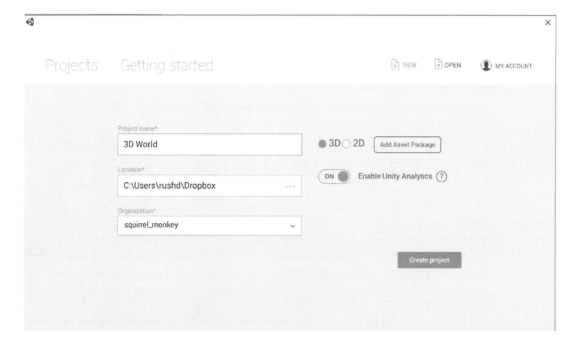

Figure 11-1. *Create your new 3D project*

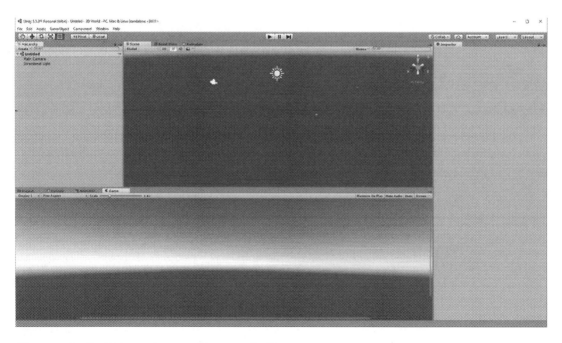

Figure 11-2. *The Unity you know and love, now in 3D*

The UI essentially behaves the same as before. The main difference is the inclusion of the perspective widget in the top right of your Scene window. Click this and you can change the angle of the view to top-down (Figure 11-3), side-on, and so forth. Working with 3D objects can be tricky at first, and you can find yourself constantly struggling with perspectives. A quick tip is that there is nothing to stop you from opening up multiple Scene windows: right-click any tab and then choose Add Tab ➤ Scene. This way you can have multiple windows, each with different perspectives (top-down, side-on, and so on). But it's up to you to decide what setup works best for your work flow, as ever.

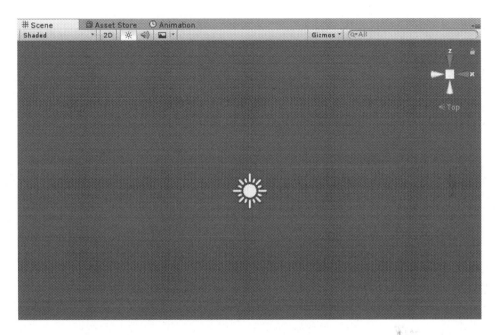

Figure 11-3. *This angle can be useful for aligning ground tiles for instance*

Otherwise, you can still drag the view around with the hand tool, or zoom in with your scroll wheel as before.

The first thing we're going to do, though, is to drop a 3D object into this world. Navigate to GameObject ➤ 3DObject ➤ Plane. This will drop—you guessed it—a 3D plane into the scene (see Figure 11-4). We'll then be able to change the size of said plane, move it around, or change its attributes through the Inspector, just as we could with our 2D sprites before.

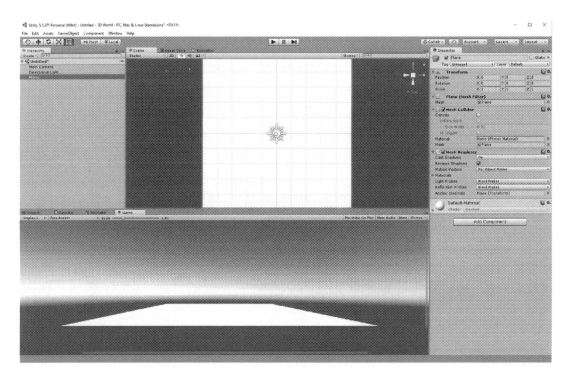

Figure 11-4. *Let there be a plane*

Now drop another element into the game. How about a cube this time? Click GameObject ➤ 3DObject ➤ Cube, and a cube will appear in your scene (see Figure 11-5).

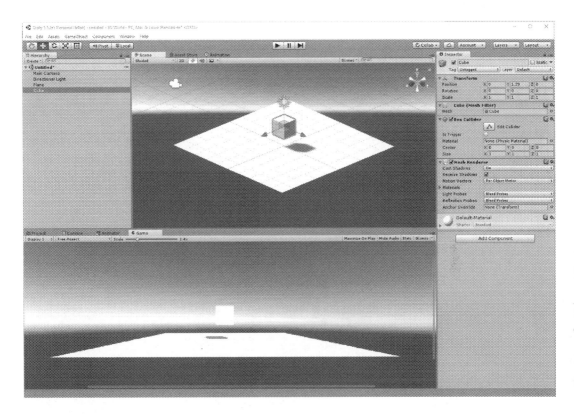

Figure 11-5. *And now a cube*

So far, so simple. But hit play and you'll see that the cube simply hovers in the air indefinitely. As before, then, we need to apply some physics. So select the cube and then Add Component ➤ Physics ➤ Rigidbody. Notice there is no *2D* suffix this time. Unity was originally developed *specifically* for 3D development, so the "default" scripts and objects are all 3D without needing to explicitly state the fact.

As soon as the game objects were added, they already had a mesh collider attached, so if you press play *now*, the cube will drop onto the plane and stop in its tracks. Awesome.

Sprites and Skybox

To make the world look a little nicer, you can create a subfolder in your Assets directory called Textures and drop some sprites in. Now drag the sprites from there onto your GameObjects and expand the Shader menu in the Inspector. Here you can set how much you want the texture to repeat (Tiling) as well as the reflectiveness (Metallic), smoothness, and more.

In Figure 11-6, I've done this using sprites from the 2D version of the game.

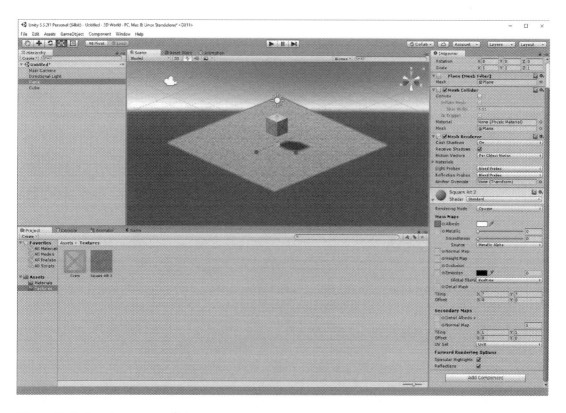

Figure 11-6. *A crate over some dirt*

Now we want to add a better background for our world. To do that we need to create a *lightbox*. Find the Materials folder in your project and right-click anywhere there to create a new material called Sky. In the Inspector, set the Shader to Skybox using the dropdown menu and then choose Procedural. This will; change the color and appearance of the sky in the background, so set the Atmosphere Thickness, Exposure, Sun Size, and so on, just as you want them. I'm going to set my scene at a beach-type location during twilight.

Now select Window ➤ Lighting and use the Scene tab to set the Skybox to the Sky material you just created. You should instantly see the look of your game change (see Figure 11-7). Note that if you chose 6 Sided for your skybox, you could use any texture you wanted for your backdrop.

Figure 11-7. *Setting up some mood lighting*

Adding a Player

Prepare to be impressed with Unity again: adding a player to our game world is *supremely* easy because there is another ready-made asset available to help us do it: the FPSController. This handles controls, physics, and more for a first-person player.

Right-click the Assets folder and select Import Package ➤ Characters. Leave everything selected as it is and hit Import. This will take a couple of seconds, but once it is done, you'll have a new folder in your project called Standard Assets, and inside that will be various subdirectories. The one we're interested in for now is FirstPersonCharacter. Later, to reduce the size of your project, you can choose to only import the elements you need.

Locate Standard Assets ➤ Characters ➤ FirstPersonCharacter ➤ Prefabs and then choose FPSController. You know what a *prefab* is by now, so you may have guessed that this is essentially a ready-made FPS character that we can just drop into our scene. Do that, making sure the character is above the ground, and then delete the superfluous `Main Camera` GameObject. Then hit play. You should have something like Figure 11-8.

Figure 11-8. *A strangely serene view...*

It's a Christmas miracle! That easily, we have a FPS game up and running. You can look around with the mouse, around with the W, A, S, and D keys, and jump with the spacebar. There are even walking sound effects, and you can interact with the box to push it around. To exit hit Esc, then you can move the mouse pointer up to the stop button.

If you feel like experimenting, bring back the `Main Camera`, delete the FPSController, and drop in the ThirdPersonController. This is a much more detailed 3D object with complex animations but no shaders, and it can be moved around with the same controls so you can get a feel for what it might be like to create a 3D platformer. This combination of assets makes for a pretty weird-looking game, though (Figure 11-9).

For now, we'll be sticking with the FPSController.

Figure 11-9. *If Damien Hirst made computer games …*

Touch Controls

Be prepared to be impressed *yet again*: adding touch controls is just as streamlined in Unity. Once again, we have a ready-made prefab; this one's called DualTouchControls. That's in CrossPlatformInput ➤ Prefabs, and all you need to do is to drop it into your scene and add an Event System. You'll also need to switch the platform to Android in the Build Settings for this to work.

You can set these touch areas on the screen as you like by using the canvas and anchoring to the screen, just as you did before (Figure 11-10). Once that's ready to rumble, try building and running the app on a smartphone to see what it's like to actually use. If everything has gone to plan, you should be able to walk around by dragging around the left portion of the screen and look at the same time using an invisible touchpad on the righthand side of the screen. The bar along the bottom is for jumping. You can see how it has all come together in Figure 11-11.

Figure 11-10. *Set up touch controls on the canvas as you want them to appear*

Figure 11-11. *Not exactly easy controls, but controls nonetheless*

Note that as soon as you set the platform to Android, the game will stop responding to your keyboard and mouse inputs. So you may want to switch this back while you're developing.

Using 3D Models

When we were building our 2D platformer, we would take breaks from coding every now and then to create a sprite of some sort. This is what brought our game world to life, and of course we wouldn't want to limit our 3D efforts to simply cubes and spheres.

Instead of sprites, though, now we're going to add 3D models into our game world, which will open up limitless opportunities for what we can create. Free3D.com is a site that offers a ton of license-free 3D models for you to download and drop into your game, including furniture, monsters, wildlife, and so on. You can also find a ton in the Assets Store, of course, and many of these are free from Unity itself. Do make sure that whatever you use, you're certain that the license extends to commercial use—if you plan on selling your final creation, that is.

Using assets from Free3D.com, I've recreated my living room in 3D (see Figure 11-12). My wife and I are going to use this to try out wall colors before making a selection. It needs a little work first, though.

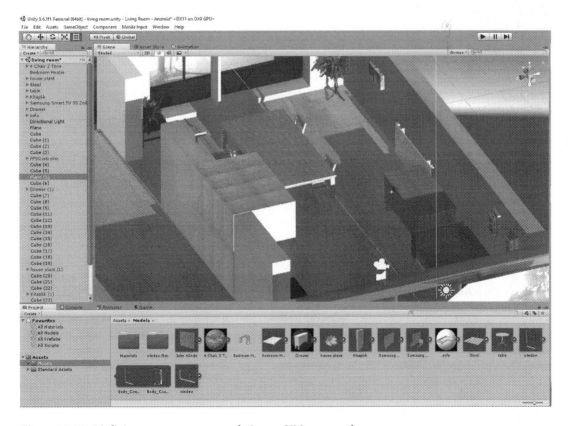

Figure 11-12. *My living room, or near enough. I am a SIM apparently*

Excuse my poor organization in the Hierarchy there. This was just a bit of fun.

Make yourself at home! Remember, it's very important to always ensure that you're legally allowed to use, distribute, and profit from any potentially copyrighted work such as 3D models—before you finalize your apps.

Want to make your own 3D models? The best way to do so is by using the free software called Blender. It's rather tricky to get to grips with, but once you know what you're doing, nearly anything is possible, and you can even start creating animations. Before you know it, you'll be working for Pixar.

Figure 11-13. *But which is the real world?*

Another New Terrain

Alternatively, another way you can create a world that's a little different and more interesting is by using some of Unity's built-in features to create lush natural landscapes.

Start a new scene or a new project and this time choose GameObject ➤ 3D Object ➤ Terrain. You'll be greeted with another plain, though this one is *significantly* larger than previous attempts. What's really neat about terrain, though, is that it will let you insert mountains, hills, trees, and more to create something that looks a lot more organic and natural.

You'll need to import another package for this. Click Assets ➤ Import Package ➤ Environment. Here you'll find trees, grass, and all kinds of other environmental objects for you to play around with.

Now select the terrain object in your scene and you'll notice some interesting icons in the Inspector. These feature mountains, paintbrushes, trees, and more. Try clicking the icon with the mountains and the arrow pointing up (see Figure 11-14) and then drag your mouse pointer around the terrain—rather natural-looking mountains start bursting forth depending on the speed and pressure you apply.

Figure 11-14. *These are fun*

You can also try painting trees onto the landscape, first by selecting the type of tree you want to add (this is where those assets come in handy) and then by painting them on in different densities. You can also paint textures on with the paintbrush tool, again after first selecting something that looks the part from the assets. Have a little go and you'll quickly get an idea of how quickly you can create worlds that are just begging to be explored. See Figure 11-15.

Figure 11-15. *Breath of the Wild, eat your heart out*

Adding a Gun

Nearly every first-person game involves shooting of some description, so how might you go about adding a gun?

It's actually very simple and it basically involves the same skills that you're already familiar with from working with 2D. There are just a few changes that you should familiarize yourself with. We could start by creating/locating a 3D model of a gun and then making it a child of the Player character. We'd align it so that it was in the correct position, as though the character were holding it.

From there, we would go on to add a script to that gun object so it would respond to a mouse click. This would correspond with a tap anywhere on the screen (or the side button on a Gear VR).

Then we would instantiate a bullet *inside* the gun at the same angle:

```
if (Input.GetKeyDown(KeyCode.Mouse0))
    {
        Instantiate(blast, gameObject.transform.position, gameObject.transform.rotation);
    }
```

The bullet would have its own script to make sure it destroyed itself after a set period of time and to keep it moving forward. The only difference would be that the bullet would be moving in three dimensions now. We'll use `transform.forward`, and this way the bullet will move forward at whatever angle it's currently facing (which in turn is the same as the gun):

```
public class Forward : MonoBehaviour {
    private float timetodestroy;

    void Start () {
        timetodestroy = 3;
    }

    void Update () {
        timetodestroy = timetodestroy - Time.deltaTime;
        gameObject.transform.position += transform.forward * Time.deltaTime * 30;
        if (timetodestroy < 0)
        {
            Destroy(gameObject);
        }
    }
}
```

From there, we can use `onTriggerEnter` or `onCollisionEnter` just as we normally would (minus the 2D) to get our bullet to explode items, flip switches, and do whatever else.

As you can see, it's a fairly simple matter to take this basic setup and build it into a full game just as you did last time. You can extrapolate from these instructions to make your AIs, springs, and other things.

Stepping into Virtual Reality

But you know what? First-person shooters (also known as FPS) just aren't that much fun on a mobile phone using touch input. So what's the point of familiarizing yourself with 3D at all?

Of course, you may find there are other types of 3D game you can make. Perhaps you're interested in making a pinball game or a racing game using tilt controls. Or maybe you're just stubborn and you're making an FPS anyway. The *N.O.V.A.* series seems to be doing okay after all...

But what you could *also* make—and what's way more exciting—is a virtual reality app (check out Figure 11-16).

Figure 11-16. *Developing for the Gear VR in a library in Radolfzell, Germany. Good times!*

Thanks to the Samsung Gear VR and the Google Daydream Headset, virtual reality is quite a big deal on mobile. In fact, I rather predict that this might well be where the future of VR lies (Figure 11-17). Adoption is greatest on mobile already (owing to the prohibitive cost and technical challenge associated with PC VR), but what's even more exciting is that mobile is now able to solve one of the biggest challenges facing VR: positional tracking.

Figure 11-17. *Is mobile VR the future?*

Positional tracking refers to the ability to not just look around but actually get up and *walk* around in a 3D space. To jump, duck, run, and tilt. The Oculus Rift and HTC Vive get around this using elaborate "outside in" solutions that involve sensors rigged around the room. The Gear VR and Daydream currently only offer head tracking.

But at the most recent Google I/O conference, HTC unveiled a "standalone" headset that would use something called WorldSense to offer a completely untethered positional tracking solution with no setup and no external sensors. This is *inside out* tracking. The device will be linked with the Daydream experience, so we can expect that it will likely run Android or at least be very similar to the current setup.

This device isn't out yet, and it's not entirely new technology. It's most likely an evolution of Google's Project Tango—an effort to create phones with enough built-in sensors to be able to see the world we do. The technology is already available in the Lenovo Phab Phone 2 and is going to be coming to many more devices in the very near future (it may already have as you read this).

In short, phones will soon have the ability to use "computer vision" in order to sense what's in front of them and how you're moving through space—thereby being able to track movements in VR *and* ensure that players aren't putting themselves in any danger.

But who knows, maybe mobile VR won't be the next big thing. Maybe VR won't take off at all. Whatever happens, we can certainly all agree that making virtual worlds and then stepping into them is *cool*.

Creating Gear VR/Google Daydream Ready Apps

So how might we turn one of the 3D landscapes we've just created into a VR app that will run on the Gear VR (see Figure 11-18) or Google Daydream?

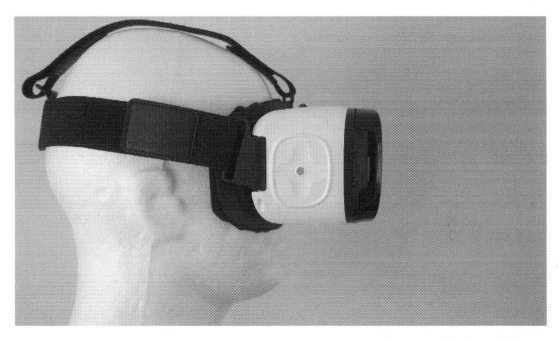

Figure 11-18. *Insert your head here*

It actually couldn't be simpler—as long as it's working, that is. Actually, at the time of writing, Unity has got some bugs to iron out, so things aren't completely smooth. Attempting to build apps for the Gear VR results in an issue where the AndroidManifest files can't be merged (these are files that contain information about your app, such as the version, the name, and so on — see Figure 11-19). The team is promising to fix this, so *hopefully* everything should be up and running by the time you read this. For Google Daydream or Cardboard, no such issue exists. I'm sharing this with you because it's the reality of coding. Sometimes there's a workaround, but other times you're forced to wait for the pros to come up with a solution. Fortunately, Unity tends to be pretty quick at delivering fixes.

EVALDAS_UNITY MAY 11, 2017 16:24

Hello everyone,

The issue has been fixed and the issue tracker above has been updated as to not cause confusion.

However, with the newest SDK/Build tools we have another issue - Merging manifest files.
https://issuetracker.unity3d.com/issues/the-project-does-not-build-on-android-platform-using-the-updated-android-sdk-tools-26-dot-0-during-the-merging-manifest-files

We patched it up a bit in 5.6.0p4, but building Android Oculus is still a no go : (
We are working on it :)

Figure 11-19. *Gee thanks, Unity. At least the frowny face shows true remorse.*

Assuming Unity is playing nice, you simply need to make a couple of changes in your Player Preferences. Specifically, you'll want to tick the box that says VR Supported and then choose Oculus or Daydream as your SDK (Figure 11-20). Of course, you can also try the others, including Cardboard, if you prefer. Unity will know what it needs to download and add to the plugins to get things working.

Settings for Android	
Resolution and Presentation	
Icon	
Splash Image	
Other Settings	
Rendering	
Color Space*	Gamma
Auto Graphics API	☑
Multithreaded Rendering*	☐
Static Batching	☐
Dynamic Batching	☑
GPU Skinning*	☐
Graphics Jobs (Experimental)*	☐
Virtual Reality Supported	☑
Virtual Reality SDKs	
≡ Oculus	

Use DX11/ES3 GPU Skinning

Figure 11-20. *Pretty simple!*

This is *literally* all you need to do in order to get your app to run on VR hardware and try exploring your landscapes in virtual reality. Hit Build and Run and then plug in.

Figure 11-21. *The VR version is much tidier*

Getting Your Oculus Signature File

Things are just a *tiny* bit more complicated if you're developing for the Gear VR. That's because Oculus is a little protective over its platform and doesn't want people to distribute their own apps through channels other than the Play Store. Thus, it has introduced a system to prohibit wanton sharing of apps, which is their "signature file." Basically, each APK can only work on *one* device, which will be defined by a file you add at build time.

To get the Oculus signature file, you'll first need to get your Device ID. This is the identifier for your specific piece of hardware, so any time you want to test your app on a new device, you'll need to go through this process again. To do it, navigate to the platform-tools folder of your Android SDK installation on your PC. Here, you'll find an executable called adb.exe, which is an acronym for *Android Debug Bridge*. Hold down Shift, right-click anywhere in this folder, and choose Open Command Line Here. In the shell that opens up, you're now going to type *adb devices* with your Android device plugged in. This will list the Device IDs of all connected hardware, as seen in Figure 11-22.

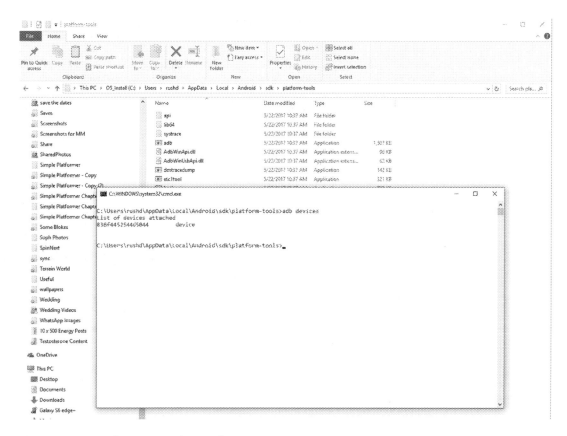

Figure 11-22. *My device ID. Don't ... steal it?*

ADB is a handy thing to familiarize yourself with anyway, because it has a number of other uses.

Now head over to developer.oculus.com and find the Oculus Signature File (osig) Generator. At the time of writing, this is at `https://dashboard.oculus.com/tools/osig-generator/`. Enter your Device ID number into the box as indicated and then click Download File (Figure 11-23). Now you simply need to place this file into a specific directory within your project:

```
Assets > Plugins > Android > assets
```

Yes, it is case-sensitive, and yes, that means that you need one capitalized Assets folder and one lowercase version. And no, these folders won't already exist, so you'll have to create them.

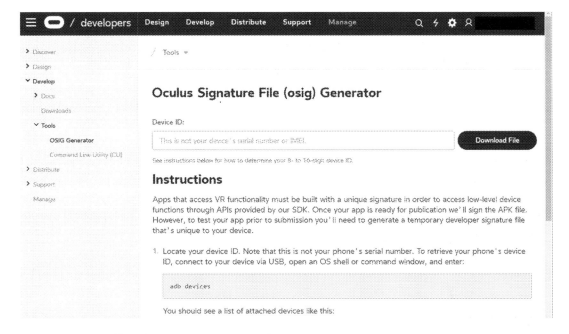

Figure 11-23. *You'll need to create a new account first*

It's a hassle but once that's done, you'll be able to start testing your new VR app on your own hardware and you won't need to worry about it again for a while.

Endless Possibilities

There is an art to creating VR content, and it's an art form that is very much still growing and developing. Things that work well on a screen don't necessarily translate well to VR and vice versa. Then there are issues like input and nausea. But the fact that this space is so unexplored is what makes it so exciting. The possibilities here are limitless, and there's every opportunity for you to stumble upon something game changing.

And with that, your repertoire of skills is pretty much where it needs to be. You'll learn by doing and you'll grow into your abilities as a developer as you go. But I feel you're ready to take on those challenges and start finding your own way. There's just one more thing we need to do: get your creations up and running on the Google Play Store so other people can enjoy them.

■ ■ ■

CHAPTER 12

How to Publish and Promote Your Android App

You've successfully made it this far, and now you're at the final hurdle. You know how to make apps, you know how to get them running on your smart phone ... and heck, you even know how to explore them in VR. Now all that's left to do is release said apps so that you can share them with the rest of the world and receive the adulation/remuneration you so rightly deserve.

This might be a nerve-wracking process. Releasing your app out into the wild makes you vulnerable to criticism, and there's always the possibility that it's going to flop and not get a single download. But don't let that fear freeze you. The great thing about Android apps is that they're never finished: you're free to keep uploading updates and keep iterating on (updating) your product after it's released. There's nothing to be afraid of then: if you don't get it right first time, you just keep trying and eventually evolve your app into something that people love.

Anyway, the success of your app is only partly to do with its quality. Just as important—if not *more* important—is the way you market it and write your store listing. And we're going to be looking at how to do all that right here.

Creating Your Signed APK

Once you've finished your game and you're happy with it, the first thing you need to do is to create your signed APK. The APK is the package file that Android uses to install your app on other people's phones, and you've already built several already while testing your game.

Up until now, though, if you've been using the Build and Run option and leaving the Player Settings mostly as default, you will have been running debug versions of the app. In order to actually publish your creation, you'll need to head back to Build Settings ➤ Player Settings in order to "sign" it to be ready for the big time (along with doing some other changes).

First, add some icons to go with your app. Then make sure you have a package name you're satisfied with. The package name is the internal filename that other Android apps will see (such as the homescreen launcher), but your users *won't* see it for the most part, unless they get technical. Nevertheless, this should be something sensible, because you won't be able to change it later on. This can all be found under the Other Settings heading in the Inspector (Figure 12-1), and the usual format is to include your company name and then the app name.

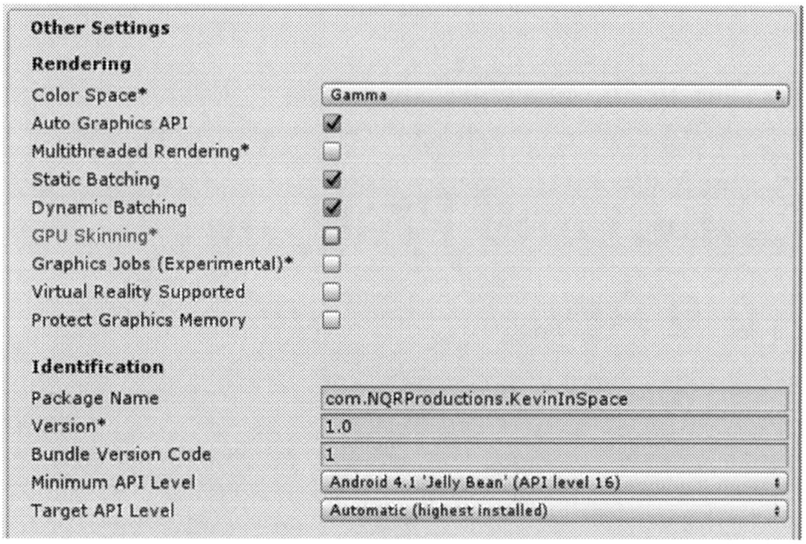

Figure 12-1. *Setting a package name for the platformer*

The Product Name is what your users will see (also called the *label*). This is where your branding will go, and this bit *is* changeable later on. In other words, this is the title for your game, but you don't need to worry if you change your mind later.

Your Version code is for you and your users. It's the version number that they will see, and you'll likely want to update this incrementally each time you roll out newer versions. Bug fixes and small tweaks might result in an incremental tweak (1.0.1), but large changes that add new features and levels might result in a whole version upgrade (2.0). Note that alpha and beta products should have version codes that are *lower* than 1.

The Bundle Version Code, on the other hand, is an internal counter that keeps track of your app version. Every time you upload a new version of your APK, this must go up by 1. This allows Google to keep track and ensure that your users are being pushed the very latest version. Thus your users might see version 1.1.4, but your bundle version code might be 8.

You also need to think about the version of Android you want to target. Some plugins and features will require you to target higher versions of Android or set a higher minimum API. This is true for VR apps, for example. But allowing as many people as possible to install and use your app is good for business where possible. A surprisingly large number of users are still on older versions of Android, so to maximize your reach, a low API is advisable. You can check out the statistics on this at https://developer.android.com/about/dashboards/index.html.

Try installing the new APK on your device and you should see that it now has the correct name and icon in your app drawer. We're getting close now—I can taste it!

Creating a Keystore

Under Publishing Settings you'll see the option to create a *keystore*. This is a special kind of digital certificate that will identify and authorize your APK files. In other words, it will be a file with a password and a username that you'll need to include in every new version of your app to *prove* it is really your app. If you lose this file, you'll never be able to publish future updates—so put it somewhere very safe! (There is an option to let Google store this on the cloud, which I discuss later on.)

Although the keystore scheme might sound strict, it's an important security measure for users *and* developers alike. Otherwise, someone with the password to your developer account could potentially upload a new "version" of your app that simply replaces it with malware. That could harm your users, ruin your reputation, and destroy your business.

So it's frustrating, but just make sure you remember where you save the file and you shouldn't have any issues.

To create your keystore, just choose Create New Keystore, enter a username and password, and select a destination to save the file in (Figure 12-2).

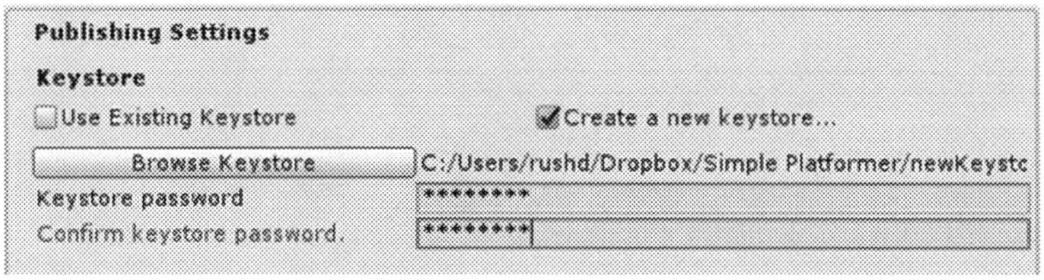

Publishing Settings
Keystore
☐ Use Existing Keystore   ☑ Create a new keystore...
          Browse Keystore   C:/Users/rushd/Dropbox/Simple Platformer/newKeystc
Keystore password   ●●●●●●●●
Confirm keystore password.   ●●●●●●●●

Figure 12-2. *Never lose this!*

Uploading Your App

Once you have your APK and it's properly signed, you'll be able to upload it to the Play Store. To do that, head over to `https://play.google.com/apps/publish` or search for the Google Play Developer Console.

If you haven't already signed up, you'll need to do that. Fortunately, you can use your Google account which will make things nice and easy. There is currently a registration fee of $25, but this is a one-off fee and is certainly preferable to the more expensive *annual* fees that iOS developers have to live with. Hopefully, this will be one of the best $25 you ever spend in terms of return on your investment. Even for a vanity project, $25 isn't exactly going to break the bank.

The developer console (Figure 12-3) is where you'll be able to see your apps and their stats once you have a few live. You'll be able to check user reviews, apply updates, and check out revenue and bug reports. You don't have any apps yet, though, so this is going to be pretty empty for now.

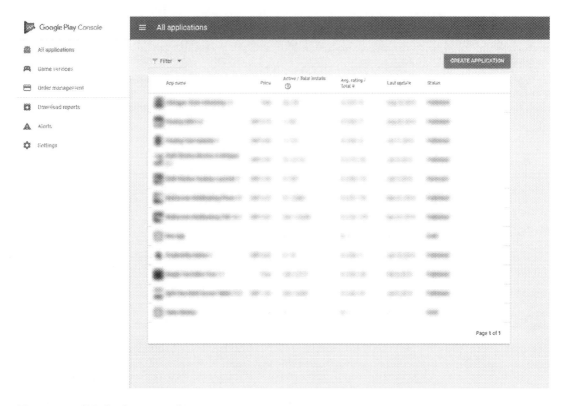

Figure 12-3. *My developer console*

Creating Your Store Listing

To get started, find and click Create Application. You'll be asked to choose a language and give it a title and then you'll be taken to another page where you can enter lots more details, including a description, translations, and various graphical assets (see Figure 12-4). We're going to fill this out first.

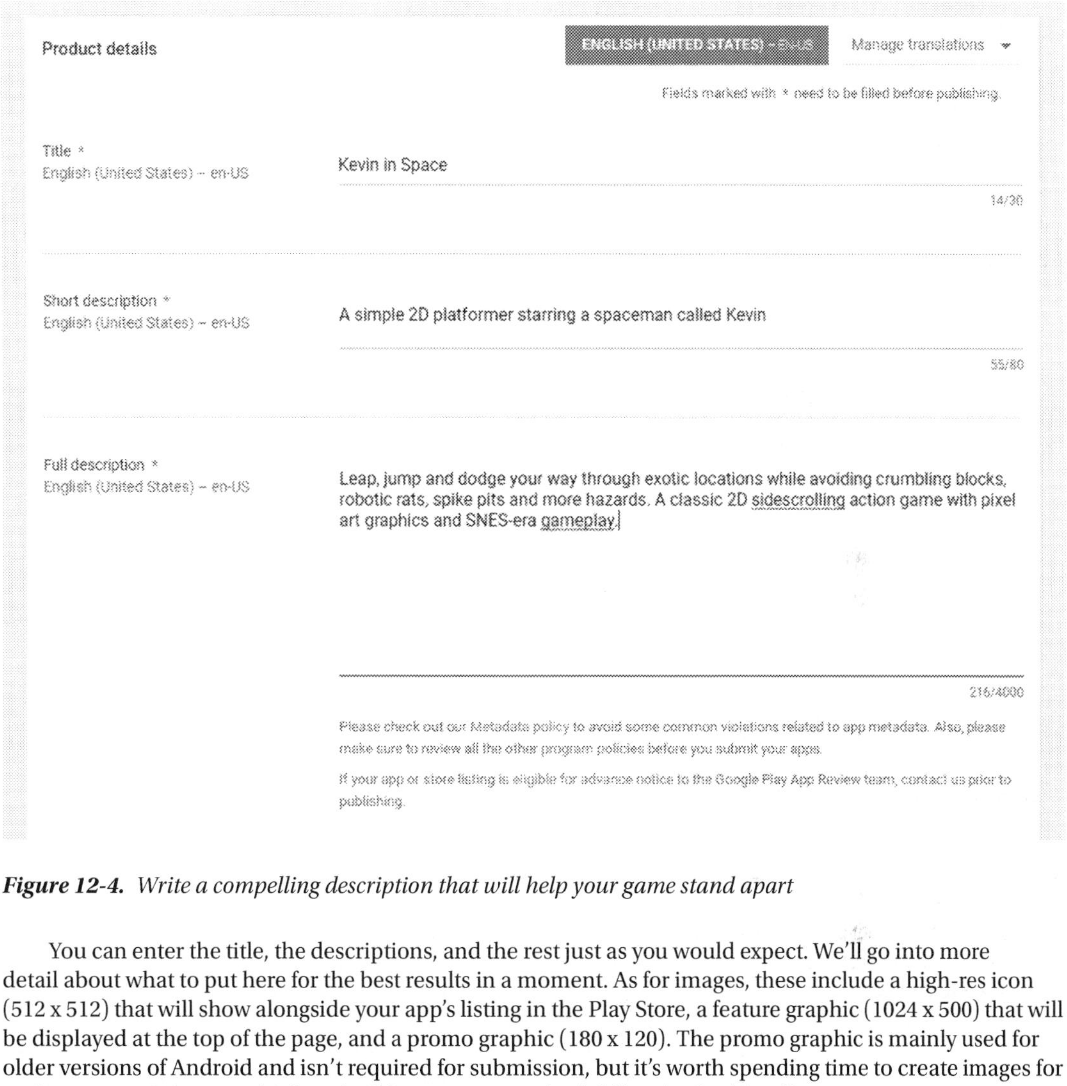

Product details ENGLISH (UNITED STATES) – EN-US Manage translations ▾

Fields marked with * need to be filled before publishing.

Title *
English (United States) – en-US

Kevin in Space

14/30

Short description *
English (United States) – en-US

A simple 2D platformer starring a spaceman called Kevin

55/80

Full description *
English (United States) – en-US

Leap, jump and dodge your way through exotic locations while avoiding crumbling blocks, robotic rats, spike pits and more hazards. A classic 2D sidescrolling action game with pixel art graphics and SNES-era gameplay.

216/4000

Please check out our Metadata policy to avoid some common violations related to app metadata. Also, please make sure to review all the other program policies before you submit your apps.

If your app or store listing is eligible for advance notice to the Google Play App Review team, contact us prior to publishing.

Figure 12-4. *Write a compelling description that will help your game stand apart*

You can enter the title, the descriptions, and the rest just as you would expect. We'll go into more detail about what to put here for the best results in a moment. As for images, these include a high-res icon (512 x 512) that will show alongside your app's listing in the Play Store, a feature graphic (1024 x 500) that will be displayed at the top of the page, and a promo graphic (180 x 120). The promo graphic is mainly used for older versions of Android and isn't required for submission, but it's worth spending time to create images for each category. You spent this long building your app—don't fall at the final hurdle.

If you use a promo video as well (which is worth doing), then your feature graphic will have a play icon over the top. For those creating Daydream apps, you'll need to create a stereoscopic 360-degree video. Good luck! Android TV apps need a 1280 x 720 banner image.

You'll also notice that you can add screenshots of your game and you can select different ones for phones, tablets, TV, and Android Wear. This is where you're going to put shots of your game in action. You can see the images I'm using in Figure 12-5.

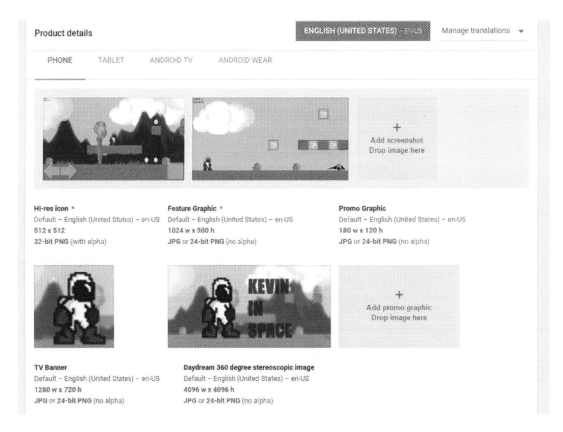

Figure 12-5. *How could anyone not want to download and play all two levels?*

Continue scrolling down the page and you'll be able to choose the application type (Game) the category (probably 'Action' in this case), the content rating and your contact details. You'll need to come back to the content rating later on and to get your certificate, you'll have to fill out various questions.

Enter your contact details next. I recommend setting up a new email address if you think there's *any* chance of your game becoming a massive hit. Anyone can contact you through here, and you can expect to get a *lot* of correspondence if your app takes off. That includes nice compliments as well as some completely inane criticisms and plenty of nonsense. So be careful when giving out your personal details.

You can then choose to submit a privacy policy if you want, or just leave it blank for now. If you're creating a mobile game that doesn't collect any private data from your users, you may have no need to go through this step.

Uploading an APK

To upload your APK, go to App Releases (on the left) and click Manage Production. Of course, this is subject to change, but one way or another you should have an option to Create Release.

Here you can click Upload APK, and if everything has gone according to plan, it should pass the test and be uploaded to the store (it isn't live just yet, don't worry). You should be able to see the correct version code and release name, corresponding to what you put into Player Settings. The title of your app should be at the top left of the page, alongside the icon you chose. You'll come back here when you want to add updates and you can add details of "What's new in this release?" to tell your users what has changed. If this doesn't work for whatever reason, the problem is likely due to your keystore, so take another look at the first section of this chapter. It should look like Figure 12-6 at this point.

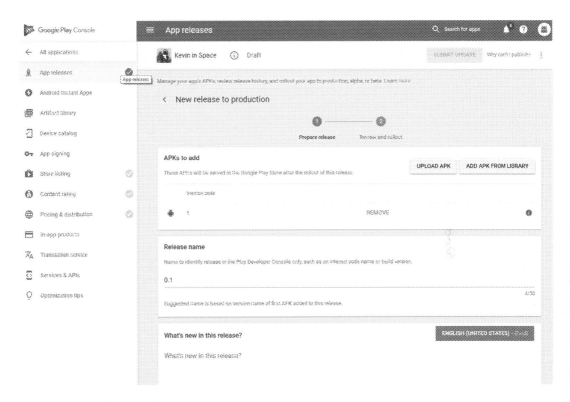

Figure 12-6. *So far, so good*

For now, you're just going to save this as a draft. You'll be able to come back in a moment when it's time to go live.

More Settings

There are a bunch of other settings to consider in the Console too, both compulsory and optional. We'll quickly go over a few of them in this section.

Content Rating

In order to make your game widely available, you'll need to complete the content rating process. Click Content Rating on the left, choose Continue, and answer the questions. They're pretty self-explanatory (Figure 12-7).

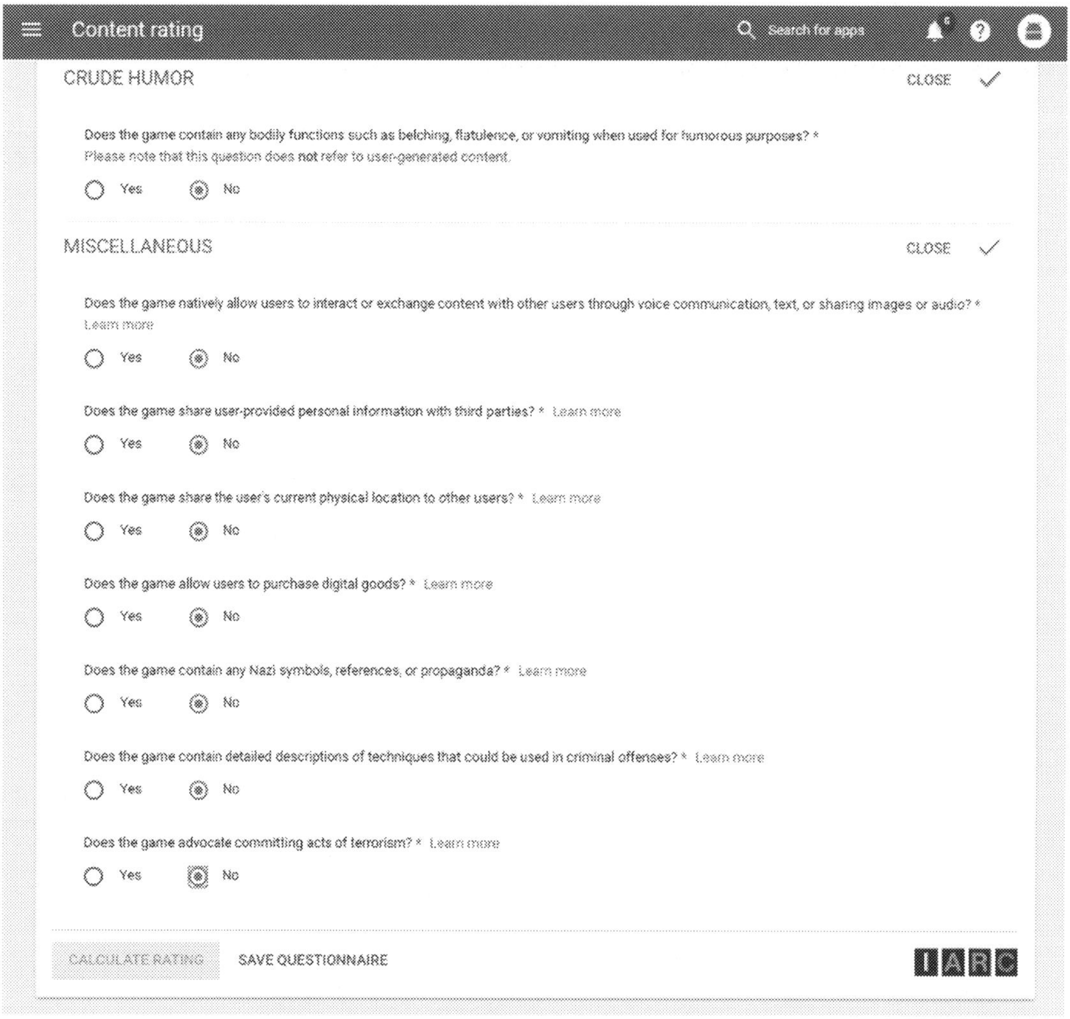

Figure 12-7. You might want to reconsider those Nazi references

Click Save Questionnaire, and then Calculate Rating to get your classification in various different regions, and finally Apply Rating.

Pricing and Distribution

You also need to decide how much you want to charge for your app, or whether you want to make it free. Note that if your app is sold for money, you can always make it free later on down the line. But once you make it free though, there is no turning back unless you upload a an entirely new store listing (Figure 12-8).

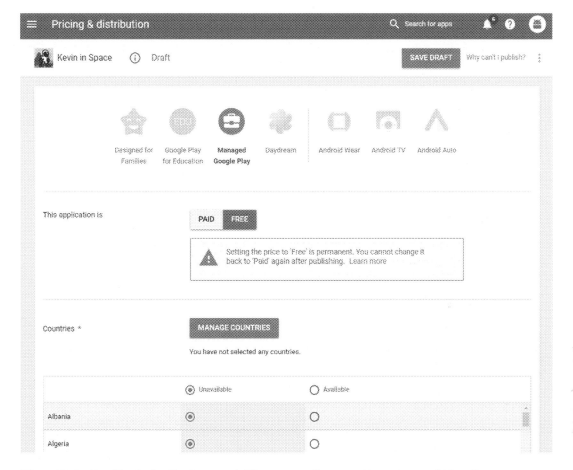

Figure 12-8. *Consider the best business model for your app if you want to make a profit from it*

The other part of this page allows you to choose the countries you want your app to be made available in. You'll probably want to make it available everywhere, because that way the maximum number of people will be able to enjoy your creation (and pay you).

You'll also need to answer some more questions below that screen, such as whether or not the app contains ads and whether it meets the Android Content Guidelines and U.S. export laws. Again, this should all be self-explanatory.

The Rest

Nearly there. Once you've completed the App Releases, Store Listing, Content Rating, and Pricing and Distribution sections, your app will then be ready to publish. But in case you were wondering what the other sections were for, read on.

The Device Catalog shows which devices can run your app, and you'll have the option to filter some out if you would prefer it were not available on them. Translation Services allows you to translate your app for other regions. Services and APIs is for accessing external tools like Firebase (Google's "backend service"—don't worry about it), and Optimization Tips just shares advice based on your current listing (worth reading). In-App Products is where you can manage your in-app purchases, but if your app doesn't have any, there's nothing to do here. Artifact Library allows you to download your APK and other bits that you may have uploaded to the Play Store.

Android Instant Apps is a relatively recent feature that allows users to run apps without having to permanently download and install them, but it won't apply here. Not only is the feature not available for everyone yet, but the large file sizes involved with most games (not to mention their very nature) means that it won't be wholly appropriate for most devs. Finally, App Signing is where you can enroll in Google's App Signing scheme to store your keystore in the cloud so that it never gets lost. A handy option, but it's not compulsory, so it's up to you whether you want to take this extra step. You can always decide to do this later if you choose. Once you go this route however, you won't be able to turn back.

When your app is live, you'll be able to return to the Console at any time to see all your published projects. Clicking one will let you see a whole host of data, including revenue, number of downloads, and more.

Go Time

With that, you're ready to publish. This is a momentous occasion, especially if you've been working on your app for months or years, so go pour yourself some bubbly.

Head back to App Releases ➤ Edit Release, scroll down to the bottom, and hit Start Rollout to Production (Figure 12-9).

Figure 12-9. *Do it!*

Confirm, and with that … your app is released! Or, almost....

Actually, your app will now be subject to review, and you'll see that it says "Pending Publication" at the top of the page. The publication process is automatic, meaning that it's handled by an algorithm rather than by actual human curators (unlike Apple's App Store). This is good news because it means your app *should* be live within the next few hours, ready for people to start downloading and reviewing. It's very rare that anything should be rejected at this stage. Of course, that's not a license to ignore the terms and conditions—your app can still get taken down later on.

Congratulations, dear reader! You just became an official game developer.

Creating More Downloads

Once your app is live, your job is far from over. Not only is it your moral obligation to keep updating and improving your apps as you go, but you also need to ensure that you're actively promoting your creations and encouraging downloads. This is *not* a case of "build it and they will come." Today there are simply *too many* great apps on Android, and the market is highly saturated. Rather, it's up to you to get the word out and ensure people are excited to check out your creation. You owe it to yourself.

So, how can you make sure people actually find and download your apps? This section talks about a few marketing tips that may help.

Think About SEO

SEO stands for *Search Engine Optimization*. This is a big deal in the world of Internet marketing, but it also has a role to play among developers. That's because the Google Play Store is essentially a search engine itself, and people will often find new apps *by searching* (see Figure 12-10).

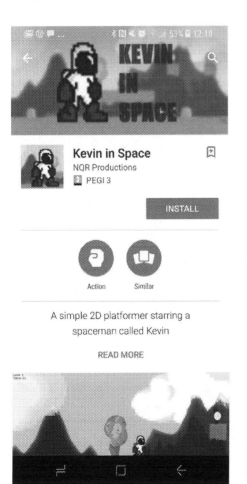

Figure 12-10. *Kevin in Space is open for business*

The key concept to understand here is the use of keywords. *Keywords* are words or phrases that someone might search to find your app. In our case, good examples might include the following:

- 2D platformer

- Sidescrolling game

- Pixel art

- Retro game

In order to increase our chances of being found, we might aim to try and include those terms a couple of times in the description. Don't overdo this, because that looks spammy and could get your app removed. Just try to include a few mentions naturally. The more you write in the full description, the easier this will be, and adding longer descriptions is also a practice that is encouraged by Google. Really sell your app and tell people why they should be interested.

Also consider that a term that's *too* popular is going to be harder to rank, due to the amount of competition. Look for that sweet spot: terms that are in demand but obscure enough that there isn't a wealth of content available already.

Choose Your Name Wisely

And of course, one of the very *best* ways to ensure you'll rank highly for a key term is to name your app using that phrase. For instance, you could actually *call* your game Retro 2D Platformer or something along those lines.

Be careful, though: doing this also means your app won't have the same amount of personality or a strong brand for you to promote. It can also be off-putting for users and can make it much harder for you to promote *outside* the Play Store.

A name that communicates something about your game isn't a bad idea, but try to be creative and interesting. Choose a name that conveys an *emotion* (like *Limbo* or *Angry Birds*) and that provokes interest (*VVVVVV* or *Thomas Was Alone*). Ideally, someone should instantly have an idea of what your game might be about or want to learn more as soon as they hear what it's called.

Find Routes to Market

Marketing also means occasionally getting out there and shouting about your amazing new game (Figure 12-11). The best way to do that is to find a *route to market*, which is essentially any place that people who are likely to be interested hang out. For example, this might be a Facebook group or Subreddit dedicated to a certain genre of game (also try `www.reddit.com/r/playmygame/`).

Figure 12-11. *Your game is now available for millions of people to download*

Route to market is something to think about in the early design stages of your game too. Of course, you should make the game you want to make and that gets you excited, but think as well what marketing opportunities will exist for your game. By targeting a specific niche you can avoid being a little fish in a big pond and sidestep the competition. More importantly, by targeting a certain *user* (called a *persona*) you can give yourself more specific routes to market.

As it is, *Kevin in Space* is rather hard to market because it doesn't stand out and it doesn't appeal to anyone in particular. But if this were a game about a free-running hero, we could post it in a forum aimed at free runners. If it were a game with an awesome synthwave soundtrack, we could try and get publicity from a synthwave website.

Likewise, think about the contacts and resources you currently have available to you. Of course, you should try and get your friends to download your app (and leave good reviews!), but perhaps you know someone who writes for a big website, for example?

Gain Good Reviews

SEO on the Play Store is a little different from SEO on Google.com because it takes into account a range of additional factors. Among these are the reviews left by your users, and more positive reviews = more downloads. Getting good reviews is a matter of creating a great game that you're proud of, but it's also a good idea to ask your users to review it with the occasional pop-up. Explain how it will really help you out, but don't try any underhanded tactics to force a positive review—Google frowns on that.

If you get a *bad* review, it's always a good idea to respond quickly. Not only will doing so show you are an attentive developer who actually cares about your users, but if you offer a solution, you might even find that the user changes their score.

Never pay for reviews. This practice can get your app removed and it will only lead to unhappy users.

Update Regularly

Updating your app regularly is also important. Not only does it encourage more positive reviews, it also gives your app a moment in the sun under the New + Updated Games section of the Play Store. More exposure like that means more opportunity for people to discover your app and give it a try.

Choose the Right Images and Text

If someone *should* stumble upon your app unexpectedly, they will have the option to either click and read more or just pass you by without stopping to read. The biggest factor influencing this decision is likely to be the icon you've chosen, so it should go without saying that this needs to be *good*. The aim is to stand out from the crowd and attract interest while also communicating precisely who your game is for. Don't try to appeal to everyone but embrace the genre, niche, and style you've chosen.

Think about your own habits: what kind of image would pique your interest while browsing for something new to play? For me, it would definitely be a game that looks futuristic, action-packed, and indie. I stay away from things like *Clash of Clans* or other polished-looking freemium games that are clearly aimed at the casual market. That's just me—but by knowing what *your* users are looking for, you can home in on what to communicate through your images. Of course, you then need to knock it out the park with your feature image and screenshots too.

The same goes for your description. Using a few keywords can be a good strategy, but it's *much* more important to write for the user. Doing so means capturing attention quickly with a strong opening statement, using bullet points to sell the key features of your game, and using emotive language to try and encourage a quick click. Read up on persuasive writing because that can make a real difference. And again: know your user and aim your pitch at them. Appealing to everyone means appealing to no one.

Create a Buzz

Finally, try to create a buzz for your app by submitting press releases to gaming websites and Android/mobile channels. Try offering free APKs to YouTube personalities in exchange for a review or a "let's play" video. Aim for smaller personalities and channels that are more likely to respond, and if your game is good, the bigger channels will take notice.

Consider creating a website for your own games that you can promote separately. Ditto for social media pages. Creating a website is surprisingly easy these days using WordPress (www.wordpress.com).

Also think about creating a buzz *prior* to your release as well. You can do this by creating a developer blog and talking about the creation of your app, or by releasing teasing news to small sites and channels.

If you're *really* ambitious, try running a campaign on Kickstarter or Indiegogo, crowdfunding sites where people will provide financial backing to help you get your game finished. Not only can crowdfunding pay for your project, it also ensures there's a big, active, and engaged community around the launch of your game. Plus it makes it easier to get noticed by the gaming media. Remember, sites and magazines don't want to offer you free promotion, but they *do* want to cover interesting *stories*.

Again, though, in order for this to work you need a compelling USP—whether that means creating a spiritual successor to a beloved franchise, reviving a forgotten genre, or trying something incredibly new and compelling. Give people a reason to get behind your game by making it into a movement rather than just another product. - make it something that they can believe in and get excited for!

Closing Comments

And with that, you're on your own. I've taken you as far as I can, and the rest is up to you. I trust that you will find your own way and create something you're proud of and that gets the attention and accolades it deserves.

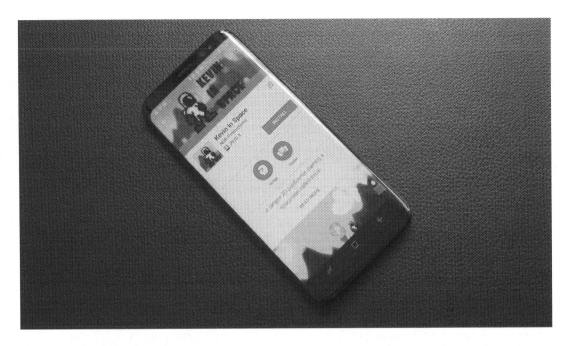

Figure 12-12. *The rest is up to you*

Just remember to start out small and build up from there. Create something different and unique. And most of all, have fun doing it. If you really enjoy the creation process and if you pour your heart and soul into your own passion project, it will show in the final product. Make the game that *you* want to play and don't be afraid to embrace your own identity.

And if your game isn't a massive hit? Move on to the next product. There is a *lot* of chance that goes into making a smash hit as well.

I wish you the best of luck with your projects and hope you absolutely knock it out of the park. Remember me when you're rich and famous!

Index

A. Sinicki, *Learn Unity for Android Game Development*, DOI 10.1007/978-1-4842-2704-6

Get the eBook for only $5!

Why limit yourself?

With most of our titles available in both PDF and ePUB format, you can access your content wherever and however you wish—on your PC, phone, tablet, or reader.

Since you've purchased this print book, we are happy to offer you the eBook for just $5.

To learn more, go to http://www.apress.com/companion or contact support@apress.com.

Apress®

31901060982461

Printed in the United States
By Bookmasters